The Ancient World

Prehistory to the Roman Empire

Senior Consultant
Dr. Judith Irvin
Florida State University

HOLT, RINEHART AND WINSTON

A Harcourt Classroom Education Company

Austin · New York · Orlando · Atlanta · San Francisco · Boston · Dallas · Toronto · London

Staff Credits

EDITORIAL

Manager of Editorial Operations
Bill Wahlgren
Executive Editor
Patricia McCambridge
Project Editor
Victoria Moreland
Component Editors: Scott Hall, Stephanie Wenger
Assistant Editor: Tracy DeMont
Writers: Terra Brockman, Rose Sallberg Kam, Mara Rockliff
Copyediting: Michael Neibergall, *Copyediting Manager;* Mary Malone, *Copyediting Supervisor;* Christine Altgelt, Joel Bourgeois, Elizabeth Dickson, Emily Force, Julie A. Hill, Julia Thomas Hu, Jennifer Kirkland, Millicent Ondras, Dennis Scharnberg, *Copyeditors*
Project Administration: Marie Price, *Managing Editor;* Lori De La Garza, *Editorial Operations Coordinator;* Heather Cheyne, Mark Holland, Marcus Johnson, Jennifer Renteria, Janet Riley, Kelly Tankersley, *Project Administration;* Ruth Hooker, Joie Pickett, Margaret Sanchez, *Word Processing*
Editorial Permissions: Susan Lowrance, *Permissions Editor*

ART, DESIGN AND PHOTO

Book Design
Richard Metzger, *Design Director*
Graphic Services
Kristen Darby, *Manager*
Design Implementation
The Format Group, LLC
Image Acquisitions
Joe London, *Director;* Jeannie Taylor, Tim Taylor, *Photo Research Supervisors;* Rick Benavides, Terry Janecek, Cindy Verheyden, *Photo Researchers;* Sarah Hudgens, *Assistant Photo Researcher;* Michelle Rumpf, Elaine Tate, *Art Buyer Supervisors;* Gillian Brody, Joyce Gonzalez, *Art Buyers*
Design
Isabel Garza Design
Cover Design
Curtis Riker, *Director;* Sunday Patterson, *Designer*

PRODUCTION

Belinda Barbosa Lopez, *Senior Production Coordinator*; Beth Prevelige, *Prepress Manager*; Carol Trammel, *Production Supervisor*

MANUFACTURING/INVENTORY

Shirley Cantrell, *Supervisor of Inventory and Manufacturing*; Wilonda Ieans, *Manufacturing Coordinator*; Mark McDonald, *Inventory Planner*

Cover Photo Credits: (mummy), Gerard Rollando/The Image Bank; (terra cotta army of Emperor Qin), Stock Boston, © Michele Burgess; (Tholos, Sanctuary of Athena, Delphi, Greece), © SuperStock

All art, unless otherwise noted, by ArtToday.com.

Contents

CHAPTER 6
The Classical World: Ancient Greece and Rome 165

CHAPTER 1

Before History Began
Prehistory   2 million B.C.–4,500 B.C.

State Song, State Bird, State . . . Fossil?

You might already know your state's flag and its official
state flower and bird. You might even be able to hum your
state's official song. But did you know that you might
also have an official state *fossil*? If you live in Colorado,
the stegosaurus is your state fossil. Wyoming claims
another dinosaur fan's favorite, the *Triceratops
horridus*. Not every state is lucky enough to have an
official dinosaur fossil—in fact, not every state has
any kind of official fossil yet—but there are plenty of
other kinds of fascinating fossils around, too. Indiana's
(and Nebraska's) state fossil is the mammoth. Idaho
claims an extinct breed of prehistoric horse. And California boasts
the *Smilodon fatalis*—better known as the saber-toothed tiger.

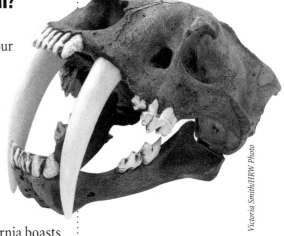

Victoria Smith/HRW Photo

The Great Hominid Hoax

In 1912, a lawyer and amateur geologist named Charles Dawson
found fossilized skull fragments in the Piltdown quarry in Sussex,
England. When Dawson presented the discovery to A. S. Woodward
of the British Museum, Woodward claimed that the strange skull
seemed to belong to a creature halfway between a human and an
ape—the "missing link."

Some scientists were always skeptical of Dawson's "Piltdown
Man," but it wasn't until 1953 that the fraud was revealed beyond
a doubt. The recently discovered carbon-14 dating technique
showed that the Piltdown Man's skull bone was not 500,000 years
old, as claimed, but was no more than 600 years old. Someone
had simply taken an oddly shaped human skull and the jaw of
an orangutan and made them look like ancient fossils by stain-
ing, filing, and smashing them.

INVESTIGATE: What
kinds of fossils have been
found in your home
state? Does your state
have an official state fossil?

Memorable Quote

"I dug things up. I was
curious. And then I liked to
draw what I found."

—Anthropologist Mary Leakey,
describing her work

Hominid (häm′ə•nid) is the broad term used for all members of the human family, going back to the earliest humanlike creatures who walked upright on two legs. The name comes from the Latin words *homo* ("human") and *-id* ("belonging to"). Every human being (yes, even you!) is a hominid.

Who was behind the hoax? People suspected both Dawson and Woodward—and practically everyone else associated with Piltdown Man. Then, in 1996, some suspicious stained and aged bones were found in a trunk in the British Museum. The bones had belonged to a man named Martin Hinton, who had worked as a volunteer under Woodward in 1912. Hinton may have set up the hoax as a way to ruin Woodward's reputation. Why? Revenge may have been a motive: Woodward had refused Hinton's request to be paid a salary for all his work!

▲ Charles Dawson with Piltdown Man skull.

Bettmann/CORBIS

We Love Lucy

On November 30, 1974, Donald Johanson and Tom Gray were looking for fossils at the Hadar site in Ethiopia. In a gully they had never visited before, Johanson spotted what turned out to be a hominid *ulna*—a bone from the forearm of an early human. He then found a skull bone and a leg bone, and, finally, a pelvis and a lower jaw.

That evening, back at their camp, the scientists celebrated their discovery. The Beatles' song "Lucy in the Sky with Diamonds" kept playing over and over in the background, and the skeleton was affectionately named "Lucy."

Lucy, a member of the species *Australopithecus,* lived at least 3.5 million years ago. Lucy would have been only about four feet tall, and she probably weighed about fifty pounds. She walked upright, and her brain was about the size of an orange. Lucy's bones showed no teeth marks or other damage, so scientists think she died either from a disease or from drowning. She was probably only about twenty years old.

THE FAR SIDE © by Gary Larson © 1986 FarWorks, Inc. All rights reserved. Used with permission.

Primitive spelling bees

Not many people get to see, touch, and even *smell* an extinct creature from 23,000 years ago—but that's exactly what the writer of this article was able to do. Get the sense of "being there" as you read this excerpt from a series of day-by-day accounts of the author's experiences helping to dig up and transport a frozen woolly mammoth.

The Permafrost Crumbles

from *Raising the Mammoth,* a Discovery Channel Web site

by DIRK HOOGSTRA, correspondent

Jarkov Mammoth Site,[1] *Oct. 4, 1999—*

Now we're making progress. Over the weekend, thanks to a pair of now-functioning jackhammers, we have chopped through the permafrost[2] so that now we have cut a trench all the way around the buried mammoth. I can tell you from my experience in digging through the ice with a pick and shovel that without the jackhammers, we'd have been at it for months to get this far.

At this point it looks like we should finish the digging within 48 hours. The next

You Need to Know...

In 1997, a boy from a tribe called the Dolgans, in remote Siberia, found the tusk of a prehistoric woolly mammoth sticking out of the ice. Fifteen feet under the ice lay a frozen giant woolly mammoth over 20,000 years old.

A scientific expedition, led by French explorer Bernard Buigues, set out in September of 1999 to do the seemingly impossible. Their goal was to get the mammoth out of the rock-hard icy ground and then use a huge helicopter to transport the creature—still in its block of ice—to an ice cave near Khatanga, Siberia. In the ice cave, a team of scientists would carefully thaw the mammoth and study every aspect of the ancient creature. The scientists hoped to learn why mammoths became extinct. Their greatest hope, though, was that they might be able to extract enough DNA from the mammoth to—yes—clone it.

---

1. **Jarkov Mammoth Site:** This is a place in the remote Taimyr Peninsula of Siberia where the Jarkov family discovered the frozen mammoth.
2. **permafrost:** subsoil that is permanently frozen.

step will be to drill under the mammoth and the block of permafrost surrounding it, then build an enclosure around it. Finally we'll need to construct the harness that will allow us to lift the mammoth out of the ground where it's spent the past 23,000 years.

Soon the pilot of the helicopter that will lift the frozen block of earth and mammoth will arrive at the site. And he'll make his estimate of what the load will weigh. He specializes in heavy lifting like this and should be able to determine if the total weight is more than 26 tons once the mammoth is lifted. If so, the helicopter will have to fly with less than a full tank and refuel along the way back to the ice caves in Khatanga. If the load weighs less than 26 tons, the flight can be made in one hop, which obviously makes the trip much less complicated.

What makes this mammoth so special?

If all goes as planned, the carcass[3] of this mammoth will be in the ice cave by the end of next week. And then its true value will become apparent. The difference between this mammoth and other preserved carcasses that have been discovered is that this one will be kept frozen until the scientists are ready to begin their research. That's never really been done before.

Not that there haven't been some remarkable mammoth discoveries in Siberia. The famous "Beresovka Mammoth," named after the river near where it was found, was a truly impressive specimen. Dug up in 1902 it was intact enough for scientists to determine that its stomach contained more than 33 pounds of grass when it died. But in their effort to dig it out, the excavation team melted most of the permafrost around the specimen with hot water. And in doing so they lost valuable clues about the mammoth's world, including pollen that was washed out of its hair.

_____

3. carcass (kärʹkəs): the dead body of an animal.

estimate (esʹtə•mit′): a rough or approximate calculation.

preserved (prē•zʉrvd′): unspoiled; undamaged.

specimen (spesʹə•mən): sample of something or one person or thing of a group.

That's why expedition leader Bernard Buigues is going to such lengths to have our specimen, the Jarkov mammoth, extracted and carried to a sub-freezing environment. Once it's there, scientists will use hair dryers to defrost the block millimeter by millimeter so they can examine the creature in a condition as close as possible to how it was when it died.

Scientists will use hair dryers to defrost the block millimeter by millimeter so they can examine the creature in a condition as close as possible to how it was when it died.

Scientist Dick Mol, here on site, believes this frozen block of earth may contain both of the mammoth's rear legs, the midsection of the animal including most of the vertebrae and ribs, and possibly internal organs, skin and hair. He thinks this specimen has the potential to be a gold mine for researchers who have long studied these extinct creatures, opening up an ancient world much more than any other mammoth find.

Eventually, scientists from all over the world and of many different specialties could come here. With luck, they'll be able to take an unprecedented[4] look into the past.

Out of the Earth

The workers have used their jackhammers to finish digging out the permafrost that connects the Jarkov mammoth to the ground. It now sits completely on the iron support platform that's been built underneath the animal.

We've also taken another step. Bernard Buigues, the man behind this ambitious project, has had the mammoth's tusks reattached to the block of frozen earth. These tusks

---

4. **unprecedented:** (un·pres'ə·den'tid): unheard-of.

Some scholars think that the word *mammoth* comes from an ancient word, *mama*, meaning "earth." This probably stems from a belief that these ancient creatures could burrow into the ground. Today, we use the word *mammoth* to mean "gigantic," and it's easy to see why. Some of the mammoths that roamed the northern parts of the earth during the Ice Age stood 15 feet high at the shoulder. (Modern elephants, their closest relatives, stand 8 to 14 feet high at the shoulder.)

ambitious (am·bish'əs): challenging; requiring much effort.

▲ A reconstructed mammoth skeleton. **?** **Why is it so important to scientists to have an intact prehistoric creature?**

Snug as a Bug?

Scientists studying a mastodon, a prehistoric relative of the mammoth, found *live* bacteria in the mastodon's stomach. The bacteria had survived over 11,000 years, making them the oldest living organisms ever found.

pungent (pun'jənt): giving a strong, sharp sensation of smell.

were actually removed by the Dolgan nomads[5] who discovered this creature a few years ago. Since then Bernard has been keeping them in storage. But he feels it's important, during the lift, for people to be able to visualize how the animal is positioned in the block in which it's been encased for the past 20,000 or so years. So, for now at least, we've reunited the mammoth with its tusks. Later, they will be kept on display in Khatanga, the nearest town to our camp.

A strong animal odor

Inside the tent that's been erected over the block of earth to protect it from snow, Bernard has been using a hair dryer to expose more of the mammoth's hair. As soon as I enter the tent, I noticed a strong animal odor all around me. It's not a foul smell, but it is pungent. And I have to say it is bizarre to be able to smell an animal at least 20,000 years old. I realize how lucky I am to be one of the few people ever to experience such a sensation. . . .

5. **Dolgan nomads:** A group of nomads who live in Siberia, often herding reindeer. Nomads are people with no permanent home; they wander from place to place looking for food and land. The Jarkov family, who discovered the mammoth, are Dolgan people.

Now all that's left to do is wait for the helicopter to lift the mammoth out of the hole. Bernard seems to have worked out a way for us to get the kerosene we need to operate the copter. But we're in waiting mode. We're all getting antsy and not just to see this mammoth raised from the ground. With the work done, there's not much for us to do here now.

Not to mention that, with the wind chill, it's close to 100 degrees below zero.

✓ Reading Check

1. Why are the workers using a jackhammer? How long has this mammoth been frozen?

2. What is the difference between this mammoth and previous ones that have been discovered?

3. How did scientists excavate the mammoth found in 1902? What was the problem with that method?

4. What parts of the mammoth do scientists think are in the frozen block?

5. Who removed the mammoth's tusks? Why does the team reattach the tusks before they lift the mammoth?

MEET THE *Writer*

Dirk Hoogstra joined explorer Bernard Buigues's expedition in September 1999 to keep a detailed journalistic record of the Siberian woolly mammoth discovery.

When Mammoths Roamed the Earth

Woolly mammoths were well suited to life during the Ice Age. They had a warm undercoat of fur and a long, hairy overcoat that nearly touched the ground. In addition, they had an insulating hump of fat on their backs and heads, and a three-inch layer of fat all over their bodies.

Mammoths were essential to Stone Age people. They provided food to feed many people for a long time—and they provided much more. Mammoth tusks, bones, fur, and fat were used for everything from housing, bedding, and fuel to jewelry and musical instruments. Hard as it is to imagine, mammoths used to roam North America, and they were probably hunted by ancient Native Americans.

Tar pits were deathtraps for many unsuspecting animals of the Ice Age. Now, however, tar pits are treasure-troves for scientists studying the animals, plants, and climate of southern California from about 40,000 to 10,000 years ago, when the last Ice Age ended. In this article, a reporter interviews a scientist working in the famous Rancho La Brea Tar Pits in Los Angeles.

Summer in the Pits— Going for the Goo

by MARK WHEELER from Discovery.com

extract (ek•strakt′): to pull out using great force or effort.

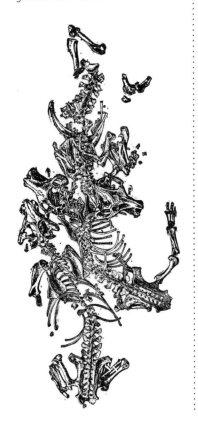

Jerry Smith digs 40,000 years into the past. Fourteen feet deep in the ground, he struggles to <u>extract</u> the skull and bones of a dire wolf.[1] Well, pry is more like it. The wolf, long dead, is putting up a fight.

Smith, a senior excavator with the Page Museum,[2] together with colleagues and volunteers, is digging and pulling through black, sticky, so-called tar. For two months this summer, they will search the gooey stuff for pieces of ancient residents, such as the wolf, of what is now a tony neighborhood about a mile from downtown Los Angeles—home of the Rancho La Brea Tar Pits.[3]

The goo isn't literally tar or oil. It's asphalt—degraded oil that for hundreds of thousands of years has welled up from a large, naturally occurring body of petroleum deep in the Earth.

---

1. **dire wolf:** Bones from more than 1,600 dire wolves have been found at Rancho La Brea—more than from any other single animal. These animals lived all across North America during the Ice Age, hunting in packs and chasing their prey until it was so tired it could run no longer. (The word *dire* means "causing terror.")
2. **the Page Museum:** This is the George C. Page Museum of La Brea Discoveries in Los Angeles, California, part of the Natural History Museum of Los Angeles County.
3. **Rancho La Brea Tar Pits:** *Brea* is a Spanish word meaning "tar." California was once part of Mexico, and the area around the tar pits was called Rancho La Brea (Tar Ranch).

Free meal to die for

Pooling on the surface, the stuff has trapped countless hapless animals in a flypaper-like grasp for tens of thousands of years. These pit captives died a cruel death from slow starvation or from the teeth and claws of a predator taking advantage of a "free" meal, thus leaving a rich, buried legacy for science. It's one that researchers have been digging through since 1908,[4] when excavation of the pits began.

"Obviously these animals didn't recognize asphalt for what it was, plus it was likely covered over by dirt, leaves, or a little water," says Smith, who has been excavating this particular hole, called Pit 91, since the 1980s. "It wouldn't take much to trap them; just a few inches of this stuff would be enough to hold something even as large as a mammoth."

Smith speaks from experience. He once stepped into the goo by mistake. "I didn't sink at all, but still needed a couple of people to pull me out."

One of 100 such pits on the museum's property, Pit 91 is the only one still actively excavated. It is a huge hole, the size of a generous garage; a metal ladder, roped to a railing on top, provides the only way up and down. Heavy beams, soaked through with

legacy (leg′ə•sē): something handed down from the past.

excavation (eks′kə•vā′shən): act of digging; something uncovered by digging.

You Need to Know...

Usually archaeologists unearth fossils from rocks, sand, or soil. In southern California, though, the best source of fossils is a series of huge tar pits called Rancho La Brea. (Read on to find out why they aren't really "tar" pits!) Oil deposits lie under much of California. Back in the Ice Age, some oil seeped to the surface and eventually became a thick mass of sticky petroleum products. (The process continues today.) Over time, these "tar pools" were covered with plant debris and water. Animals that wandered into them rarely made it out again. After the trapped animals died and their flesh decayed, their bones sank to the bottom of the pits and were perfectly preserved.

Many of the scientists who study the La Brea fossils are not archaeologists but paleontologists (pā′lē•ən•täl′ə•jists)— geologists who study the fossils of prehistoric times. The word *paleontology* comes from *paleo-*, meaning "ancient or early"; *onto-*, meaning "organism"; and *-logy*, meaning "science or study of." Like many of the words you encounter as you read about prehistory, it's easier than it looks once you break it down into its Greek and Latin word parts.

---

4. 1908: For hundreds of years before 1908, Native Americans and then early European settlers in California used the tar at Rancho La Brea for a number of practical purposes, among them to glue baskets and tools and to waterproof boats and the roofs of houses.

▲ A reconstruction of what it was probably like for animals trapped in the tar pits. ❓ **Why was it so easy for even enormous animals like mammoths to get trapped in the tar pits?**

asphalt, wall off the pit, preventing its collapse. Wooden catwalks crisscross the floor, allowing the researchers access to the 3-foot grids they excavate, one at a time.

Summer heats things up

Over the decades, researchers like Smith have extracted more than 1 million richly preserved Ice Age fossil bones. Because of budget constraints, though, these days the pit is only worked for two months in the summer—the hottest ones. This is when the asphalt is at its most viscous,[5] but still not viscous enough to allow someone to simply stick a hand into the muck and yank out a bone.

The work, carried out in part by a league of trained volunteers, is hard and sweaty, hot and dirty—old clothes are a must, and Smith's boots, he says dryly, have "gained weight" from their permanent coating of asphalt.

---

5. **viscous** (vis′kəs): having a sticky, fluid consistency.

Lester V. Bergman/CORBIS

The tools the researchers use haven't changed much from the ones used by their colleagues back in '08; they just use fewer of them. In the early days, the paleontologists used picks and shovels, and didn't sweat the small stuff. They were interested in the big bones of mastodons and mammoths, huge ground sloths and the so-called short-faced bear. Everything else—leaves, stems, the "matrix" (the mix of dirt and asphalt)—was tossed.

Not today. "We save everything," says Smith, "including every bit of asphalt we dig up. That's where we find our microfossils."

Sorting through the muck

Once they've siphoned[6] off the liquid asphalt, called the "glop," the excavators sit, squat, or lie on the catwalk, bending over their entombed targets. Backs aching by the end of the day, using one hand for support, they work the end of a chisel or screwdriver into the matrix nearest a bone, prying it loose, then toss the detritus[7] into buckets. Later, it's brought to the museum's lab, where the asphalt will be chemically dissolved and sifted. Whatever's in the goo— bits of leaves, seeds, stems, insects, perhaps a tiny mouse

▲ Sorting through tar pit discoveries.

Whatever's in the goo—bits of leaves, seeds, stems, insects, perhaps a tiny mouse bone or a random tooth or two—is saved and examined.

---

bone or a random tooth or two—is saved and examined. These microfossils help scientists determine what the climate was like in Southern California 40,000 years ago— namely, wetter and cooler, more like San Francisco's.

---

6. siphoned (sī′fənd): drawn off by a siphon (a tube or pipe used to draw liquids).
7. detritus (dē·trīt′əs): loose particles of rock.

Tiger, Tiger

Actually, the saber-toothed tiger wasn't a tiger at all. This cat was the size of a lion, but with more powerful front legs and weaker back legs. It moved more slowly than lions of today and hunted slower prey such as the mammoth, mastodon, and ground sloth. Once it caught an animal, however, the victim's fate was sealed. The saber-tooth held the victim tightly with its powerful front limbs. Then it used its strong head and neck muscles to repeatedly stab the prey with its incredibly long, saber-like teeth. (A *saber* is a kind of sword with a blade that curves slightly.)

intact (in·takt'): whole or entire, with no part damaged or removed.

protruding (prō·trōod'iŋ): sticking out from the surroundings.

It's exacting work. Heat builds up in the pit, and if the diggers want water, they must go topside. "We used to keep bottles of water down here," says staff excavator Meghan Meyer, laughing. "But since we always get asphalt on our gloves, the water bottles would get stuck to our hands."

Of course, while the excavators are careful to preserve every microfossil, it doesn't mean they've lost interest in big bones (every bone, by the way, is permanently stained brown and wonderfully preserved by the asphalt). In the summer of 1997, the paleontologists extracted over 1,000 new fossils, including skulls and bones of the saber-toothed cat, a horse and ground sloth, a lion and coyote.

Fossil display

Smith notes, though, that entire skeletons are rarely found intact. "Winter rains would wash the bones downstream, a lucky predator probably grabbed a bone and escaped,

earthquakes would have caused the asphalt to shift," he says.

That's why in the museum, a display of a saber-toothed cat, say, may actually be comprised of the bones of 20 different cats. All the skeletons exhibited by the museum come from the pits.

Once a bone is ready to be removed from the pit, says Smith, a careful plot is made of its precise location and its depth within the pit. Eventually, the museum hopes to develop a computer database, where the pit and the location of every bone found can be seen in 3-D on screen. That big picture will make it easier for scientists to develop scenarios as to what exactly got trapped first and why, as in the case of the dire wolf now being "ungooed," along with another large bone nearby, probably that of a bison.

No one really knows, of course, how these particular protruding bones wound up in the pits, but the paleontologists have a likely theory. "In most sites where fossils are abundant, it's normal to find few predators and more prey," says Smith. "Here it's exactly the opposite—what probably happened, over and over, is that an animal would be trapped, attracting a predator. That animal would be trapped as well. More predators would come, and get stuck."

More goo than time

The result for researchers like Smith is almost an overabundance of fossils, each with its potential clues. And there appears to be at least another 4 feet left to unearth in Pit 91—"work beyond my professional lifespan," says Smith.

Just this month, new construction on the museum's grounds unveiled at least three new pools of asphalt buried 8 feet in the ground. And there's still the 99 other existing pits to be exhumed[8] and examined further. One hundred years from now, paleontologists could still be being gooed by the glop of La Brea.

---

8. **exhumed** (eks·hyōomd′): dug out of the ground.

✓ Reading Check

1. Even though the pits at Rancho La Brea are called tar pits, the author says they aren't tar. What are they made of? Where did the substance come from?

2. In what two ways did animals probably die after becoming stuck in the Rancho La Brea pits?

3. How many inches of tar does Jerry Smith say it would take to trap a mammoth? What happened when Jerry Smith stepped into the tar?

4. What two reasons are given for why people work at La Brea for only two months in the summer?

5. The author says that the first excavators only wanted to save the large animal bones. What do today's excavators save? Why?

An obituary is a short article that appears in newspapers and magazines to announce a person's death. Many obituaries are like short biographies, highlighting the achievements and importance of a person's life. This obituary from *Newsweek* magazine focuses on the lasting contributions made by anthropologist Mary Leakey.

Mary Leakey, 1913–1996

by SHARON BEGLEY

from *Newsweek* magazine

impression (im•presh'ən): visible mark made on a surface by pressing something hard into something softer.

encased (en•kāst'): enclosed; closed in on all sides.

For all the ancient skulls and prehistoric-stone tools that Mary Leakey chiseled out of the rocks of East Africa, what this accidental anthropologist will be best remembered for are feet. Feet prints, actually. One day in 1978, on the arid Laetoli plain of Tanzania, Leakey bent over an impression that looked as if it had been made by a human heel. With a dental pick and brush she painstakingly cleaned away the 3.75 million-year-old, hardened volcanic ash that encased the print. Three hours later, convinced that the print had indeed been left by human ancestors, she stood up . . . and announced, "Now this really is something to put on the mantelpiece."

Or in a museum. The 75-foot-long trail of crisp footprints had been made

You Need to Know...

Some people recognize the name of the Olduvai Gorge in Africa, but fewer know about Laetoli, just 30 miles from Olduvai. Mary Leakey set up her camp there in 1976. It was not a pleasant place. Buffalo and elephants chased people, the nearest water was ten miles away, and the area was crawling with poisonous snakes and bothersome ticks. But Mary Leakey did not let these things get in the way of her work.

On July 27, Leakey found some tracks that were obviously those of an early human. After careful study, she realized that she had discovered something of enormous scientific importance. Until Mary Leakey's discovery, people had assumed that what first happened to make modern humans—well, human—was the development of a larger brain. Leakey's discovery showed that before the larger brain came bipedalism (bī•ped'əl•iz'əm), the ability to walk on two feet. Bipedalism freed the hands to make tools—and then brain capacity began to expand. Leakey considered the discovery of the hominid footprints to be the most important breakthrough in her entire career.

by three lithe[1] hominids (members of the human family) who <u>ambled</u> across the volcanic plain at the dawn of humankind. One of them seemed to pause and turn left, briefly, before continuing north. This relic[2] of a behavior from eons back brought the find to life in a way that mere bones could not. As Leakey wrote, "This motion, so intensely human, <u>transcends</u> time. A remote ancestor . . . experienced a moment of doubt." The find helped overturn the prevailing wisdom that the seminal[3] event in human evolution was the development of a big brain. Instead, it was standing up, which freed the hands to make tools. Toolmaking stimulated growth in the size and complexity of the brain. "This new freedom of fore-limbs posed a challenge," Leakey wrote soon after the discovery. "The brain expanded to meet it." And humankind was born.

Without Leakey, who died last week in Nairobi[4] at 83, the family tree of mankind would have been quite short of branches. In 1936 she married African archeologist Louis Leakey. . . . Though she was trained as an artist, as soon as she joined him in Africa she began making discoveries that would change the whole field of human evolution. In 1948, on an island in Lake Victoria, she uncovered a piece of the skull of a Proconsul, an apelike creature that is ancestral[5] to both humans and apes and that lived some 25 million years ago. The find was the first to support Darwin's[6] <u>notion</u> that Africa, not Asia, was the cradle of mankind. In 1959, in Tanzania, she found teeth and part of the jaw of

ambled (am'bəld): walked at an easy pace.

transcends (tran·sendz'): goes beyond; is not limited.

Bettmann/CORBIS

▲ Mary Leakey at work, with two canine friends.

notion (nō'shən): belief.

---

1. **lithe** (līth): graceful.
2. **relic:** a remaining trace.
3. **seminal** (sem'ə·nəl): highly influential; providing a basis for further development.
4. **Nairobi:** the capital and largest city in Kenya. From 1905 until 1963, it was the capital of British East Africa.
5. **ancestral** (an·ses'trəl): of, having to do with, or inherited from ancestors.
6. **Darwin:** Charles Darwin (1809–1882) was a British naturalist who revolutionized biology with his theory of evolution based on natural selection.

an ancestor new to science. The 1.8 million-year-old creature, *Australopithecus boisei*, so captured the public's imagination that it secured essentially permanent research funding for the Leakeys. She and Louis, who died in 1972, discovered the scattered remains of *Homo habilis* ("handy man") in 1960. Actually, son Jonathan was the first to spy the fossil fragments; she habitually dragged along her three small sons to dig sites.

By 1968 Leakey had broken with her headline-seeking husband and decamped to Olduvai Gorge in Tanzania, where she directed research. "We would do well," she wrote, to "spend less time in putting forward our own, personal interpretations" and more on adding to the fossil record. Luckily for science, she did just that.

✓ Reading Check

1. What does the writer say Mary Leakey will be most remembered for? What other discoveries does the author mention?

2. What was Leakey originally trained to be? How did she end up in anthropology?

3. What action shown by one of the hominids' footprints does Leakey identify as "intensely human"?

4. Which of Leakey's early discoveries supported the theory that Africa was the cradle of humankind?

5. What important discovery did the Leakeys' young son Jonathan make?

MEET THE *Writer*

Sharon Begley has worked for *Newsweek* for many years and has received numerous awards for her work. She joined *Newsweek* as an editorial assistant in 1977 and has been a senior science writer since 1990.

We know that there are caves containing art from the Ice Age, but how on earth could there be an *underwater* cave with Ice Age art? (Did cave people go scuba diving?) Read on to find out more about this amazing discovery and to learn how prehistoric people entered and worked in this cave approximately 18,000 to 28,000 years ago.

Swimming into the Ice Age

by DAVE GETZ

from *Muse*

Though he didn't know it, Henri Cosquer was about to scuba dive into a place where human voices hadn't been heard for 18,000 years. It was the summer of 1991 and Cosquer was 120 feet beneath the surface of the Mediterranean Sea. He was swimming toward the entrance of a small cave just off the coast of Marseilles, France. After passing through a 450-foot-long tunnel that sloped gently upward, Cosquer emerged in an immense air-filled cave. Climbing out of the water onto the dry ground, he removed his scuba equipment and breathed the air that seeped in through tiny cracks in the ceiling of the cave.

He had been here before.

emerged (ē·mŭrjd′): came out.

You Need to Know...

Henri Cosquer, the discoverer of this Ice Age cave, wasn't an archaeologist. Instead, he was a professional diver who made his incredible discovery quite by accident after swimming through a treacherous underwater passage. Cosquer took photographs of his discovery, but he kept it a secret—until he heard about three divers who were missing, last seen near the same underwater passage. Cosquer was called on to help with the search and rescue, but the three divers were found dead. Cosquer then decided to tell the world his secret—and make certain that the entrance to the cave would be blocked so that future adventurers would not be endangered.

Archaeologists at first didn't know what to make of the photographs Cosquer had taken. Some of them thought that the paintings and engravings were forgeries. Perhaps Cosquer was trying to start a hoax and cash in on the public's fascination with cave art. Besides, whoever heard of an underwater cave filled with prehistoric art? Fortunately, they were wrong about Cosquer. His discovery was very real.

For six years he had kept his knowledge of this cave a secret. Surrounding him was a room of dazzling beauty. Columns of amber-colored stalagmites[1] rose up from the floor. Fantastic stalactites[2] hung from the ceiling. The ground was encrusted with crystals, and curtains of transparent minerals were draped over the cave walls.

Cosquer began to explore, as he had so many times before. Then he came upon the red hand prints. He was stunned and disappointed. Another diver was here before me, he thought. I wasn't the first. Somebody else knows my secret!

For six years he had kept his knowledge of this cave a secret.

It wasn't until Cosquer returned again, this time with a team of divers and more powerful lights, that he discovered that there were paintings and engravings[3] of animals all over the cave's walls. There were images of deer, bison, reindeer, and what looked like penguins. There were walls covered in the outlines of human hands. Some of those hand prints appeared to be missing fingers or parts of fingers. There were strange geometric shapes, and odd signs.

Cosquer's team sent some photos of the paintings to the French Ministry of Culture. They in turn sent the photos to Jean Clottes, their scientific advisor on prehistoric art. Cosquer claimed to have discovered a cave that had been decorated by prehistoric people. But could this be true? Could ancient people have reached an underwater cave?

When French scientists learned of Cosquer's claims, many said it was a hoax. But Clottes suspected Cosquer had made a great discovery. How could Clottes be sure? "I couldn't go there. I'm not a diver," Clottes recalled.

transparent (trans·per′ənt): clear; easily seen through.

geometric (jē′ə·me′trik): based on simple shapes such as a line, circle, or square.

1. **stalagmites** (stə·lag′mīts): cone-shaped stone columns that rise from the floors of caves.
2. **stalactites** (stə·lak′tīts): stone formations resembling icicles that hang from the roofs of caves.
3. **engravings** (en·grāv′iŋz): designs or pictures cut into a surface.

"We needed to send somebody who was both an archaeologist and a diver. So we decided to send Jean Courtin."

Jean Courtin knew that exploring the cave was a dangerous assignment. Just a month earlier, four inexperienced divers had entered the cave, curious to see what Cosquer had discovered. As they returned, the divers touched the cave's walls with their flippers, releasing a black cloud of mud. Trapped in an underwater tunnel 120 feet beneath the surface and unable to see anything, they panicked. Three of them drowned.

Courtin was codirector of the French Department of Underwater Archaeological Research, and so he was able to use the *Archaeonaute*, a ship specially designed to support divers during underwater archaeology. He and his team ran

Alan Atkins/Wood River Gallery/Picture Quest

▲ Not all cave art is painted. In this artist's rendering, an Ice Age artist is shown chiseling the image of a bison.

Hold Your Breath

The Cosquer Cave is closed to the public—not only because it is dangerous, but also because the paintings must be protected from potential damage from, of all things, human breath. It turns out that breathing can be hazardous to paintings—especially prehistoric ones in damp caves.

The breath from a million tourists nearly destroyed the paintings in Lascaux Cave in France—sometimes called the Sistine Chapel of prehistoric art. The magnificent cave had been discovered by accident in 1940 when four boys found the partially hidden entrance to an art-filled prehistoric cave that had been undisturbed for 20,000 years. Soon the boys were charging a fee to anyone who wanted to visit the cave. The crowds grew, and then the owner of the land began advertising the cave and charging admission as well.

Between 1948 and 1963, over a million people visited Lascaux Cave. During that time, the carbon dioxide and moisture in their breath reacted with the cave wall, eventually covering the cave paintings with white calcite and threatening to damage them beyond repair. Lascaux Cave had to be climate-controlled and closed to the public in 1963. It didn't seem right that people be prevented from seeing the cave's amazing artwork, so in 1980 the French came up with a clever solution: They built an exact replica of the most representative parts of the cave nearby. Here, at Lascaux II, the tour guides will assure you that you are allowed to breathe!

electrical and phone lines from the ship to the cave. Divers also set up a lifeline, a thin nylon cord that stretched from the entrance of the cave to the large chamber Cosquer had discovered. Even though they put lights in the tunnel, the lead divers kicked up so much mud, the divers who followed couldn't see. Each diver had to blindly pull himself along the lifeline for 12 unnerving[4] minutes to reach the cave's entrance.

SIPA Press

▲ Detail of artwork in the Cosquer Cave. **❷ Why were scientists so doubtful about Cosquer's discovery?**

Once in the cave, Courtin's team took off their diving equipment and put on dry clothes they had brought with them in waterproof cases. Then they got out their work equipment, cameras, and drawing materials, and set off to observe, measure, map, and record their findings.

They soon realized that Henri Cosquer was right: the paintings had to be very old. Some lay beneath transparent sheets of the mineral calcite.[5] As ground water drips down the walls of limestone caves, it leaves behind microscopic amounts of the mineral. Slowly, over a period of thousands of years, these tiny deposits form a transparent curtain that drapes the cave's walls. If there were paintings under calcite, the artwork had to be thousands of years old. But exactly how old was it?

Courtin collected small samples of charcoal from some animal paintings, from a few hand stencils,[6] and from the cave's floor. This charcoal was later sent to a laboratory for carbon-14 dating, a technique that can be used to

---

4. **unnerving:** losing strength or courage; nerve-racking.
5. **calcite** (kal′sīt): a form of calcium carbonate found in marble and limestone.
6. **stencils** (sten′səlz) : designs or pictures made by dabbing paint through a cut-out pattern so that an image is left underneath.

find out how long ago something died. If scientists could determine when the tress were cut to make the charcoal, they could get a pretty good idea when the charcoal paintings and hand prints were made.

The carbon-14 dating confirmed both Courtin and Clotte's suspicions. The charcoal from the paintings of animals was approximately 18,500 years old. The charcoal from the drawings of hands and symbols was roughly 27,500 years old. Since there was no evidence that anyone had been in the cave in the years between, the cave must have been abandoned and then rediscovered 9,000 years later.

They soon realized that Henri Cosquer was right: the paintings had to be very old.

Who were the people who painted the walls? "Well, they were people like us," says Clottes. "Same brain. Same physical appearance. Same nervous system. They were our great-great-great-grandparents." We know from examining what they left behind at other sites that they used stone tools, and that they hunted and ate wild horses, bison, reindeer, caribou, and other large game.

But how did they get in the cave? They walked. The people who painted the cave lived during the last ice age, when the world was much colder, and ice caps several thousand feet thick covered much of North America, Europe, and Asia. With all of this water trapped as ice on land, the seas didn't come as far up the shore as they do today. Eighteen thousand years ago, the Mediterranean was miles away from the entrance to Cosquer's cave. "They entered at the bottom of the cliff," explains Clottes. "There was a hole and no sea. They had to have wooden torches, and we found the remains of those torches." The torches came from Scotch pine, a wood that burns long and brightly, perfect for lighting a dark cave.

Why did they enter the cave? We're not sure. We know they didn't use it as a home. If they had, there would have been thousands of broken bones from the animals they had killed and cooked. But no remains of animal bones were found.

Why did ice-age people make the paintings? "We can be sure that the chances of people wandering into a cave and making very good paintings are very faint," Clottes explains. "The artists who made these works were trained and highly skilled." He believes that the paintings were part of a ritual, some religious or magic ceremony. The act of painting on the wall was intended to cause something to happen. Will we ever find out what these artists hoped to accomplish? "Well, they are no longer here to tell us," says Clottes. "These people have disappeared. Their tradition is lost. The only thing we can do is make guesses."

What the art in Cosquer's cave can tell us clearly is how much our world has changed, and how much it's still the same. The reindeer, red deer, and the horses that run on Cosquer's walls are all cold-loving animals that hint that this warm Mediterranean region was once as cold as Alaska. The "penguins" depicted on its walls are now thought to be auks that migrated to the northern arctic regions at the end of the ice age. Auks, seabirds that were massacred[7] by the millions by fisherman and sailors in the early 1800s, are now extinct. Another animal depicted on Cosquer's walls is the megaloceros, an immense, ice-age deer whose antlers could span nine feet. The megaloceros has long been extinct. The type of bison depicted on the walls is also extinct. So is the aurochs, a bison-like animal that stood over six feet high at the shoulder, was 13 feet long, and weighed more than a ton.

Perhaps most alarming of all these paintings however, is the "killed man." The man is lying on his back, and a spear-like object pierces his back and skull. This image is mysterious. Is this a depiction of a real killing, or could it be a symbol, meant to stand for something else? Either

extinct (ek·stiŋkt′): no longer alive and having no descendants.

depiction (dē·pik′shən): picture; representation.

---

7. **massacred** (mas′ə·kərd): killed in large numbers, often carelessly or cruelly.

way, Clottes says, "the idea of killing one's fellow creature with a weapon was there 15,000 years ago."

The people who painted Cosquer Cave left us hints of what was important to them. And they left us images of their own hands. Perhaps those images, some of which appear to have missing fingers, were some sort of sign language. What are those hands trying to say? We'll probably never know. They've left us to wonder.

✓ Reading Check

1. Explain how air got into the underwater cave that Cosquer discovered. Why did Cosquer think that someone else had found his secret cave? What did he find when he investigated further?

2. What were some of the ways the researchers decided that the paintings must be very old? In what two time periods had people worked in the cave?

3. How did the painters get into the cave? How was this possible?

4. Why do scientists think prehistoric people did not use the cave as a home? What does Clottes think the paintings were made for?

5. The author says that the cave paintings show us both how things have changed and how things have stayed the same. What are some things that are different? What things are the same?

MEET THE *Writer*

Dave Getz is the author of a number of popular nonfiction books for young people, including *Frozen Man, Floating Home, Life on Mars,* and *Frozen Girl.* When he's not writing, he works with science teachers in the New York City public school system.

VISUAL ART •

HISTORY •

Sometimes it seems like all the major discoveries about prehistoric times have already been made. Such thoughts did not stop three old friends from hiking around southeast France, where many caves used by prehistoric people have been found. In her award-winning book *Painters of the Caves*, Patricia Lauber tells the story of an important cave art discovery and offers some ideas about why Ice Age people created their cave paintings.

What the Art May Tell
from *Painters of the Caves*

by PATRICIA LAUBER

Cave paintings were not a way of decorating shelters, for people seldom lived deep within caves. Nor were the paintings done for fun. Dark, damp, and slippery, the caves were not pleasant places to work. Some pictures were painted in nooks and crannies that were hard to squeeze into. Ceilings and other high places required ladders or <u>scaffolds</u>. Art must have played an important part in the lives of modern humans and had meaning for them.

scaffolds (skaf′əldz): raised platforms or frameworks to support people working high on a wall or a building.

What did it mean?

Because the art shows mostly animals, some people have thought that the paintings were hunting magic. There may be some truth in that idea, but it cannot be the whole story. It does not, for example, explain why there are so few reindeer and birds, both of which were important foods. One cave has more horses than any other

You Need to Know...

In December 1994, three friends—two men and a woman—went cave exploring in limestone hills near Avignon, in southeast France. They followed an ancient mule path up a cliff and arrived at a narrow ledge, where they could feel air coming out of a pile of rocks—a sure sign of a cave. Removing some rocks, they squeezed inside the opening and found an enormous cave filled with more than 300 paintings of animals that lived some 32,000 years ago, in the late Stone Age, or Pleistocene era. The cave, named Chauvet (after Jean-Marie Chauvet, one of the three explorers), proved to be one of the biggest, best, and oldest sources of prehistoric art—art that had been hidden from human eyes for thousands of years. Patricia Lauber's book *Painters of the Cave* tells the story of the Chauvet cave.

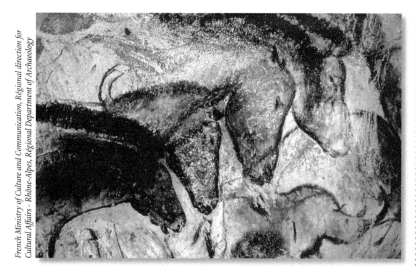

French Ministry of Culture and Communication, Régional direction for Cultural Affairs - Rhône-Alpes, Régional Department of Archaeology

▲ Detail from Chauvet cave painting. The most common images in the cave are stenciled human handprints and drawings of animals—especially bison, horses, cattle, goats, and mammoths. ❓ **Why do you think cave people painted mainly animals?**

animal: yet bones at the nearby campsite show that the people ate mostly reindeer. At another cave, the paintings show horses and mammoths; again, bones tell of reindeer. Also, hunting magic does not explain rhinos and lions, which were not food.

Another idea had to do with beliefs. The moderns[1] almost certainly believed in powerful spirits. Actions of these spirits would explain many mysterious things: thunder and lightning, the coming of spring, good or poor hunting, the rising and setting of the sun.

There are tribes today with such beliefs. They have an important member called a shaman. A shaman is a person with spiritual powers who serves as healer, priest, and, most important, a link between this world and the spirit world. Shamans reach the spirit world when they are in a trance,[2] and they see spirits in animal form.

Perhaps the cave animals stand for spirits being asked

spiritual (spir′i•chōō•əl): relating to the spirit or soul; supernatural.

---

1. **moderns:** The "moderns" are the painters of the cave at Chauvet: the Cro-Magnons, the first *homo sapiens sapiens* ("very wise people"). They were modern humans, like us.
2. **trance:** a dreamlike, semiconscious, or hypnotic state.

appealed (ə·pēld′): made a plea to; requested something of.

for help. Perhaps the spirits represented by horses and bison were the ones shamans most often appealed to.

Some scientists think that shamans may have done some of the paintings while in a trance. They think, too, that shamans are shown in cave art—they are the figures that seem to be part animal, part human, or a human wearing an animal mask and skin.

A third idea is that the painted caves were places where ceremonies were held, where young people were accepted as adults.

To keep memories alive, people must pass them down.

Still a fourth idea is that the cave paintings were aids to memory. People who cannot read and write—who cannot look something up in a book—must depend on memory. The history of the group, its beliefs and myths, its rules, its hunting methods and places—everything is stored in memory. To keep memories alive, people must pass them down.

SIDELIGHT

"Prehistoric paintings don't have to be masterpieces to be moving; the mystery's the thing. Two hours southeast of Lascaux, a cave called Pech-Merle is open to the public, and it contains, among other things, a very nice pair of ponies. More striking than the animals themselves, however, are the half-dozen hands that surround them—negative handprints of the artists, outlined in black. What were they trying to say with those? What were Cro-Magnon painters ever trying to say?

Maybe they were reaching through the cave wall to the spirit world beyond. But today, looking at the Pech-Merle handprints, one gets the spooky sense of people reaching out as they fall away into the chasm of time. One hears their voices calling, but can't make out the words."

—from "Virtually Cro-Magnon"
    by Robert Kunzig
    from *Discover*, November 1999 (Vol. 20, Issue 11)

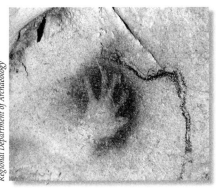

French Ministry of Culture and Communication, Régional direction for Cultural Affairs - Rhône-Alpes, Régional Department of Archaeology

Cave paintings may tell a story or remind the viewer of a story. Perhaps this is how young people learned about their history. Imagine you are led into a cave. Darkness swallows you. Every sense in your body is alert. The shaman starts to speak. Suddenly there is light. Adults have arrived with torches. In the flickering light, animals on the walls seem to move. You are sent on alone in the dark, crawling through narrow passageways, wading through water, stumbling over blocks of stone. Suddenly you round a corner and a moving bear appears on a wall, lighted by a lamp on the cave floor. The shaman's voice follows you, telling of the time when . . .

What you hear will make an impression on you. And each time you look at a painting, you will hear the shaman's voice again.

Today's scientists think there is probably some truth in all of these ideas. But we may never know the whole truth. Cave paintings and signs hold messages that were not addressed to us, and the time of great cave paintings came to an end before people had learned to record their beliefs in writing.

Life changed at the end of the Ice Age[3] when a warm period began, the one in which we still live. The mile-high sheets of ice and the mountain glaciers melted and shrank. Over the next few thousand years, some animals, such as the mammoths, died out. Trees and forests came back and spread north. Animals moved with the plants.

Daily life became harder than it had been during the Ice Age. Hunting large game on open grasslands had been much easier than hunting deer and boars in the woods. Ways of life changed. Around this time another group of

The Picasso Connection

The great twentieth-century artist Pablo Picasso once visited the famous Lascaux caves in France to see the treasury of prehistoric paintings. Humbled by what he saw, he commented, "We have invented nothing." One of the greatest developments in art in the twentieth century was the movement toward making art abstract—showing things in their basic underlying geometric or organic forms, instead of showing them realistically. Ice Age painters were creating "abstract art" tens of thousands of years ago. Picasso realized that these unknown cave painters, armed with only primitive tools and limited colors (they used only red, yellow, black, and brown), were truly "modern" artists.

impression (im·presh′ən): impact; effect; feeling.

glaciers: (glā′shərz) huge masses of ice that flow very slowly down a mountain or over land.

---

3. **Ice Age:** the most recent glacial period, which occurred during the Pleistocene epoch, from two million to 11,000 years ago.

modern humans to the south and east took a different kind of big step forward. They discovered how to raise crops and herd animals. With this discovery people could settle in one place. First towns and then cities grew. People discovered metal. They invented writing.

The art of the Stone Age was forgotten, lying hidden in caves, where rockfalls often blocked the entrances. It was only in the 1860s that the world began to learn that great artists had worked in Europe thousands of years ago.

Much has been learned since then, and much remains to be discovered. . . .

✓ Reading Check

1. The author says that cave paintings were not done for decoration or for fun. What reasons does she give to support this claim?

2. What four ideas does the author present to explain why the cave art may have been created?

3. What is a shaman? What would a shaman's role have been in cave society?

4. Why don't we know for certain what the cave paintings mean?

5. What happened at the end of the Ice Age to bring an end to the era of cave paintings?

MEET THE *Writer*

Patricia Lauber (1924–   ) has written more than a hundred books for young people, on subjects ranging from earthworms to hurricanes—and just about everything in between. When Lauber is not writing, she enjoys hiking, dancing, reading, listening to music, seeing plays, and talking. To Lauber, one of the best things about being a writer is that practically everything she does—even the fun stuff—can be considered "research" for her work.

There's an old saying that "dead men tell no tales." Yet, some ancient bodies found in certain wetland areas called bogs definitely do have tales to tell, and we're only just beginning to understand them.

A Bundle of Bog Bodies

from *Bodies from the Bog*

by JAMES M. DEEM

The Grauballe Man[1] was not the first bog body ever discovered. In fact, the earliest written reports of such discoveries come from the 1600s. When these bodies turned up, they were usually reburied, sometimes in cemeteries, sometimes right where they were found. Some bodies were dried and <u>ground</u> into "mummy pow-

ground (grŏund): crushed into a fine powder.

der" and sold as medicine. A few bodies, or parts of them, were taken home by their discoverers as additions to their own "antique" collections. At least one was sold at an auction in London. Because of the way they were treated, almost all of the bodies discovered up to the late 1800s no longer exist.

By then, scientists began to take an interest in bog bodies. They studied them and their clothing; guesses were made about the reasons for their deaths. A few were put on display in

> ## You Need to Know...
>
> Bogs are wetlands. At first sight, they seem to be made of solid ground, but underneath they are almost completely water. Peat moss—also known as sphagnum moss—grows at the upper level of a bog. Underneath, at a deeper level, is peat—an important source of heat and fuel in many parts of the world. Bogs are drained by peat diggers so that they can get at the peat, cutting it into chunks and drying it so that it can be processed.
>
> Most bog discoveries have been made in areas of northern Europe. Over the centuries, peat diggers have found everything from tools and swords to bowls and even jewelry in bogs. They've also found the bodies of men, women, and children. Many of these discoveries give us important information about early northern Europeans. Until the last century, however, these bodies were just objects of curiosity, not important archaeological finds.

---

1. **Grauballe Man** (grä•bôl′ə): This famous bog body was found in Grauballe, Denmark in 1952. (See the photograph on page 31.)

For Peat's Sake

Why are bog bodies so well-preserved? Bog water is the answer. Most bacteria and other microorganisms that cause flesh to decompose need oxygen in order to live, and they just don't get enough of it in the motionless, low-oxygen waters of a bog. Even bacteria that don't need much oxygen can't survive the second ingredient in bog water: acid. The plants in a bog release an acidic substance that makes it impossible for bacteria to grow. Finally, there's the great "secret ingredient" in bogs—sphagnum moss, also called peat moss. This moss contains a chemical called tannin, which is the same chemical used to tan hides for leather. It turns out that tannin is a great preservative—it mummifies flesh into a leathery consistency.

mortally (môrt′l·ē): fatally; causing death.

museums, generally as curiosities.[2] A German scientist named Alfred Dieck even tried to compile a list of all the bog bodies ever found. After fifty years of work, he was able to record about 1,850 cases. Unfortunately, many of these are no more than "paper" bog bodies—that is, bodies that were mentioned in newspaper articles and other written accounts. Because these bodies were "discovered" long ago and never saved, they may never have really existed. That may explain why many paper bog bodies are much more dramatic than the bodies that have been found and studied. For example, one paper account reported that the body of a spear-holding female warrior, killed by arrows, had been found in Germany in 1906. Near her were the bodies of six men, all shot by arrows and slashed with swords. Scientists doubt that such a startling discovery was ever made.

A few bodies, or parts of them, were taken home by their discoverers as additions to their own "antique" collections.

Most scientists were much more interested in real, not paper, bog bodies. In the six years before the Grauballe Man was discovered, a series of bog bodies were found. This time, however, archaeologists and other scientists were ready to study the finds.

In 1946, the skeleton of a thirty-five- to forty-year-old man was found in the Porsmose Bog near Naestved, Denmark. He had been killed by arrows in about 3500 B.C. One arrowhead pierced his nose and mouth, but this shot did not kill him. Instead, he was mortally wounded by an arrow that went through his breastbone into his aorta.[3]

Also in 1946, a 2,500-year-old bog body was found in Borremose, Denmark. The next year, another was

---

2. **curiosities:** items arousing interest for their strangeness.
3. **aorta** (ā·ôr′tə): the large vessel that carries blood out of the heart to all the rest of the body except the lungs.

uncovered in the same bog. And in 1948 a third body was discovered there. The first two showed signs of a violent death. Because they were found over a half-mile area, scientists doubted that their deaths were related. When the local museum curator[4] sent the third body to the National Museum in Copenhagen, he included a note that read, "I have great pleasure in sending you the <u>customary</u> annual bog body."

customary (kus′tə•mer′ē): usual.

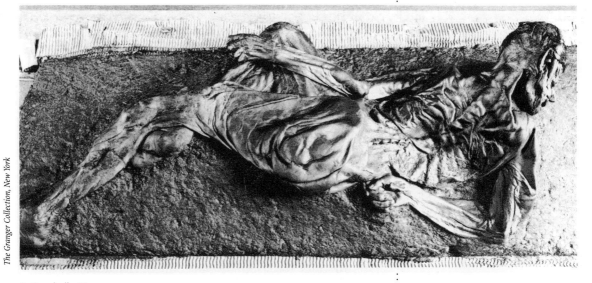

The Granger Collection, New York

▲ Grauballe Man.

In May 1948, a <u>grisly</u> discovery was made near Osterby, Germany. Two peat cutters uncovered a human head wrapped in a deerskin cape. Although the men looked for the rest of the body, they could not find it. Scientists concluded that the Osterby Head had been <u>deposited</u> in the bog by itself and had belonged to a man about fifty or sixty years old. Only a small amount of skin remained on the skull, but what intrigued the scientists was his hairstyle: the Osterby Head displayed a Swabian knot, a figure-eight twist held without any fasteners. The Swabians were a group of German tribes of 2,000 years ago who wore their hair in such a fashion.

grisly (griz′lē): horrifying; frightening.

deposited (dē•päz′it•id): put into.

---

4. curator (kyoo•rāt′ər): person in charge of a museum.

The Granger Collection, New York

▲ Tollund Man. This remarkable bog body of a thirty- to forty-year-old man is probably the best preserved of all the bog bodies. ❷ **What theories might explain why so many of the bog bodies show signs of violent death?**

In 1950, about eleven miles from Grauballe, a bog body that is still considered the best preserved was unearthed. Called Tollund Man for the bog in which he was found, he was so fresh-looking that peat cutters called the police; they were certain they had stumbled across a murder victim. It turned out that he had been lying in the bog about 2,000 years. And although he looked as peaceful and calm as if he were sleeping, a plaited[5] cord around his neck showed that he had probably been hanged.

In 1951, Dutch peat cutters discovered the body of the Zweeloo Woman. Her "body" consisted of a skeleton, along with skin and intestines. Her skeleton revealed a rare condition: the bones from her elbows to her wrists and from her knees to her ankles were very short. Her arms and legs would have looked unusual; she may have had difficulty walking. The contents of her intestines showed that she had eaten a gruel[6] made from millet[7] and a few blackberries shortly before she died.

And in May 1952, about a month after the Grauballe Man was found, the bodies of a man and a fourteen-year-old girl were found in a bog near Schleswig, Germany. Scientists don't know if their bodies were deposited in the peat at the same time, but the man's body was pegged down with eight stakes, and the girl had been blindfolded with a woolen headband and a large stone had been placed beside her. Scientists could not find any signs of violence on the girl's body, but they believed that the man may have been strangled by a thin hazel rod, which had been wound around his neck.

---

5. **plaited** (plāt′id): braided.
6. **gruel** (grōō′əl): cooked mixture of water and grain.
7. **millet:** a kind of grain used for cereal.

No matter how these people died, their bodies would have decayed and never been seen again once they were buried, except that something amazing happened in their cold watery bog graves, something that allowed them to tell the stories of their deaths.

Michael Holford

◀ Lindow Man. This bog body was found in 1984 near Cheshire, England. Like many other bog bodies, this one shows evidence of possible murder.

You Think *That's* Old . . .

All bog bodies are ancient, but some bog bodies are more ancient than others. The most "recent" bog bodies go back to the Middle Ages or so, but the oldest bog bodies go all the way back to the Neolithic ("New Stone") Age, from about 4500–2000 B.C. The next-oldest bodies are from the Bronze Age, about 2000–800 B.C. Bodies from the Iron Age (about 800–1 B.C.) and Roman period (about A.D 1–400) are among the most famous: Grauballe Man, Lindow Man, and Tollund Man are all from these periods. These famous bog bodies are probably the remains of men from the "barbarian" northern tribes known to the ancient Romans, whose historians wrote about the human sacrifices and strange rituals of these early Germans and Danes.

1. The author says that bog bodies were discovered as long ago as the 1600s, but the only ones existing today are those found after the late 1800s. What happened to the earlier bog bodies?

2. According to the author, what is a "paper" bog body?

3. How did the man found in Osterby, Germany, wear his hair? What did this hairstyle reveal to scientists?

4. What did the cord around the neck of Tollund Man tell scientists about his death?

5. What was unusual about the body of Zweeloo Woman? What did scientists conclude from this?

MEET THE *Writer*

James M. Deem says that he became a writer in the fifth grade after discovering some strange tracks in the snow. That night he opened a notebook, wrote "The Strange Tracks Mystery" at the top, and began his writing career. Since then he has written both fiction and nonfiction, choosing to write about nonfiction subjects that fascinated him as a child, such as ghosts, UFOs, treasures, and mummies. His regular job is teaching reading and study skills to underprepared college students.

Cross-Curricular ACTIVITIES

■ ART/HISTORY

Caving In to Art Cave people painted images of the world they knew, especially animals. Their images were simple and abstract, but graceful and lively. They used a limited number of colors: black, red, brown, and yellow. Make your own cave art mural of images from your own world. Work on a roll of brown craft paper using paints, pastels, or crayons in "earth" colors. Try to make your images look like ancient cave paintings.

■ MUSIC/DANCE/DRAMA

Performing an Ancient Story Believe it or not, the story of Lucy, the ancient hominid (see page 2) has been made into a ballet. Shirl Jae Atwell, a composer and amateur scientist, and choreographer Alun Jones worked together to create a ballet, *Lucy,* which imaginatively recreates the life of this early human.

   From the readings on prehistory in this chapter, or some additional research, find another story from prehistory that you think would make a good performance piece. Work with a partner or small group to develop either a drama or a music/dance piece that tells this story. Perform your work for the class.

■ HEALTH/SCIENCE

They Were What They Ate Some scientists today think that prehistoric hunter-gatherers, like the Cro-Magnons, actually ate rather well. In fact, they argue, a hunter-gatherer diet is actually the healthiest diet for a human being. What exactly did early hunter-gatherers eat? How did their diet affect their health? What changes took place in the human diet once agriculture got started? Research the answers to these questions with a partner or small group, and report your findings to the class. (You might even want to make a "hunter-gatherer menu" to share with classmates!)

■ SCIENCE/SPEECH

Start Cloning Around One reason some scientists are excited about the discovery of the Siberian woolly mammoth (see page 3) is that they think it might be possible to eventually clone the mammoth. Would it actually be possible to clone an extinct creature? Would it be *wise* to try cloning such a creature? With a partner, research more about the Siberian mammoth study, as well as current scientific views of cloning. With one of you taking a "pro" position and the other taking a "con" position, hold a debate about the scientific possibilities of successfully cloning a mammoth. Be sure to address whether or not you think it would be wise to do so. What could we learn? What could go wrong?

■ LANGUAGE ARTS/ART

Reading the Past Imagine that an archaeologist one thousand years in the future finds the remains of your backpack, locker, or even your room. From the archaeologist's point of view, write a brief report of the findings. What would most puzzle the archaeologist? What inferences would he or she make about your way of life and what you valued? Before you begin, make a list of the most important objects your archaeologist would find. You may want to draw these things and use the pictures to accompany your report.

READ ON: FOR INDEPENDENT READING

■ NONFICTION

Eyewitness: Early Humans by Nick Merriman (Dorling Kindersley, 2000), full of photographs and illustrations, is a visual reference book for anyone wanting to actually *see* the difference between an *Australopithecus boisei* and a *Homo habilis*.

The Mystery of the Mammoth Bones and How It Was Solved by James Cross Giblin (HarperCollins, 1999) tells the story of America's first paleontologist, Charles Willson Peale, who in 1801 excavated the skeletons of two mammoths.

Painters of the Caves by Patricia Lauber (National Geographic Society, Washington DC, 1998) tells the story behind the discovery of the famous Chauvet cave in France and the treasure-trove of prehistoric art uncovered there.

Skara Brae: The Story of a Prehistoric Village by Olivier Dunrea (Holiday, 1986) gives a detailed portrait of life in the Neolithic "village of hilly dunes": a 4,000-year-old archaeological site on the Orkney Islands.

The Stone Age News, edited by Fiona Macdonald (Candlewick Press, 1998). The topics in this "newspaper" weren't taken out of today's headlines, but they're still newsworthy—if you want to know more about what life was like in prehistoric times. In this humorous account of Stone Age life, learn about the ten possible uses for a mammoth, keep up with "new" farming methods, and learn a few tips about how those cave paintings can add a special touch to your dwelling.

■ FICTION

A Bone from a Dry Sea by Peter Dickinson (Laureleaf, 1995). Li is an early female hominid whose intelligence is far beyond that of the rest of her tribe. Vinny is a modern-day girl accompanying her father and a team of archaeologists as they excavate the site in Africa where Li and her people once flourished. In alternating chapters, this novel explores strange parallels in the lives of these two characters separated by thousands of years.

The Boy of the Painted Cave by Justin Denzel (Philomel Books, 1988). Fourteen-year-old Tao, an orphaned Cro-Magnon boy with a twisted foot, yearns to be a cave painter, but orphans are forbidden to become image makers. See how Tao follows his dreams in this book and its sequel, ***Return to the Painted Cave***.

The Magic Amulet by William Steel (Harcourt, 1979) tells the story of Tragg, a boy in prehistoric times who tries to cope with rejection and survival when his family clan abandons him because his wounded leg slows their hunting and gathering.

Maroo of the Winter Caves by Ann Turnbull (Clarion, 1984). In what is now the south of France, Maroo, a teenage girl, must save her family from the onslaught of an icy winter during Europe's last Ice Age.

Warrior Scarlet by Rosemary Sutcliff (Oxford, 1958) explores the world of prehistoric Britain as a boy named Drem struggles to find a place for himself in his tribe. Drem is determined to become a warrior so that he can wear the scarlet cloak signifying manhood in his tribe. Drem has only one good arm, though, and it seems impossible that he will ever achieve his goals.

CHAPTER 2

Between Two Rivers
Ancient Mesopotamia   5000 B.C.–500 B.C.

Crescent and Cradle

Ancient Mesopotamia, home to the world's first known human civilizations, is often called the "Cradle of Civilization." Located in the heart of what is now Iraq, Mesopotamia was about the same size as Maine. Beginning about 5000 B.C., many civilizations, including those of the Sumerians, the Akkadians, the Assyrians, and the Babylonians, rose and fell in this region.

Mesopotamia is in an area that is sometimes called the "Fertile Crescent." The term was coined by American archaeologist James Breasted in 1916. He noticed that the piece of land extending along the valley of the Euphrates and Tigris rivers, west of the Mediterranean, was in the shape of a crescent moon.

Erich Lessing/Art Resource, NY

▲ Mesopotamian winged human-headed bull.

Inventions That Rocked the Cradle of Civilization

The world's first cities were probably located in southern Mesopotamia in an area known as Sumer. The Sumerians may have contributed many other "firsts" to the world, including

- the invention of the wheel
- the first system of writing
- the twelve-month calendar
- the development of bronze and iron
- the first irrigation system

The Sumerians may also have been the first people to develop office supplies. Their "stationery" was clay tablets, and the Sumerians "filed" these tablets in baskets, organized by content and neatly labeled.

The British Museum

INVESTIGATE: What other "firsts" have the ancient Mesopotamians been credited with inventing?

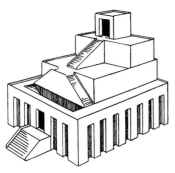

▲ Sumerian ziggurat.

The World's First Skyscrapers?

The largest building in a Sumerian city was a huge "temple tower" called a ziggurat (zig′ōō·rat′). Ziggurats were similar in shape to pyramids, but they were flat-topped and stepped, like a six- or seven-layer wedding cake. Some ziggurats were as tall as a seven-story building, with a base as big as two football fields! Ziggurats were probably decorated with colorful glazed tiles, and each level may have been painted in a different color. The topmost part of the ziggurat was the sacred dwelling place of the city-state's patron god or goddess. Only priests, the most powerful members of Sumerian society, could enter this sacred place.

The word *ziggurat* translates roughly as "hill of heaven" or "god's mountain." With their great skyward reach, ziggurats were thought to link heaven and earth.

Built on Mud

Ziggurats may have had a lofty purpose, but they were made of a lowly material: river mud. In the river delta region of the Tigris and Euphrates, there was little stone and almost no timber, so Sumerians used mud to make bricks for their buildings. The same river mud was used to make pottery and the clay tablets on which the Sumerians wrote. In a way, you could say that ancient Mesopotamian civilization was built on mud.

It's a Wonder . . . or Is It?

One of the Seven Wonders of the ancient world—the Hanging Gardens of Babylon—was thought to be in ancient Mesopotamia. These amazing, lush gardens were supposedly built at the palace of Nebuchadnezzar II (604–562 B.C.). A Greek historian in the first century A.D. described the gardens as a series of high-rise terraces planted with tropical plants and trees and irrigated by water pumped from the Euphrates River. Strangely enough, clay tablets from the time of Nebuchadnezzar do not mention the gardens. In fact, the Greek historian who wrote about them never actually saw them with his own eyes; he was just reporting what he had heard. (An earlier Greek historian who had actually visited Babylon never mentioned the Hanging Gardens.) Were the gardens only a myth? We may never know for certain.

You may have heard the expression "an eye for an eye" used to describe a particular kind of harsh justice in which the punishment fits the crime. In this excerpt from Elaine Landau's book *The Babylonians,* you'll learn where that ages-old expression comes from as you read about the legacy of one of the ancient world's greatest rulers: King Hammurabi.

Hammurabi's Babylonia

from *The Babylonians*

by ELAINE LANDAU

While Hammurabi remained on the throne, Babylonia thrived. Babylonian scientists made important strides in astronomy. Mathematicians achieved advances in algebra and geometry and devised tables to quickly calculate the square and cube roots of numbers. Babylonian writers composed epics and poetry, while sculptors created statues and scenes in stone and clay depicting the Babylonian way of life.

Agriculture and trade were strong in the area as well. Hammurabi maintained the region's complex irrigation systems, ensuring that the farmlands stayed fertile. With the ample crops produced, there was more than enough food. The excess was usually stored for later use or traded for the raw materials that the Babylonians needed.

Although the region had long-established trade routes, trade flourished

thrived (thrīvd): grew, flourished, or prospered.

You Need to Know...

Around 1792 B.C., a strong ruler named Hammurabi (hä'mōō•rä'bē) came to power and reigned over the first Babylonian empire. During Hammurabi's time, the arts, sciences, and commerce of Babylon flourished. Today, though, Hammurabi is mostly remembered for developing his famous collection of laws, often called the "code of Hammurabi."

Hammurabi's list of 282 laws dealt with almost every part of daily life, including marriage, divorce, business contracts, theft, property damage, wages, and trade. The laws of Hammurabi set fines and punishments for crimes. There were laws aimed at helping victims of crime and natural disasters. (Flooding was common in the Tigris-Euphrates region.) Ultimately, Hammurabi's laws helped life run smoothly as ancient communities grew larger and human relationships became more complex.

Gianni Dagli Orti/CORBIS

▲ This stone sculpture is probably a portrait of Hammurabi, the law-giving king of Babylonia.

artisans (ärt′ə•zənz): persons trained to work at a trade requiring skill with the hands.

during this period. Located on the banks of the Euphrates River, Babylonia's capital city of Babylon became an important trading center. Babylonian traders regularly traveled west to Syria and other lands as well as south to regions along the Persian Gulf. They traded grain and woven cloth for wood with which to build furniture and ships. The traders also returned from their journeys with gold, silver, precious gems, and livestock.

The profitable trade market helped Babylonia's economy grow and prosper. A wide assortment of craftspeople did quite well there. Metalworkers used imported copper, iron, and tin to construct farm equipment, building parts, and weapons for war. Since there were few trees in the region, Babylonian carpenters relied on the wood brought in by traders to build a broad range of items. Other Babylonian craftspeople included leather workers who made shoes, belts, and water bags, and basket weavers who produced containers, mats, bedding, and even small boats. Babylonian jewelers designed beautiful necklaces, bracelets, earrings, and decorative daggers, while other artisans created magnificent wall murals and a variety of decorative items.

Elaborate ornaments were essential to enhance the spectacular temples and palaces existing in Hammurabi's Babylonia. Kings, high priests, wealthy upper-class families, and some well-placed government officials had splendid homes and wore the finest garments. But, of course, not everyone lived in luxury—the various craftsworkers, tradespeople, clerks, farmers, and merchants lived considerably less lavishly. Their more modest homes stood along the narrow twisting streets of Babylon and other Babylonian cities. These houses usually consisted of several rooms built around an open courtyard.

Slaves were on the lowest rung of Babylonian society. But Babylonian slaves did enjoy some rights. Once their duties for their masters were completed, they were permitted to work elsewhere and keep their wages. Slaves were also allowed to own property and enter into business agreements. If they were able to save enough money, they could even buy their freedom.

Babylonian women also had more rights and freedoms than females in other ancient societies. While their fathers still usually picked their husbands, married Babylonian women remained somewhat independent. They were permitted to have their own property and money.

In many ways Hammurabi strove to make Babylonian society just.

In many ways Hammurabi strove to make Babylonian society just. Besides uniting Mesopotamia during his reign, Hammurabi is best known for the legal code he devised. The ancient ruler claimed that the gods had instructed him to write these early legal statutes (laws) "to make justice appear in the land," and so that "the strong may not oppress the weak."

Hammurabi's detailed code covered a broad range of situations. The complete legal code consisted of about 280 sections and dealt with such issues as trade disputes, wages for herdsmen and farm laborers, penalties for destroying or stealing property, and rates for renting a boat, wagon, or farm animal for a specific time. There also were portions covering marriage, divorce, adoption, inheritance, and assault. Still other sections delved into penalties for unsatisfactory professional services, and the treatment and sale of slaves.

The following are some examples from Hammurabi's code of justice:

- A builder who sells a poorly constructed house that collapses and kills its owner may be put to death. If the owner's son rather than the owner is killed in the collapse, the builder's son may be put to death.
- A surgeon who operates on a gentleman (a member of the wealthy upper class) and saves the patient's life will be paid ten shekels (coins) of silver for that service. If the patient is a commoner, the surgeon will be given five shekels. If the patient is a slave, the surgeon can

code (kōd): a body of laws, principles, or rules.

Death Pits

In early Mesopotamia, when rulers died, their servants and slaves were buried alongside them. Excavations have unearthed such "pits of death." Dressed in fine burial clothes, the servants and slaves were probably given poison to drink and then buried next to their masters.

Signed, Sealed, and Delivered

Legal agreements in ancient Mesopotamia were written on clay tablets. Still, like legal documents of today, they often had to be signed by witnesses. These "signatures" were often made by cylinder seals: small, spool-shaped stones with designs carved into them. When it was rolled across a wet clay tablet, a cylinder seal left an image that was as unique as a modern individual's signature.

Important "letters" were written on clay tablets that, believe it or not, were often enclosed in "envelopes" also made of clay. The name and address of the recipient were written on the outside of the envelope, which was simply sealed with more wet clay. The lucky recipient cracked open the envelope to read the letter inside.

expect to receive two shekels of silver. However, if the doctor makes a surgical error resulting in the patient's death, the surgeon's hand may be cut off.

- Someone who steals another person's slave or hides a runaway slave intending to keep that individual as his own slave may be put to death.
- If someone helping to put out a fire loots (steals something from the premises), that individual may be thrown into the fire.
- A man who lies while serving as a witness in a court case involving the death penalty may also be put to death. If a witness lies while testifying in a property dispute, that individual may have to pay the same costs as the person who loses the case.
- If, due to crop failure resulting from either a flood or drought, someone is unable to pay interest on debt, he may be excused from the interest payment that year.
- If a son strikes his father, his hand may be cut off.
- If a person destroys a gentleman's eye, his eye may be destroyed in turn. If he breaks a gentleman's bone, the same bone in his body may be broken. However, if a commoner's eye is destroyed or his bone broken, the offender may only be required to pay a fine. If a slave's eye is destroyed or his bone broken, the guilty person must pay half the slave's sale price to his owner.
- If a slave strikes a free man, his ear may be cut off.
- If two equals engage in a fair fight and one is injured, the person causing the injury may have to pay for the other's medical treatment. However, he cannot be punished further for having caused the injury.
- If an ox unexpectedly gouges a man, causing his death, no claim may be made against the animal's owner. However, the owner of an animal that habitually gouges must restrain his animal's movement or remove or cap the ox's horns. If the owner fails to take these precautions and the animal gouges someone, the owner must pay a substantial fine.
- If a wife's poor behavior publicly disgraces her husband, he can be rid of her with no penalty to himself.

However, he must first prove his claim in court. Once his claim is recognized, he can either divorce her or marry another woman, reducing the status of his first wife to that of household slave girl.

- If a woman is disgraced by her husband, she can also go to court. If her <u>accusations</u> are adequately proven, she can leave her husband and take her dowry (the property or sum of money a wife brings to her husband in marriage) with her.
- A husband cannot divorce a sickly wife because of her illness. He is required to care for her in their home for the rest of her life. But if the woman wishes to leave on her own accord, she is free to do so and can take her full dowry with her.
- A man can leave property to his wife rather than his son. However, a woman is not allowed to sell property willed to her by her husband. At her death, all she owns goes to her sons.

While Hammurabi's laws covered numerous specific incidents, no legal code could possibly deal with every dispute or problem that might arise. Hammurabi intended that the reasoning behind his <u>prescribed</u> legal penalties would extend to similar situations arising at that time and in the future. The ancient ruler wanted his code to be the law of the land in the broadest sense of the word. He advised all future Babylonian rulers to refer to his regulations in their decision making. He wrote:

To the end of days, forever, may the king who happens to be in the land observe the words of justice which I have inscribed. . . . If that man has the sanction [of the gods] and so is able to

accusations (ak′yo͞o•zā′shənz): charges of wrongdoing.

prescribed (prē•skrībd′): authorized; established.

Gianni Dagli Orti/CORBIS

▲ All sections of Hammurabi's code were carved into tall stones. At the top of this stone marker, Hammurabi stands before Shamash, the god of the sun and justice. ❷ **What message do you think this image conveyed to the ancient Mesopotamians about the code written underneath it?**

give his land justice, let him pay heed to the words which I have written . . . and let that show him the accustomed way, the way to follow, the land's judgments which I have judged and the land's decisions which I have decided.[1]

Some of Hammurabi's laws may seem particularly harsh by present-day standards. Depending on the offense, people might be put to death, lose an eye or limb, have their bones broken, be tortured, or have their children put to death. Yet it's important to view these laws within the framework of the time and place in which they were written. Hammurabi unified legal practices throughout Babylonia. This was an important step toward creating a society in which everyone's rights were recognized to some degree, regardless of class.

---

1. FROM H.W.F. Saggs, *Everyday Life in Babylonia & Assyria* (New York: G. P. Putnam's Sons, 1967), p.146.

✓ Reading Check

1. Did Babylonia prosper or suffer under Hammurabi? Give three details from the text to support your answer.

2. Where was Babylonia's capital city located? Why was its location important?

3. What were some of the rights that Babylonian slaves possessed? In what ways were married Babylonian women given some independence?

4. About how many sections made up Hammurabi's code? If a situation that was not described in the code arose, what did Hammurabi intend be done?

MEET THE *Writer*

Elaine Landau (1948–   ) has written a number of award-winning books on a variety of subjects, from dinosaurs to ancient civilizations. Landau also presents writing workshops for children and young adults.

Right now, as you're reading this page, you are relying on one of the most important inventions in human history—the alphabet. In this chapter from *Alphabetical Order: How the Alphabet Began*, author Tiphaine Samoyault explains the significant contributions the ancient Mesopotamians made to the development of writing—and the invention of the alphabet.

from Writing and Alphabets

from *Alphabetical Order: How the Alphabet Began*

by TIPHAINE SAMOYAULT

Why Did People Begin Writing?

Alphabets didn't just appear. The earliest writing started long before alphabets, when people began to connect meaning with natural or manmade markings. We have found forms of writing from as far back as around 3400 B.C. in Mesopotamia and China.

In almost every civilization, the earliest writing was connected to religion and magic. Priests were always looking for signs from the gods—literally. They looked on tortoise shells or inside animal livers, and they found them! Perhaps a squiggle or circle—anything that looked like a distinctive mark—could be seen as a message from a god, which had to be interpreted. Ultimately, these interesting shapes and patterns or "divinations"[1] may have been the inspiration for developing written language. In

> ### You Need to Know...
> Sumerian writing developed slowly. The first writing was basically a tool for accounting—a way to keep track of business activities. This early form of writing was not based on an alphabet. Instead, it used pictures and symbols.
>
> We are lucky that the Mesopotamians wrote on clay tablets and stone, since thousands of these ancient records have survived to modern times. These enduring records give us a keen insight into the lives and times of this ancient civilization.

literally (lit′ər•əl•ē): based on exactly what is said.

distinctive (di•stiŋk′tiv): clear; marking a difference from others.

inspiration (in′spə•rā′shən): a bright idea or impulse.

---

1. **divinations** (div′ə•nā′shənz): omens or signs.

fact, the name of one early writing system, "hieroglyphics,"[2] means "priest-writing." But writing was quickly put to use for financial life and daily activities as well.

Ideograms[3] and pictograms[4] were some of the earliest writing systems. These systems do not use an alphabet: they use pictures and symbols and represent more complicated ideas by combining signs.

The oldest known writing system is called cuneiform. It was invented by the Sumerians, who lived in Mesopotamia (part of modern-day Iraq) more than 5,000 years ago.

What were the conditions in Mesopotamia that gave its citizens a need for writing? It is helpful to look at the whole picture. Mesopotamia was a civilization rich in certain raw materials. They had plenty of corn, vegetables, meat, leather, and especially clay. But they were almost entirely lacking wood, stone, and metal, which were

2. **hieroglyphics** (hī′ər•ō′glif′iks): pictures or symbols representing words or syllables in ancient written languages.
3. **ideograms** (id′ē•ō•gramz′): two or more pictures or symbols used to represent single things or ideas.
4. **pictograms** (pik′tə•gramz′): pictures or symbols used to represent things or ideas.

  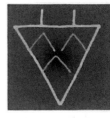

▲ Combining the pictograms that stand for "ox" and "mountain" creates the ideogram that stands for "wild game."

 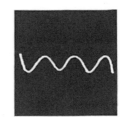 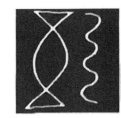

▲ Combining the pictograms that stand for "jug" and "water" creates the ideogram for "fresh."

"Writing and Alphabets," from ALPHABETICAL ORDER: HOW THE ALPHABET BEGAN by Tiphaine Samoyault, translated by Kathryn M. Pulver, copyright © 1996 by Circonflexe. Translation © 1998 by Penguin Books USA Inc. Used by permission of Viking Penguin, an imprint of Penguin Putnam Books for Young Readers, a division of Penguin Putnam Inc.

needed to maintain a successful society. Mesopotamia needed to trade with other cultures, to acquire the things they lacked in exchange for what they had too much of. In order to keep track of what they traded, they started marking symbols for numbers and items in clay tablets, which then hardened. We call the system "cuneiform," meaning "wedge-shaped," because when a stick or reed was pressed into the clay to make the mark, it left a <u>triangular</u> shape.

Cuneiform was not in any particular language. The symbol for an object could be understood by different cultures as whatever their particular word for that object was. From the Sumerians, cuneiform writing spread to Akkadians, Babylonians, and Assyrians, and eventually became the writing system of the entire Middle East.

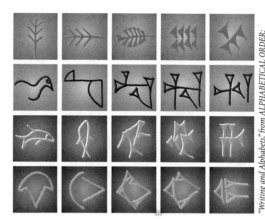

▲ From 3300 to 700 B.C., the cuneiform system evolved from pictograms to abstract signs, as shown here with the changing signs for "barley," "bird," "fish," and "cow."

triangular (trī·aŋ'gyə·lər): shaped like a triangle, a three-sided figure.

SIDELIGHT

"In ancient Mesopotamia, most clay tablets were not fired in a kiln. After being inscribed, they were dried in the sun, which means that once they are excavated at a modern archaeological site, they begin to deteriorate. Those tablets that were fired in a kiln—a privilege usually reserved for important documents, such as those in a library—or were burned in a subsequent fire are stabilized and generally need no further preservation. But those that were not baked in any way must be preserved if they are to survive in the modern world.

As scholars at Yale research their collection, they identify those tablets that need immediate attention. These items are dried in a kiln for three to four days and then fired at high temperatures for several hours. After cooling, the tablets are removed and soaked in water to remove impurities. They are left in ordinary tap water inside a family-sized picnic cooler for up to three weeks for a final cleansing."

—from "The 5,000-Year-Old Recipe: Ancient Tablets Offer a Taste of Everyday Babylonian Life" by Hayes Jackson, from *Humanities* (January/February 1997)

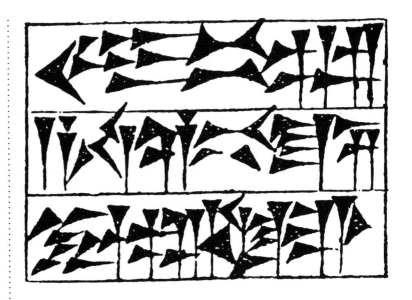

✓ Reading Check

1. What came first, alphabets or writing? Explain.

2. What did priests look for in the lines and shapes on tortoise shells and in animal organs? How might these lines and shapes be related to writing?

3. What was writing first used for?

4. Why did the Mesopotamians need to trade with other cultures? How was trade related to the development of writing?

5. According to the author, what made it possible for the cuneiform system of writing to spread throughout the Middle East?

MEET THE *Writer*

Tiphaine Samoyault (1968–   ) is a professor of literature near Paris, France, where she lives. *Alphabetical Order: How the Alphabet Began,* from which this selection was excerpted, was chosen as a Notable Book by the NCSS (National Council of Social Studies) in 1999.

Famous women from ancient times are few and far between. Who would have guessed, then, that the world's first "non-anonymous" author would be a woman? Read on and meet the most famous ancient woman writer you never heard of.

BIOGRAPHY

LANGUAGE ARTS ●

HISTORY ●

Enheduana of Sumer

from *Outrageous Women of Ancient Times*

by VICKI LEÓN

▲ King Sargon established a great Akkadian empire.

Erich Lessing/Art Resource, NY

You might call Enheduana one of history's first bookworms. Perhaps she brought books to the dinner table. If so, they looked like small clay pillows, not paperbacks. In her day, almost 4,300 years ago, "books" were written on soft clay with a pointed tool called a stylus. It was a big deal, learning to read back then. Enheduana not only read well, she wrote well. In fact, she became the world's first bestselling author as well as the most famous poet from the ancient land of Sumer.

Enheduana, her twin brothers Rimush and Manishtusu, and her father Sargon lived in a spanking-new big palace, surrounded by the city-state of Akkad in Sumer (located about where Baghdad is today). King Sargon, an ambitious boy from a family of Mesopotamian farmers, began his rise to the top as a humble cupbearer for the king of Kish, a nearby city-state. No one knows how he managed to grab the throne for himself, but he did. Soon he expanded his rule over Kish and Akkad and made them important cities of Sumer, a flat and fertile <u>crescent</u> of land between two great

You Need to Know...

Sargon was considered the greatest of all the Akkadian kings. He ruled from 2334 to 2279 B.C. and had twin sons and a daughter, Enheduana (en•hā′dōō•ä′nə). As the daughter of a powerful king, Enheduana learned to write at a time when only a few people—mostly men—had this ability. Perhaps Enheduana was proud of her writings, or perhaps she felt she had the right to include her name because of her status as a high priestess. Whatever the reason, Enheduana was the first person to use her own name in her writings. She thus became the first known author in the entire history of literature.

crescent (kres′ənt): a shape like the moon just before or just after a new moon.

rivers in what is now Iraq. (In Enheduana's day, "countries" as we know them didn't really exist yet—instead, independent cities like Akkad, Kish, and Ur fought to control larger regions of land. Political power and political boundaries changed hands all the time.)

Naturally, Sargon[1] expected Enheduana's kid brothers to follow in his footsteps as kings of Sumer and Akkad one day. Unfortunately, the twins had the yen[2] to be kings, but not the talent.

Enheduana, on the other hand, soon showed that she had talent and drive to spare. When she became a teenager, her dad thought she was ready for grownup responsibility. He appointed her to be the high priestess to Nanna, the important moon-god of Sumer.

To perform her duties as high priestess, Enheduana had to leave her hometown of Akkad and move south to Ur, one of the most <u>sacred</u> cities in Sumer. Ur sat near the Persian Gulf, its houses and buildings clustered around a tall ziggurat, a temple that looked like a pyramid with steps. Each of the ziggurat's seven stories was painted a different color. The top story was painted blue. Enheduana used the room at the very top, nearest the heavens.

Enheduana's people believed in many gods and goddesses. Only through the priestess's hard work would the higher powers smile on the land and keep the crops, animals, and people well and prosperous. Wearing her special cap, carrying a mace,[3] and dressed in a long embroidered gown with rows of ruffles, Enheduana offered prayers and carried out rituals throughout the year. On the altars at the top of the ziggurat, she made animal <u>sacrifices</u>. To please the gods and goddesses, she also burned incense and other perfumed resins,[4] sending the sweet-smelling smoke through the clear blue skies of

sacred (sā′krid): holy.

sacrifices (sak′rə•fīs′iz): something precious, such as animal or human lives, offered to a god.

---

1. **Sargon** (sär′gän): considered the greatest of the Akkadian kings; legend says soon after he was born, he was put in a basket on the Euphrates River and raised by a gardener who found him. As a young man, Sargon overthrew the king and seized power.
2. **yen** (yen): a desire or longing.
3. **mace** (mās): an ornamental staff or scepter.
4. **resins** (rez′ənz): sticky gums given off by certain plants.

Sumer. (Our word "perfume" actually means "through smoke.")

Her most important ritual duty was the annual New Year celebration each spring. (Early religions often celebrated the new year in the spring because people wanted to encourage the growth of crops.) The ceremony retold the story of a sacred marriage between a shepherd named Dumuzi and the moon-goddess Inanna. Inside her blue room high in the ziggurat, Enheduana as the goddess-bride and one of the reigning kings or high priests would reenact the marriage of a goddess and a human each year, to keep the gods happy.

Besides her spiritual duties as high priestess, a position she kept for nearly twenty-five years, Enheduana channeled much of her religious feeling into her writing. She wrote a set of forty-two poems or hymns to the temples of Sumer and Akkad. Although a priestess of the moon-god originally, Enheduana began to identify more with the moon-goddess Inanna. She wrote a great cycle of poetry to her, which was probably sung and performed, called the Exaltation of Inanna. Thanks to her influence, Inanna (later called Ishtar) gradually became the supreme being in the land of Sumer.

Enheduana's poems were very popular in her day and long after. Because she wrote on clay tablets, which were much more durable than paper, archaeologists have found over fifty tablets with the same poem on them. For Enheduana's time, this

David Lees/CORBIS

▲ These statues were placed in temples to serve as permanent worshipers. **?** **How would you describe their appearance, and why do you think the sculptor created the statues to look this way?**

▲ The ziggurat was the most important structure in Mesopotamian cities. The ziggurat at Ur (shown above) is the most preserved of all Mesopotamian ziggurats and has been partially restored.

composing (kəm·pōz′iŋ): creating or producing, usually a musical or literary work.

was like going platinum or making the bestseller list.

Enheduana's writings tell us much about herself, the Sumerian religion, and even politics. For instance, she wrote an exciting account about her father. At one point, the city-states that Sargon had taken united in revolt against him. They besieged[5] the city of Akkad and exiled the goddess Inanna from her temples. Sargon finally broke the siege, beat the rebels, and made them recognize the goddess Inanna as all-powerful.

Enheduana kept on composing poetry and taking care of her religious responsibilities, even after her father died. Her brother Rimush, the older twin, ruled first. Then Manishtusu (named "who is with him?" by the surprised midwife who delivered the babies) took over. Both brothers loved bloodshed; both were killed in turn by palace enemies who hated them. Then a nephew of Enheduana's came into power. In spite of her long experience, popularity, and royal background, Enheduana lost her priestess post. Her nephew kicked her out, possibly exiling her to the desert. Then he installed his own daughter as high priestess.

But Enheduana ended up having the last laugh. And the last word, literally. No one remembers her nasty nephew King Naram-Sin today. Enheduana, however, has become a famous first: she is the very earliest author, male or female, to be known by name. Her poems, written around 2300 B.C., are the first creations anywhere in the world credited to an individual person. A verse from one of them shows her spirit:

The first lady of the throne room
has accepted Enheduana's song.
Inanna loves her again.
The day was good for Enheduana, for she was dressed
  in jewels.

---

5. besieged (bē·sējd′): tried to capture by surrounding and isolating.

She was dressed in womanly beauty.
Like the moon's first rays over the horizon,
how luxuriously she was dressed!
When Nanna, Inanna's father, made his entrance
the palace blessed Inanna's mother Ningal.
From the doorsill of heaven came the word: "Welcome!"

There is a proverb from Enheduana's day, written in a dialect used by women only, called Emesal. It says: "My mouth makes me comparable with men." That proud statement, written by an unknown woman, could have come from the smiling lips of Enheduana herself.

✔ Reading Check

1. What did books look like during the time that Enheduana was writing? How were these books written?

2. Where did Enheduana and her family live? What did her father do?

3. What was Enheduana's job? List three of her duties. How did she lose her job?

4. The author says that Enheduana's poems were so popular that they were like bestsellers today. What evidence does she use to support this claim?

5. Enheduana's writings are hymns of praise, but they also tell us about the times she lived in. Describe one "current event" that Enheduana wrote about.

Ringing in the New Year

The New Year was a very important celebration for the ancient Mesopotamians—but they didn't stand around singing "Auld Lang Syne" and setting off fireworks. The Mesopotamians believed that each New Year the gods decided peoples' fate for the coming year. During the eleven-day New Year's festival, ordinary people, as well as priests and priestesses, offered food and incense to the gods. A sheep was killed in a special ceremony. The people believed that the sheep absorbed the evil of the old year. When the dead sheep was thrown into the river, all the evil floated away with it.

MEET THE *Writer*

Vicki León (1942–   ) is a writer, editor, researcher, and photographer. She has written books for both children and adults. León's interest in historical women has led her to research, rediscover, and write about forgotten women of the past.

LINKING PAST AND PRESENT

We often assume that science as we know it today began with the Greeks and the Romans. As this excerpt from *Greek and Roman Science* suggests, though, there's more to the story. If you look hard enough, you'll see the shadow of those ancient Mesopotamians standing right behind the Romans and Greeks, laying the foundation for mathematics and science in the Western world.

The Patient and Persistent Babylonians

from *Greek and Roman Science*

by DON NARDO

The Babylonians were not nearly as advanced in medicine as the Egyptians. But the scholars of the Tigris-Euphrates region made significant contributions in the areas of math and astronomy. Like the Egyptians, the Babylonians used a simple decimal[1] system for counting, but only for numbers from 1 to 59. For numbers higher than 59 they employed a sexagesimal[2] system—a counting method based on the number 60. Apparently the Babylonians chose 60 because it is easily <u>divisible</u> by 2, 3, 4, and 5. Trying to express numbers using a combined decimal and sexagesimal system was often complicated. For instance,

divisible (də·viz′ə·bəl): capable of being divided.

You Need to Know...

Ancient Mesopotamia was an almost forgotten world until European archaeologists started making startling discoveries when they began excavations in the Middle East. It wasn't even until the 1850s that cuneiform tablets could be translated. Even so, long before modern people knew anything about ancient Mesopotamia, they were unknowingly using Mesopotamian advances and discoveries. We are indebted to the ancient Mesopotamians for numerous inventions, such as the wheel, as well as some basic concepts of math and science.

Whether Mesopotamian scientists were motivated by curiosity, by religion, or by necessity—or all three—we will probably never know. What is certain is that they paved the way for the thousands of years of scientific inquiry that followed.

1. **decimal:** based on the number ten.
2. **sexagesimal** (sek′sə·jes′i·məl).

the number 3,832 was expressed as 1,3,52. Reading from right to left, the second number (3 in this example) occupied an order of magnitude[3] higher than the first and the third an order higher than the second. Thus, the user understood that the 1 stood for 1 x 60^2 (or 3,600), the 3 for 3 x 60 (or 180), and the 52 for 52 single decimal units; and that the three numbers were to be added together (3,600 + 180 + 52 = 3,832).

Nevertheless, it is remarkable that the Babylonians understood and readily used square and cube roots[4] (i.e., 60^2 = 60 x 60 = 3600, and 60^3 = 60 x 60 x 60 = 216,000). Remnants of their sexagesimal system have also survived the ages. We still divide a circle into 360 degrees and count 60 seconds to a minute and 60 minutes to an hour in timekeeping, navigation,[5] and astronomy.[6]

Modern astronomers owe much more to their Babylonian predecessors than the division of the sky into degrees, minutes, and seconds. Babylonian scholars kept regular records of the movements of the heavenly bodies and compiled large archives of observations made over the course of many centuries. These scholars were priests, and they scanned the sky from towers called ziggurats. Unlike their Egyptian counterparts,[7] they carefully watched how the planets moved, noting when these objects came near to one another or to bright stars; and they also observed and recorded the occurrence of "hairy" or "guest" stars, which we know as comets, and of solar and lunar eclipses.

The Babylonian priest-astronomers had a strong influence on the later development of the science of astronomy. They originated the idea of naming the planets after

remnants (rem′nənts): traces; fragments.

predecessors (pred′ə•ses′ərz): ancestors or people who came before.

archives (är′kīvz′): documents or records that are kept as evidence.

---

3. **order of magnitude:** a mathematical term for increasing quantity; for example, in the number 43, the 4 stands for 40, which has a higher magnitude than the 3.
4. **square and cube roots:** mathematical terms in which square refers to a number multiplied by itself once (3 x 3) and cube refers to a number multiplied by itself two times (3 x 3 x 3). Root refers to the opposite calculation, so 3 is the square root of 9, and it is also the cube root of 27.
5. **navigation:** the science of getting ships (or aircraft or spacecraft) from place to place.
6. **astronomy:** the scientific study of stars, planets, and other heavenly bodies.
7. **counterparts:** people or things that closely resemble or correspond to others.

Is There a Doctor in the House?

Ancient Mesopotamians could choose between two types of doctor. The *ashipu* used magical charms and spells to treat illnesses, while the *asu* used mostly herbal remedies to cure their sick patients. The *asu* was also able to set broken bones and perform minor operations. Many Mesopotamians probably used both types of doctor, depending on their illnesses and ability to pay.

deities. For example, they named the brightest planet, often erroneously called the "evening star," after Ishtar, the Babylonian goddess of love and beauty. The tradition survived and is still in use. Following the Babylonian lead, the Greeks named the planet Aphrodite, after their goddess of love and beauty; and later, the Romans adopted many of the Greek gods, including Aphrodite, whom they called Venus—the title the planet has borne ever since.

The Babylonian priest-astronomers had a strong influence on the later development of the science of astronomy.

Through their painstaking astronomical observations, the Babylonian astronomers also determined that as the sun, moon, and planets move through the heavens they always stay within one narrow path. That path later became known as the zodiac. They divided the zodiac

Bettmann/CORBIS

▲ Babylonian priests made careful observations of the stars and other celestial objects, such as comets, or "hairy" stars. **❷ Why do you think the ancient Babylonians kept such detailed records of their heavenly observations?**

into twelve sections, each marked by a constellation that formed a distinct pattern (Cancer the Crab, Scorpio the Scorpion, and so on); and these "signs" of the zodiac are still recognized today. What is more, in the sixth century B.C. a Babylonian scholar named Nabu-rimanni made the earliest known precise calculation of the year's length. His figure of 365 days, 6 hours, 15 minutes, and 41 seconds is only 26 minutes and 55 seconds too long, an amazing feat considering that he used no sophisticated measuring devices. He and his colleagues possessed only <u>rudimentary</u> instruments, such as sundials.

rudimentary (roo′də•men′tər•ē): beginning; elementary.

✓ Reading Check

1. According to the author, which ancient culture was more advanced in medicine? Which culture was more advanced in math and astronomy?

2. What two systems did the Babylonians use for counting?

3. From where did the Babylonians observe the stars and other heavenly bodies? How long did they keep records of their observations?

4. What was the Babylonian name for the planet Venus? How is our name for this planet connected to the Babylonian name for it?

5. Who was the first person to calculate the length of a year most accurately? How accurate were his calculations?

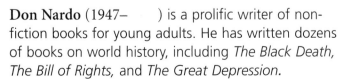

MEET THE *Writer*

Don Nardo (1947–   ) is a prolific writer of non-fiction books for young adults. He has written dozens of books on world history, including *The Black Death, The Bill of Rights,* and *The Great Depression.*

The ancient Mesopotamians may have filled thousands of tablets with lists and business documents, but they also filled a few tablets with a mythic tale that still thrills readers today. The following excerpt from Bernarda Bryson's award-winning book *Gilgamesh: Man's First Story* is a lively retelling of an episode from the world's oldest written tale—an ancient epic of heroism and friendship.

from The Monster Humbaba

from *Gilgamesh: Man's First Story*

by BERNARDA BRYSON

The Granger Collection, New York

▲ *A terra-cotta mask of the monster Humbaba.*
Mesopotamian priests often examined the organs of sacrificed animals in hopes of finding messages from the gods. Perhaps they sometimes imagined monstrous faces like this in the masses of intestines.

Gilgamesh and Enkidu walked toward the mountain of the cedar forest. At a distance of twenty double-hours they sat down beside the path and ate a small amount of food. At a distance of thirty double-hours, they lay down to sleep, covering themselves with their garments. On the following day they walked a distance of fifty double-hours. Within three days' time, they covered a distance that it would have taken ordinary men some fifteen days to cover. They reached the mountain and saw before them a towering and magnificent gate of cedar wood.

"Here," said Gilgamesh, "we must pour meal[1] upon the earth, for that will gain us the goodwill of the gods; it will persuade them to reveal their purpose in our dreams."

They poured meal on the ground and lay down to sleep. After some time Gilgamesh wakened his friend. "Enkidu, I have had a dream; it went like this: We were standing in a deep gorge beside a mountain. Compared to it, we were the size of flies! Before our very eyes the mountain collapsed; it fell in a heap!"

---

1. **meal** (mēl): a coarsely ground grain.

"The meaning of that seems very clear," said Enkidu. "It means that Humbaba is the mountain and that he will fall before us!"

They closed their eyes again and slept. After some time, Gilgamesh again awakened his friend. "I've had another dream, Enkidu. I saw the same mountain this time, and again it fell, but it fell on me. However, as I lay struggling, a beautiful personage appeared. He took me by my feet and dragged me out from under the mountain. Now I wonder what this means? Is it that you will rescue me from the monster, or will someone else come along?"

They pondered a little and went back to sleep. Next Enkidu wakened his brother, Gilgamesh. "Has a cold shower passed over us? Did the lightning strike fires, and was there a rain of ashes?"

"The earth is dry and clean," said Gilgamesh, "you must have dreamed!" But since neither of them could understand the meaning of this dream, they fell asleep again, and soon the day came.

They approached the magnificent gate. "Let's open it, Enkidu! Let's be on our way!"

For a last time, Enkidu tried to persuade his friend to turn back.

But since the King would not listen, it was he who went first and placed his hand against the gate to push it open. Enkidu was thrown backward with such violence that he fell to the earth. He rose to his feet. "Gilgamesh, wait! My hand is <u>paralyzed</u>!"

paralyzed (par′ə•līzd′): unable to move or feel.

▲ Gilgamesh is often portrayed fighting wild animals. Here, he is shown taming a lion. ❷ **What image of the hero does this drawing of an ancient statue convey?**

"Put it on my arm, Enkidu! It will take strength from my arm because I am not afraid."

When the two friends threw their weight against the gate, however, it swung inward.

They walked up the mountainside through the sacred trees. And these became closer and thicker until the sky was blotted out. They could hear the giant heartbeat of Humbaba and smell the smoke from his lungs.

To show his daring, Gilgamesh cut one of the cedar trees. The blows of his axe rang out, and from afar the terrible Humbaba heard the sound.

With a crashing of timbers and a rolling of loose stones, Humbaba came down upon them. His face loomed among the tree tops, creased and grooved like some ancient rock. The breath he breathed withered the boughs of cedar and set small fires everywhere.

Enkidu's fears now vanished and the two heroes stood side by side as the monster advanced. He loomed over them, his arms swinging out like the masts of a ship. He was almost upon them when suddenly the friends stepped apart. The giant demon lurched through the trees, stumbled, and fell flat. He rose to his feet bellowing like a bull and charged upon Enkidu. But the King brought down his axe on the toe of Humbaba so that he whirled about roaring with pain. He grasped Gilgamesh by his flowing hair, swung him round and round as if to hurl him through the treetops, but now Enkidu saw his giant ribs exposed and

---

They could hear the giant heartbeat of Humbaba and smell the smoke from his lungs.

---

he thrust his sword into the monster's side. Liquid fire gushed from the wound and ran in small streams down the mountainside. Gilgamesh fell to the earth and lay still, trying to breathe. But meanwhile Humbaba grasped the horns of Enkidu and began to <u>flail</u> his body against a tree.

flail (flāl): to move or beat wildly about.

Surely the wild man would have died, but now Gilgamesh roused himself. He lanced into the air his long spear with its handle of lapis lazuli[2] and gold. The spear caught Humbaba in the throat and remained there <u>poised</u> and glittering among the fires that had <u>ignited</u> everywhere.

The giant loosened his hold on Enkidu; he cried out. The earth <u>reverberated</u> with the sound, and distant mountains shook.

Gilgamesh felt pity in his heart. He withdrew his sword and put down his axe, while the monster Humbaba crept toward him grovelling and wailing for help. Now Enkidu perceived that the monster drew in a long breath in order to spew forth his last weapon—the searing fire that would consume the King. He leaped on the demon and with many sword thrusts released the fire, so that it bubbled harmlessly among the stones.

Humbaba was dead; the two heroes, black with soot and dirt, were still alive. They hugged each other, they leaped about; and singing and shouting, they descended the mountainside. Gentle rains fell around them and the land was forever free from the curse of the giant Humbaba.

poised (poizd): balanced.
ignited (ig·nīt′id): caught fire.

reverberated (ri·vɥr′bə·rāt′id): echoed back or resounded.

---

2. **lapis lazuli** (lap′is laz′yōō·lī′): a semiprecious stone, usually deep blue in color.

British Museum, London/Bridgeman Art Library/SuperStock

▲ This panel, found in a Sumerian grave, depicts ancient Mesopotamians in battle. The legends of Gilgamesh reflect the warlike realities of this society.

A Gutsy Monster

Humbaba was just one of many strange—and downright ugly—monsters in Mesopotamian mythology. (There were also scorpion-men, bull-men, dragons, and lion-men.) In addition to breathing fire, Humbaba is sometimes described as shooting deadly rays or bolts from his eyes. Gruesome as it sounds, most ancient images of the monster Humbaba show that his face is made from looping animal intestines. (See the picture on page 58.) No one is quite certain why he has this appearance, but the image is probably connected with rituals in which Mesopotamian priests sacrificed animals and "read" their intestines to figure out what the gods wanted or what the future held. Can there be any doubt that fighting Humbaba would take a lot of "guts"?

✓ Reading Check

1. Why does Gilgamesh pour meal upon the earth?

2. What were Gilgamesh's dreams? What did they mean?

3. How is the monster Humbaba described in this story? What aspect of nature do you think he might represent?

4. Why does Gilgamesh withdraw the sword he has used to spear Humbaba's neck? What danger does this create?

MEET THE *Writer*

Bernarda Bryson (1905–   ) is a distinguished writer and illustrator. Her illustrations have appeared in magazines such as *Harper's* and *Scientific American* and in many children's books. Bryson's *Gilgamesh: Man's First Story* won the Book of the Year Award from the American Institute of Graphic Arts in 1967 and was named as a Boston Globe–Horn Book Honor title in 1968.

Modern schools don't bear much resemblance to the harsh and tiresome Mesopotamian classroom. However, in the following conversation between a father and his son, taken from an ancient cuneiform tablet, you may find that some things have *not* changed all that much in the past 4,000 years!

from Education: The Sumerian School

from *The Sumerians: Their History, Culture, and Character*

by SAMUEL NOAH KRAMER

Gianni Dagli Orti/CORBIS

▲ Sumerian clay tablet: tally of goats and sheep (ca. 2350 B.C.).

"Where did you go?"

"I did not go anywhere."

"If you did not go any-where, why do you idle about?[1] Go to school, stand before your 'school-father' (professor), <u>recite</u> your assignment, open your schoolbag, write your tablet, let your 'big brother' write your new tablet for you. After you have finished your assignment and reported to your <u>monitor</u>, come to me, and do not wander about in the street. Come now, do you know what I said?"

"I know, I'll tell it to you."

"Come, now, repeat it to me."

"I'll repeat it to you."

---

1. **idle about:** to dawdle away time.

You Need to Know...

Thanks to extensive archaeological findings, scholars actually know a lot more about education in ancient Mesopotamia than they know about later Greek and Roman schooling. In ancient Mesopotamia, sons of wealthy families went to a school called an *edubba*, or "tablet house." There, they studied science, literature, math, and grammar. Lessons were copied on small clay tablets in wedge-shaped cuneiform writing, which was difficult to master (see "*from* Writing and Alphabets," page 45). Students spent a great deal of time practicing their writing, and the long school day lasted from sunrise to sunset.

With very few exceptions (see "Enheduana of Sumer," page 49), only boys attended the edubba. Students were known as "sons of the tablet house," and their professors were called "school fathers." Assistant professors were known as "big brothers."

recite (ri•sīt'): to answer questions orally or to read aloud publicly.

monitor (män'i•tər): a student appointed to assist a teacher; a person who warns or instructs.

They Aren't Just Chicken Scratches

When the first clay cuneiform tablets were published in Europe in the 1600s, no one thought these "chicken scratches" could be writing. However, as more and more tablets and inscriptions on statues were unearthed, it became clear that the strange symbols had to be writing. No one could understand them, however, until a British army officer, Henry Rawlinson, climbed a high cliff in Iran in the 1840s. Carved on the cliff were inscriptions in Old Persian, Elamite, and Babylonian cuneiform. Rawlinson copied the inscriptions and, by studying them side-by-side, was able to decipher the cuneiform. By the 1850s, people were finally able to read all those clay tablets, and an ancient culture came to life.

"Tell it to me."

"I'll tell it to you."

"Come on, tell it to me."

"You told me to go to school, recite my assignment, open my schoolbag, write my tablet, while my 'big brother' is to write my new tablet. After finishing my assignment, I am to proceed to my work and to come to you after I have reported to my monitor. That's what you told me."

"Come now, be a man. Don't stand about in the public square or wander about the boulevard.[2] When walking in the street, don't look all around. Be humble and show fear before your monitor. When you show terror, the monitor will like you.

(About fifteen lines destroyed)

"You who wander about in the public square, would you achieve success? Then seek out the first generations. Go to school, it will be of benefit to you. My son, seek out the first generations, inquire of them."

---

2. **boulevard** (bool′ə·värd′): a broad city street.

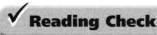

Reading Check

1. What are three things that the father instructs his son to do?

2. What does the father tell his son to do if he wants to be successful?

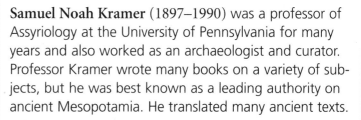

MEET THE *Writer*

Samuel Noah Kramer (1897–1990) was a professor of Assyriology at the University of Pennsylvania for many years and also worked as an archaeologist and curator. Professor Kramer wrote many books on a variety of subjects, but he was best known as a leading authority on ancient Mesopotamia. He translated many ancient texts.

Cross-Curricular ACTIVITIES

■ LANGUAGE ARTS/ART

Heroes and Villains Every age has its heroes and villains. Think about today's heroes and villains. How are they similar to and different from Gilgamesh and Humbaba, the hero and villain of ancient Mesopotamia?

Work with a classmate to make a list of real people or characters in books, movies, or video games who might be considered villains. Make a Venn diagram to show how today's villains are like or unlike the monster Humbaba. You may want to ask questions like the following to help you get started:

- What does the villain look like?
- What is his or her personality?
- What are his or her reasons for fighting against "heroes"?
- What weapons (if any) does she or he use?

After you complete your Venn diagram, write briefly about how this villain could be compared or contrasted with Humbaba. You may want to illustrate your paper with drawings of the two villains.

■ SCIENCE/HISTORY

Who's on First? The ancient Babylonians were the first to make many significant scientific and mathematical discoveries. Re-read "The Patient and Persistent Babylonians," and then use reference books or the Internet to find out when specific discoveries such as those listed below were likely made.

- the discovery and use of the number zero
- discovering how to make bronze
- the use of the wheel for transportation
- the first domesticated plants and animals
- calculating the length of a year
- the discovery of some of the planets

Create a time line to record the results of your research. You may also wish to research when these same discoveries were made or adopted in ancient Greece, Egypt, China, India, or Europe. If you include these dates on your time line, color-code each civilization's dates to make your time line more readable.

■ HISTORY/DRAMA

Listen Up! In the excerpt from *The Sumerians,* you read a portion from an ancient cuneiform tablet in which a father is both criticizing and giving advice to his son. With a classmate, role-play the parts of the father and the son, adding dialogue of your own to create an original performance. Before you perform your encounter for the class, review what you know about these and other factors in ancient Mesopotamia. Think about how these factors would affect what each person is likely to say.

- the power of people in authority (parents, teachers)
- the importance of learning to read and write
- the motivations of the father
- the motivations of the son

■ HISTORY/ART

Coming Soon! Many documentaries and historical movies (docu-dramas) have been made about the lives of famous men and women. You have been asked to produce a movie about Hammurabi. Sketch out a few ideas, and then choose art and words to create a movie poster about your film. Movie posters usually show a key scene or character from a movie and use words or phrases that convey the mood of the film and arouse our curiosity.

READ ON: FOR INDEPENDENT READING

■ NONFICTION

First Civilizations: Cultural Atlas for Young People by Erica Hunter (Checkmark, 1994) covers various topics and aspects of life in ancient Mesopotamia and includes many full-color illustrations.

History Begins at Sumer: Thirty-Nine "Firsts" in Man's Recorded History by Samuel N. Kramer (University of Pennsylvania Press, 1981) provides an account of the inventions and innovations of ancient Mesopotamia and includes original Sumerian myths. The book was written by one of the best-known experts on ancient Mesopotamia.

In the Land of Ur: The Discovery of Ancient Mesopotamia by Hans Baumann (Pantheon, 1969) This winner of the 1971 Mildred L. Batchelder award describes various archaeological finds in Mesopotamia and gives us a picture of what these "digs" have revealed about the ancient civilizations of this time period.

Looking Back: Mesopotamia and the Fertile Crescent by John Malam (Steck-Vaughn, 1999) is part of a series that presents various historical cultures. The text provides an overview of Mesopotamian society and has an easy-to-use format with numerous photos, maps, and a time line.

Science in Ancient Mesopotamia by Carol Moss (Franklin Watts, 1989) describes the many contributions of the ancient Mesopotamians in a variety of fields.

■ FICTION

Gilgamesh: Man's First Story by Bernarda Bryson (Holt, 1966) is a classic retelling of humankind's oldest known epic. The tales are retold with simplicity and are accompanied by reproductions of authentic illustrations. This edition was listed as a 1968 Boston Globe–Horn Book Honors title.

The Great Deeds of Superheroes by Maurice Saxby and Robert Ingpen (Bedrick, 1990) is a collection of various myths and legends of Western civilization. Traditional hero tales from the ancient Middle East to medieval Europe are retold in this volume, which is illustrated with many full-page color paintings.

The Last Quest of Gilgamesh by Ludmilla Zeman (Horn Book, Inc., 1995) is the third and final volume of Zeman's trilogy about the ancient Sumerian hero. This 1995 winner of the Governor General's Literary award is an account of the hero Gilgamesh, King of Uruk, who undertakes a dangerous journey in search of the secret of immortality. Illustrations accompany the story.

CHAPTER 3

Civilizations of the Nile
Ancient Egypt and Kush   5000 B.C.–500 B.C.

A River Ran Through It

Without the Nile River, the ancient civilizations of North Africa would never have grown to greatness. The Nile is the world's longest river, flowing north for over 4,000 miles from the mountains of central Africa to the Mediterranean Sea. Once a year, heavy rains cause the river to swell and overflow its banks. For the ancient Egyptians, the annual flooding of the Nile meant survival itself. The floodwaters dumped fertile black soil on Egypt's parched, sandy earth. The Nile transformed the broad, flat plains along its banks into the richest farmland in the ancient world. It also provided reeds for making paper and small boats, clay for making bricks and pottery, and a variety of creatures for food, such as fish, birds, and hippopotamuses.

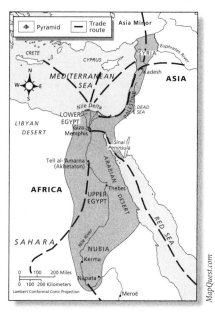

▲ Egypt: ca. 1450 B.C.

Did You Know?

In ancient Africa, the Egyptians weren't the only people with kings, pyramids, and fabulous riches. South of the major centers of ancient Egypt was the kingdom of Kush (also called Nubia). Kush was also a highly advanced civilization—and an even older one than Egypt. In fact, some historians believe that Kush may have existed as long as seven centuries before Egypt, making it the first known monarchy in human history.

INVESTIGATE: What role did the Nile play in the religion and art of ancient Egypt?

Smirking Sphinx

You've probably heard about three enormous pyramids that rise out of the desert near Cairo, the present-day capital of Egypt. You may not know that, crouching in the sand near the pyramids, is a giant figure of a lion with a human head. This kind of figure is

▲ The Great Sphinx.

In this chapter you'll see the word *pharaoh* (far′ō) in many of the selections. *Pharaoh* is the title of the kings of ancient Egypt. In ancient Egyptian, the word means "great house," referring to the ruler's palace.

known as a sphinx (sfiŋks). Along with the pyramids, the Great Sphinx at Giza is one of the most famous monuments on earth, and one of the most mysterious. It was carved from a block of left-over limestone from the same quarry used to build the pyramids at Giza. The Sphinx is almost as long as a football field, and its head is taller than a six-story building! The purpose of the Sphinx remains a riddle, which is perhaps why it still smiles at us after 4,600 years.

Egyptomania!

In 1798, the French emperor Napoleon invaded Egypt. His army began carrying Egyptian treasures back to Europe, and in this way Egypt invaded the Western world! For over two centuries Egyptian art has inspired everything from cookie jars to clocks. The discovery of King Tutankhamen's tomb in 1922 gave Egyptomania a boost. Movie theaters, libraries, and hotels were designed with an Egyptian look. Products were given Egyptian names, and fabrics for curtains and couches reproduced Egyptian paintings and designs. Egyptian images, such as the goddess Isis and Queen Cleopatra, could be found on almost everything from soap wrappers to playing cards. Look around and you'll probably see evidence that Egyptomania rages on in ads, clothing, hairstyles, and jewelry.

"Sorry, Akhet, but we've decided to stick with pyramids."

Walk Like an Egyptian

Along with pyramids, mummies, and King Tut, most people associate ancient Egyptians with the unique artwork they left behind. If you look closely at Egyptian tomb paintings, you'll notice something unusual about the way human figures are drawn. Faces, arms, hips, and legs are shown in profile (from the side), but the eye and shoulders are drawn from the front view. No one is sure why Egyptian artists began portraying humans in this way, but some historians think that each part of the body was drawn from its most commonly seen angle.

Memorable Quote

Concerning Egypt . . . there is no country that possesses so many wonders, nor any that has such a number of works which defy description.

—Herodotus, Greek historian

What do many people believe is the most amazing monument ever made? It's also the world's largest tomb—the Great Pyramid of Giza. The following article reveals some details about how and why the pyramids were built.

The Wonders of the Pyramids

from *Cricket*

by GERALDINE WOODS

In a travel guide for ancient tourists, the Greek writer Philon[1] called the Great Pyramid at Giza one of the wonders of the world. Scientists who have studied the construction of the pyramids would agree—these monumental structures are indeed one of the most remarkable achievements of ancient times.

Archeologists have identified the <u>remains</u> of over eighty pyramids in Egypt, all tombs for pharaohs and other noble Egyptians. The step pyramid built for King Djoser about 2680 B.C. is the oldest—and also the first large building ever constructed entirely of stone. According to an ancient Egyptian writing, the step design was meant to be "a staircase to heaven . . . for [the pharaoh]." As Egyptian builders

> ## You Need to Know...
>
> Stop for a moment and think about a block of stone that weighs as much as a large pickup truck. Now, imagine over *two million* of these blocks precisely cut, dragged, and placed without the use of wheels, steam engines, hydraulics, or gasoline motors. As impossible as it sounds, the pyramids of Egypt were built with nothing more than simple tools and human strength. Because such a feat is truly mind-boggling, some people have suggested that space aliens may have built the pyramids! Archaeologists, however, have several ideas about how humans built these unique structures, which are still standing after 4,500 years.

remains (ri•mānz′): ruins, especially of ancient times.

---

1. **Philon:** Greek engineer who in the second century B.C. listed the seven wonders of the world. The wonders were the Lighthouse at Alexandria, the Hanging Gardens of Babylon, the Colossus of Rhodes, the Statue of Zeus at Olympia, the Temple of Artemis at Ephesus, the Tomb of Mausolus at Halicarnassus, and the Great Pyramid of Cheops.

▲ The step pyramid of King Djoser.

exposed (ek·spōzd′): made visible or uncovered.

site (sīt): the place where something is located.

became more skilled, they changed the steps into a true pyramid, the sacred sign for their sun god, Ra.

The Great Pyramid of the pharaoh Khufu (usually known by his Greek name, Cheops) is the largest. It covers 13 acres and contains 2,250,000 blocks of stone, averaging 5,000 pounds each. It's hard to imagine how anyone could construct such an enormous building, even today. Moreover, the Egyptians employed only three simple machines in building the pyramids—the lever, the inclined plane, and the wedge.[2]

The first steps in construction were to clear the area of sand and gravel until the desert's rock floor was exposed and then to make the site perfectly level. Even a slight difference in height between one side of the pyramid and another could cause the entire structure to come crashing down.

2. **lever, inclined plane, wedge:** three simple tools. A lever is a rigid bar that pivots on a fixed point and is used to transfer weight. An inclined plane is a surface set at an angle so that heavy objects can be slid up or down. A wedge tapers to a thin edge and can be used to split something apart.

▲ Pyramids at Giza. The largest of the three, in the middle, is the Great Pyramid.

How do you make sure that 13 acres of land are perfectly flat, without modern instruments? The Egyptians used water. They knew that free-flowing water always forms a level surface, so the Egyptians dug a network of trenches that crisscrossed the base area of the pyramid. They flooded the trenches, then marked the water line on the sides. After draining the trenches, laborers cut the surface of the ground down to the watermarks and filled in the trenches with rubble.

Meanwhile, architects were drawing the plan of the building on clay tablets. Although a pyramid appears to be a solid mass of stone, it actually contains a number of tunnels and rooms. There was a chamber for the pharaoh's sarcophagus[3] (a stone coffin) and another for treasures the ruler would need in the next life. A passage from the outside was built for carrying the pharaoh's body to its resting place. In some pyramids, chambers for the pharaoh's wife were also included.

Many pyramids contained false tunnels and empty rooms to make things harder for tomb robbers. Unfortunately these chambers also created difficulties for the builders. The pyramids were constructed in layers. Once the thousands of blocks that made up each level were in place, it was almost impossible to move them. Therefore the builders had to be extremely careful to plan the proper position of openings.

The pyramids were built around a core of limestone from the western desert, only a short distance from the building site. The interior chambers were usually made of granite, which was quarried[4] at Aswan, about 500 miles upriver. The outer surfaces of the pyramids were covered with pure white limestone from across the Nile near Cairo in eastern Egypt. The architects listed the number, type, and measurements of the stones they needed. Scribes[5] sent copies to the quarries, where work gangs filled the orders.

Pyramid Security System

To protect the dead pharoahs and their treasures, the builders installed a kind of security system in the pyramids. Some built-in features designed to trick tomb robbers included hidden entrances, secret chambers, false doors, and maze-like tunnels. Huge stones were placed in passages to block them off, and some passages led straight into a wall. One deadly booby trap was a large stone balanced so that it would crash down on anyone who passed by after the tomb was sealed. Was finding the mummies and their treasures a daring job for the likes of Indiana Jones? Not exactly. For centuries tomb robbers found ways to get around this ancient security system. As a result, many pharoahs were robbed of the treasures they had hoped to take with them to the afterworld.

---

3. **sarcophagus** (sär·kăf′ə·gəs).
4. **quarried** (kwôr′ēd): obtained stone from a quarry, the open pit from which stone is cut.
5. **scribes** (skrībz): people who wrote out or copied documents by hand.

Old Hollywood movies often show hundreds of sweaty, exhausted slaves hauling gigantic stones to build the pyramids, at the mercy of cruel overseers cracking whips. In reality, the pyramids were probably built by farmers who were paid for their labor with bread, beer, garlic, linen, ointment, barley, and wheat. The workers believed the king (pharaoh) was a god, and they felt honored to build his tomb. In fact, some of them were so proud of their work, they inscribed the stones they moved with names like "Vigorous Gang" and "Boat Gang."

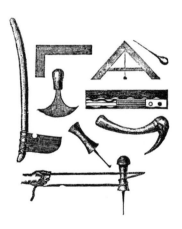

Before cutting stone, workers first drew marks on the rock to outline each block. Then, with chisels and mallets, they chipped a series of small cracks into the stone. Next, the workers hammered wooden wedges into the cracks and soaked the area with water. As the water was absorbed by the dry wood, the wedges swelled and split the rock.

Many pyramids contained false tunnels and empty rooms to make things harder for tomb robbers.

The rough-cut blocks of stone then had to be transported to the building site. To raise each block, the workers probably tied ropes of palm fiber to it and tilted one side with a lever. Or the Egyptians may have used a weight arm to lift the blocks. A weight arm is made of heavy timber. It has a central post and two arms, one short and one long. A sling is slipped under the block and attached to the short arm. Small rocks are placed on a platform attached to the long arm until they almost balance the weight of the block. The block rises when the long arm is tipped.

Once the block was raised, a wooden sled was quickly slipped underneath. A team of men pulled the sled, following a path of logs that kept the sled from sinking into the sand. The blocks were brought to the Nile and loaded on barges,[6] which carried them to the building site.

When they arrived, the blocks still had to be smoothed and cut to exact size. Workers cut away the larger bumps with saws or chisels and mallets. Then they rubbed the surface with rough stone or a lump of extremely hard rock called dolerite. The corners of each block were measured to be sure that they were perfectly square. The workers used wooden right angles and knocked away any extra rock with chisels or pieces of flint.

Many of the pyramids contained underground rooms. Before construction could begin, these chambers had to

---

6. **barges** (bärj′iz): long, large flat-bottomed boats for carrying freight.

be excavated. To make the digging easier, the Egyptians probably worked with caissons.[7] Caissons, which are still used in the construction of tunnels, are hollow cylinders made of stone and brick. The caisson is placed on the site, and the diggers work inside it. As the dirt is removed, the caisson is pushed forward. Its strong walls keep the hole from caving in.

After the Egyptians dug the underground chambers, it was time to actually move the pyramid stones into position. The blocks were dragged into place on sleds or rollers made of logs. To carry blocks to the higher layers, huge ramps made of mud and sand were built on the sides of the pyramids. Workers probably sprinkled water or oil over the stones to make them slide more easily over one another. The blocks fitted together so well that no mortar was needed to hold them in place. In most places, the seam between blocks was so tight that not even the blade of a knife could be inserted. As each layer was finished, a surveyor checked that the edges were perfectly square and that the layer was rising at the correct angle.

———————————————
7. **caissons** (kā'sənz).

excavated (eks'kə•vāt'id): dug out; hollowed out.

surveyor (sər•vā'ər): a person who takes measurement and applies mathematical principles to determine boundaries, areas, and elevations.

SuperStock

▲ The pyramid at the Louvre Museum in Paris. ❷ **Why do you think the images of ancient Egypt continue to fascinate people?**

When it was time to put a roof over an inner chamber, workers filled the room with dirt. They set the roof stones in place and then removed the dirt through the chamber's doorway. Stoneworkers finished the interior of the room, usually with granite.

The very top of the pyramid was the capstone, a perfectly pointed stone with a plug on its lower side. The plug fit into a hole on the preceding layer. Once the capstone was in place, stoneworkers began to polish the outside of the pyramid. As they traveled toward the base, workers removed the dirt ramps. When the last ramp was removed, the pyramid was finished—a path to heaven for the pharaoh, and a monument to the earthly labor of the Egyptians.

✓ **Reading Check**

1. How many pyramids have archaeologists discovered in Egypt? How old is the oldest pyramid?

2. For whom were the pyramids built? What machines did the Egyptians use to build the pyramids?

3. What principle did the Egyptians use to make the pyramid site perfectly level? How did the Egyptians put this principle into practice?

4. Why did the pyramid builders make false tunnels and empty rooms? Give three examples of the kinds of rooms often found in pyramids.

5. What kinds of rock were used to make the pyramids? Which kind of rock was brought from a long distance?

MEET THE *Writer*

Geraldine Woods (1948–   ) is the author of more than thirty-five books for children. Woods is an English teacher and has served as the director of the independent study program at the Horace Mann School in New York City.

What is the first thing that comes to mind when you think about ancient Egypt? Pyramids? The Sphinx? Maybe you think of mummies! Mummies have fascinated people for centuries. The following chart gives general facts about mummies and shows the steps of how a mummy is made.

What Was Inside a Pyramid?

from *Who Built the Pyramids?*

by JANE CHISHOLM and STRUAN REID

You Need to Know...

For the early Egyptians, death meant the beginning of a new life in another world, a world much like this one. In this earth-like afterworld, the spirit of the dead would need a body. To preserve the body for its afterlife, the Egyptians made it into a mummy. Because mummies were so important to the Egyptians, preparing them was a time-consuming process, involving many steps and rituals.

We tend to think that the ancient Egyptians were too focused on death, with their pyramids and complicated burial ceremonies. In reality, the Egyptians seemed to have enjoyed living. They loved it so much, they wanted to spend eternity in a world very similar to this one. Making bodies into mummies was one of the ways they hoped to get there.

▲ Mummy case (ca. 900–700 B.C.).

The Granger Collection, New York

The Metropolitan Museum of Art, Museum Excavations, 1928-29 and Rogers Fund, 1930.

◀ Funeral papyrus of Egyptian princess.

What was inside a pyramid?

Not much (considering how big pyramids are). The insides are mostly solid stone, with long narrow passages. The pharaohs were buried with all kinds of amazing treasures, but they were all stolen long ago.

What is a mummy?

A body that is embalmed or preserved, so it doesn't decay, even over thousands of years. The Egyptians believed that doing this would mean that the person could carry on living in the Next World.

How did they preserve the bodies?

By finding ways of drying them out. Follow the pictures to see how they did this.

These pictures show how a mummy is made. In the background, you can see an outline of the Great Pyramid sliced in half.

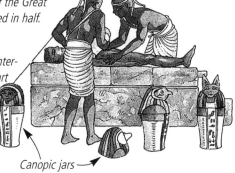

1. First, they take out the internal organs, such as the heart and lungs, and put them in jars called canopic jars.

Canopic jars

Natron

2. Then, they cover the body all over with a salt called natron, to dry it out. After several days, the insides are stuffed with linen, sawdust, natron, and sweet-smelling herbs and spices.

Burial chamber

Anubis mask

3. Next, the body is wrapped tightly with bandages, with lucky charms called amulets between the layers. They use huge amounts of bandages.

Passageways

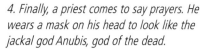

4. Finally, a priest comes to say prayers. He wears a mask on his head to look like the jackal god Anubis, god of the dead.

Why is it called a mummy?

The name comes from *mumiyah*, the Arabic word for bitumen, a sort of tar used on modern roads. When archeologists first found the bodies, they thought they must have been dipped in tar because they were so dark.

Didn't the mummies smell bad?

Not if the embalmers worked quickly before the body had a chance to decay. After it had been dried out and properly stuffed, it would have smelled lovely!

Mummies in the New Kingdom were put in a nest of two or three human-shaped coffins, like these. These were put inside a huge stone coffin, called a sarcophagus.

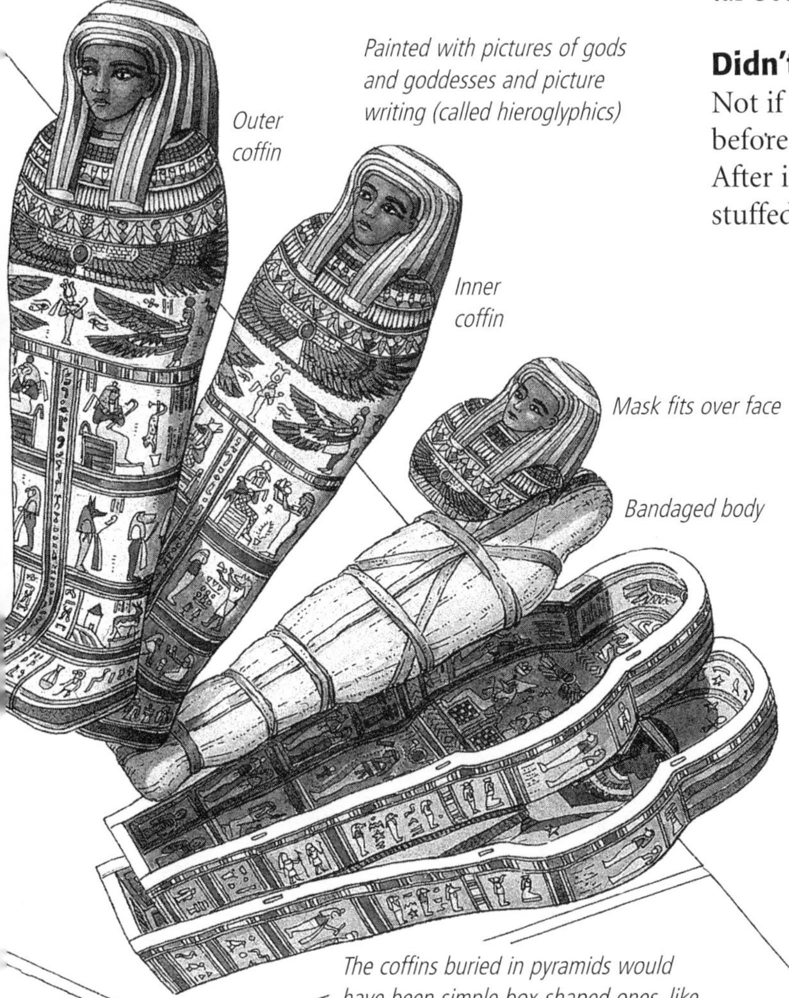

Outer coffin

Painted with pictures of gods and goddesses and picture writing (called hieroglyphics)

Inner coffin

Mask fits over face

Bandaged body

an you pot a pair f eyes on e coffin? hey allow e mummy o look out magic.

The coffins buried in pyramids would have been simple box-shaped ones, like this one, with much less decoration.

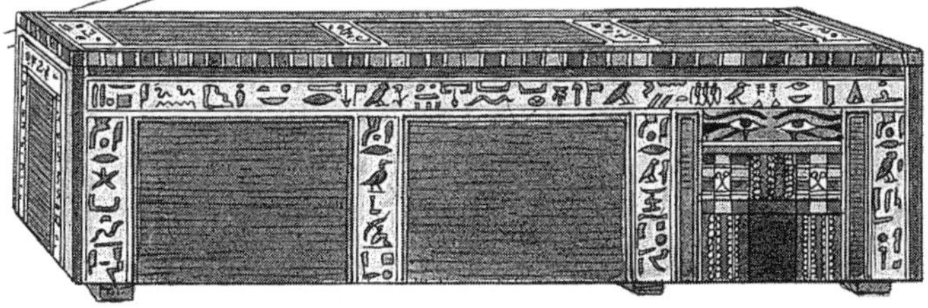

Were ordinary people mummified?

No. It was far too expensive for anyone except the royal family or top officials. But archeologists have found literally millions of animal mummies. These were animals who represented a particular god or goddess. They include cats, dogs, birds, baboons and crocodiles.

Mummified cat

Reproduced from Who Built the Pyramids, by permission of Usborne Publishing, 83–85 Saffron Hill, London EC1N 8RT. © 1995 Usborne Publishing Ltd.

"Ancient Egyptians, well-known for mummifying their human dead, also mummified their animals. They mummified so many that later generations of Egyptians and Europeans ground up the wrapped remains for fertilizer or burned them instead of firewood. A German ship once used thousands of cat mummies for ballast (weights used for stability).

When you see a mummy of a shrew, a baboon, or a fish, the overwhelming question is: *Why? Why? Why?* Why did people who lived four thousand to sixteen hundred years ago put mummified animals in the tombs of the human dead? Why did they create so many enormous animal cemeteries?

'Ancient Egyptians mummified animals for several reasons,' says Salima Ikram, who teaches Egyptology and archeology at the American University in Cairo. 'They believed that after they died, they traveled to another world. Victual (food) mummies—joints of cows or whole birds—were preserved and entombed with dead humans so the humans would have food in the next life.'

Since ancient Egyptians also believed that you CAN take it with you, they packed up pets, furniture, jewelry, and clothes that might be useful on the other side. Pets such as dogs or cats were mummified and buried with their owners when they died so they'd be able to play together in the next life. Many ancient Egyptians had good relations with their pets, says Ikram. 'It was a relationship not based on need, but on affection.'"

—from "Animal Mummies" by Jane Ellen Stevens
from Discovery.com

The Granger Collection, New York

✔ **Reading Check**

1. What is a mummy? Why did the ancient Egyptians mummify bodies?

2. What was the first step of making a mummy? What was placed between the layers of bandages?

3. What substance did the Egyptians cover the body with to dry it out when making a mummy?

4. What did the priest who said prayers for the mummy wear on his head?

In 1922 Howard Carter made an astounding archaeological discovery. In the following excerpt from *The Tomb of Tutankhamen,* Carter himself describes the suspense and excitement he felt at the moment he discovered King Tut's tomb.

▲ Art from the tomb of Tutankhamen.

plundering (plun'dər•iŋ): robbing or looting.

from The Finding of the Tomb

from *The Tomb of Tutankhamen*

by HOWARD CARTER AND A. C. MACE

As we cleared the passage we found, mixed with the rubble of the lower levels, broken potsherds,[1] jar sealings, alabaster[2] jars, whole and broken, vases of painted pottery, numerous fragments of smaller articles, and water skins, these last having obviously been used to bring up the water needed for the plastering of the doorways. These were clear evidence of plundering, and we eyed them askance.[3] By night we had cleared a considerable distance down the passage, but as yet saw no sign of second doorway or of chamber.

The day following (November 26th) was the day of days, the most wonderful that I have ever lived through, and certainly

You Need to Know...

Howard Carter spent six years digging around in the Egyptian desert, searching for the tomb of King Tutankhamen (toot'änk•ä'mən). He was convinced the tomb was located in a royal burial ground called the Valley of the Kings. Although Carter discovered many other tombs, including that of Queen Hatshepsut (see "The Other Half of History," page 86), all had been broken into by grave robbers. Lord Carnarvon of Great Britain, who had been paying for Carter's expedition, wanted to call off the search. Carter and his team were almost ready to give up. Then one day Carter's crew discovered a stone step. Digging quickly they found another, then another, until they had uncovered sixteen steps. At the bottom Carter found a door with its clay seal unbroken. Could it be? After years of searching, Carter hardly dared to hope that he had finally found King Tut's tomb.

---

1. **potsherds** (pät'shərdz'): pieces of broken pottery.
2. **alabaster** (al'ə•bas'tər): white, translucent stone that can be carved into objects.
3. **askance** (ə•skans'): with distrust or doubt.

Photograph by Harry Burton, The Metropolitan Museum of Art

The Mummy's Curse

A few months after he entered Tut's tomb, Lord Carnarvon died of an illness in Cairo. Rumors of a "mummy's curse" spread. It was said that when he died all the lights in Cairo went out due to a power failure, and that his dog back in England howled, then fell over dead. Of course, most scientists discount a curse, but some say that mold spores on mummies could have made early excavators seriously, if not fatally, ill. During a more recent excavation of an Egyptian tomb, archaeologist Zahi Hawass encountered a yellow powder with a "terrible and deadly" smell. Is it possible that this powder was a kind of poison left by those who prepared the tomb's mummy for burial?

replica (rep′li•kə): an exact or close copy.

vicinity (və•sin′ə•tē): a surrounding area.

encumbered (en•kum′bərd): blocked or obstructed.

verdict (vur′dikt): a decision or judgment.

one whose like I can never hope to see again. Throughout the morning the work of clearing continued, slowly perforce,[4] on account of the delicate objects that were mixed with the filling. Then, in the middle of the afternoon, thirty feet down from the outer door, we came upon a second sealed doorway, almost an exact replica of the first. The seal impressions in this case were less distinct, but still recognizable as those of Tut·ankh·Amen and of the royal necropolis.[5] Here again the signs of opening and re-closing were clearly marked upon the plaster. We were firmly convinced by this time that it was a cache[6] that we were about to open, and not a tomb. The arrangement of stairway, entrance passage, and doors reminded us very forcibly of the cache of Akh·en·Aten and Tyi material found in the very near vicinity of the present excavation by Davis, and the fact that Tut·ankh·Amen's seals occurred there likewise seemed almost certain proof that we were right in our conjecture. We were soon to know. There lay the sealed doorway, and behind it was the answer to the question.

Slowly, desperately slowly it seemed to us as we watched, the remains of passage debris that encumbered the lower part of the doorway were removed, until at last we had the whole door clear before us. The decisive moment had arrived. With trembling hands I made a tiny breach[7] in the upper left hand corner. Darkness and blank space, as far as an iron testing-rod could reach, showed that whatever lay beyond was empty, and not filled like the passage we had just cleared. Candle tests were applied as a precaution against possible foul gases, and then, widening the hole a little, I inserted the candle and peered in, Lord Carnarvon, Lady Evelyn, and Callender standing anxiously beside me to hear the verdict. At first I could see nothing, the hot air escaping from the chamber causing the candle flame to flicker, but presently, as my eyes grew accustomed to the

---

4. **perforce** (pər•fôrs′): by force of circumstances or necessity.
5. **necropolis** (ne•kräp′ə•lis): cemetery, especially a large and elaborate cemetery of an ancient city.
6. **cache** (kash): hiding place for valuables.
7. **breach** (brēch): an opening made by breaking.

light, details of the room within emerged slowly from the mist, strange animals, statues, and gold—everywhere the glint of gold. For the moment—an eternity it must have seemed to the others standing by—I was struck dumb[8] with amazement, and when Lord Carnarvon, unable to stand the suspense any longer, inquired anxiously, "Can you see anything?" it was all I could do to get out the words, "Yes, wonderful things." Then widening the hole a little further, so that we both could see, we inserted an electric torch.[9]

_____

8. **dumb** (dum): here, unable to speak.
9. **electric torch:** flashlight.

K. Scholz/H. Armstrong Roberts, Inc.

▲ This magnificent mask of beaten gold and inlaid jewels covered the head of King Tut's mummy.
❓ What are some of the reasons you can think of to explain why Carter was hardly able to speak when he first glimpsed Tutankhamen's treasures?

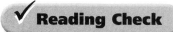

✔ Reading Check

1. Carter writes that there was "clear evidence of plundering." What two things led him to this conclusion?

2. Carter was sure that he was about to enter a *cache,* not a *tomb.* What is the difference between a cache and a tomb? Why did Carter think it was a cache?

3. Carter says that his work, even on the "day of days" when he discovered the tomb, was slow. Why was his work, and archaeological work in general, so slow?

4. What did Carter first see when he held the candle inside the chamber? What did Carter say when answering Lord Carnarvon's question?

MEET THE *Writer*

Howard Carter (1873–1939) was a British archaeologist who also served as Inspector-in-Chief of the Monuments of Upper Egypt and Nubia. Carter's hard work and determination provided a wealth of information about ancient Egypt, much of it recorded in his own words.

The ancient Egyptians were never short on gods to hear their prayers. They had literally *hundreds* to choose from! The following excerpt describes some of these gods and goddesses and the special roles they played in Egyptian life.

Multitudes of Gods

from *The Ancient Egyptians*

by ELSA MARSTON

▲ Ptah, the god of creation and crafts.

deities (dē′ə•tēz): gods or goddesses.

dynasties (dī′nəs•tēz): periods during which a certain family rules.

Some of Egypt's many, many gods came from predynastic times, such as Set and Horus. Others were local, belonging to this town or that, or even borrowed from non-Egyptian peoples. As gods were welcomed into the Egyptian collection of deities, they sometimes blended with other gods. In that way they took on a mixture of characteristics and roles.

The chief deities were the cosmic gods, who stood for the power of natural forces, especially in the sky. The sun, which gives life, was most important. Ra, the sun god, was the king of gods and the creator. He was worshiped from the earliest dynasties onward. Some other important deities were Horus, the sky god; Thoth, the God of learning; Hathor, the goddess of "all things feminine"; Ptah, the god of creation and craftsmanship; Khnum, the potter who created humans, and Anubis, the protector of the dead.

The gods and goddesses were not abstract ideas but were like real persons. They were shown vividly

You Need to Know...

A Greek traveling in ancient Egypt wrote: "There seem to be more gods than men in Egypt." Of course, this was an exaggeration, but the Egyptians did worship an incredible number of gods. The belief in many gods is called polytheism (päl′i•thē•iz′əm). Religions such as Judaism, Christianity, and Islam are based on monotheism—the belief that there is one god.

Each Egyptian god or goddess had a particular area of influence. The ancient Egyptians felt their prayers would get better results if they were addressed to the right god. For example, if they were ill, early Egyptians prayed to the god of medicine, Imhotep. If Egyptian farmers needed water for crops, they prayed to the river goddess, Hapi. Read on to find out more about the multitude of gods in ancient Egypt.

in paintings, reliefs,[1] and sculpture, each one with a special appearance. Osiris, King of the Other World, was colored green or black, symbolizing the fertility of the soil. Ma'at, the goddess of justice, carried an ostrich feather, while Isis, the wife of Osiris, wore a throne-shaped crown. Ptah was depicted as a mummy.

Many deities had a human body and the head or some feature of a particular animal. For instance, Hathor was often shown with the ears and/or horns of a cow. Khnum had the head of a ram, and Thoth had the odd-looking head of a long-billed ibis. The goddess Bastet sat with a cat's head on a female form, and Sekhmet, protector of the king, had the head of a lioness. Horus, the sky god, had a falcon's head, perhaps because the falcon could be seen soaring high in the sky; and Anubis had the head of a jackal, probably because jackals were frequent visitors to graveyards. The goddess who assisted in childbirth, Taweret, was a hippopotamus.

Each deity was associated with at least one special role or task and often several, even contradictory ones. Bastet, for example, was a goddess of love—and war. Min was a god of male fertility, the desert, and thunder. Set, the jealous brother of Osiris, was the "bad god"—but a full member of deity society. In fact, it was his job to travel every night in the solar boat with Ra. He was supposed to protect the sun god against the dragon of chaos, Apophis.

Why did the ancient Egyptians need all these gods? We may find them strange—but to their worshipers they were very real and important. Perhaps the following explanation may help us understand:

Though the Egyptians, then as now, depended on the unceasing flow and the annual overflow of the Nile, the flood was not a sure thing. Sometimes it came late, or was too low to renew the soil's fertility and supply water for irrigation. Famine could follow. Sometimes, too, the flood might be too high—and destroy whole villages. Compared with neighboring arid lands, where different

---

1. **reliefs:** sculptures in which the figures stand out from a surface.

Keep an Eye Out

You could be carrying ancient Egypt in your pocket at this very moment! If you turn over a dollar bill, you'll see a pyramid with an eye at the top. These ancient Egyptian symbols were incorporated into the design of the dollar bill because of George Washington. Our first President belonged to a society called the Masons, which based many of its traditions on ancient Egypt. The eye is the sign of the Egyptian sun-god Ra, and it symbolizes light and vision. Another Egyptian eye can be found on medical prescriptions. The Rx abbreviation used by doctors came from the god Horus. Horus's eye was torn out by Set, a god of evil. By magic, the eye was put back in place. The ancient Egyptians believed that the eye of Horus gave life and strength to everyone who saw it.

---

contradictory (kän′trə•dik′tə•rē): opposing or opposite.

chaos (kā′äs′): confusion and disorder.

famine (fam′in): a great shortage of food that can occur over a large area for a long time.

peoples competed and fought to live, Egypt appeared blessed; but there was always uncertainty. Beneath their joy in life, the Egyptians seem to have felt fear. Chaos continually threatened, they believed, and might strike if the gods did not keep the world on track. And it was up to humans to keep the deities contented and strong.

The Egyptians worked hard to make sure their gods were happy. The deities, they thought, had the same basic needs as people. In a society that greatly valued the family, the gods were married and had children. They needed homes where they could live peacefully and comfortably, so the Egyptians gave them homes—the temples. Not only did the deities receive offerings in the temples, but they were cared for like human beings. The priests would go through the daily ceremonies of getting the god's statue up in the morning, bathing and dressing it, presenting important visitors to it, providing it with good meals, and putting it to bed again at night.

In addition, the gods were treated to public festivals. The most important festival in Thebes, called Opet, lasted for twenty-four days. It honored the marriage of the chief god, Amun, and Mut, the vulture-headed mother goddess. Priests carried boats containing the two deities' statues from the Temple of Amun (Karnak) to Luxor Temple. At both temples wall reliefs still show the processions and the excited crowds along the way.

The major gods were well taken care of by the priests. Ordinary people, however, seem to have felt closer to more homey deities, such as

▲ The Egyptian goddess Isis.

Beetlemania

Scarabs (skar′əbz) are gems or ornaments carved in the form of a dung beetle, and the ancient Egyptians were wild about them. They wore scarabs as jewelry, used them as seals, and wrapped them in mummies as a symbol of immortality. Why was the image of this lowly insect so important in ancient Egypt? The *scarabaeus sacer* beetle lays its eggs in a ball of animal droppings, or dung, that it rolls along the ground to its burrow. The Egyptians associated the beetle's actions with the daily rebirth of the sun. The Egyptians saw the god Khepri as a great scarab beetle who rolled the sun across the sky each day, buried it at night, and made sure it rose again each morning.

local gods or even personal gods that individuals could choose for themselves. Probably most homes had shrines for these gods. A popularity contest would doubtless have been won by Bes, a squat, ugly, naked, but kind little god. He especially looked after women and children, and his job description included happy marriage, dance, and good times.

✓ Reading Check

1. Which Egyptian god was considered most important? Why?

2. Every god had a certain appearance. What are the distinguishing colors of Osiris, and what do they represent?

3. The author lists the animal characteristics of a number of gods, but explains only two of them. Which two does she explain and what are the explanations?

4. The author uses the Nile to explain why the ancient Egyptians needed so many gods. How was the Nile connected to religious beliefs?

5. How were the Egyptian gods like people?

SuperStock

▲ Temple of Amun in Luxor. The modern town of Luxor occupies the site of ancient Thebes, which was the capital of the ancient Egyptian empire.

MEET THE *Writer*

Elsa Marston (1933–   ) is the author of both fiction and nonfiction books for young people. She has taught at the American University of Beirut in Lebanon. Marston has also exhibited her artwork in Tunisia and New York and directed an art gallery.

Bettmann/CORBIS

▲ Queen Hatshepsut.

Cleopatra, Queen of the Nile, wasn't the only royal Egyptian woman who made headlines. The following book excerpt focuses on three powerful women in ancient Egypt and also explores some of the roles women played in this society.

from The Other Half of History: Women in Ancient Egypt

by FIONA MACDONALD

Three Famous Women Rulers

Women, by tradition, could not be rulers of Egypt. Only a man could be a divine ruler—a living god—which is what the Egyptians believed their pharaohs to be. But some royal women found ways of <u>exercising</u> power and ruling Egypt.

exercising (ek'sər•siz'ŋ): using; putting into play.

HATSHEPSUT (ruled 1473–1458 B.C.)

Hatshepsut[1] was the daughter of a pharaoh and was married to Pharaoh Thutmose II, but they had no sons. When Thutmose II died she was appointed <u>regent</u> to his son (by another wife), Pharaoh Thutmose III. It was very unusual for a woman to be given such responsibility.

regent (rē'jənt): a person who rules when the ruler is too young, too sick, or otherwise unable to rule.

Keeping control

As regent, Hatshepsut was expected to hand over power to the new pharaoh as soon as he was old enough to rule. But she had

---
1. **Hatshepsut** (hät•shep'soot).

You Need to Know...

The history of Egyptian women is mostly a mystery. We do know that their lives were filled with household duties and that they possessed some legal and economic rights. Egyptian women could travel freely, own property, and claim financial support if they were divorced.

A few women achieved high status in ancient Egypt. These women were usually the daughters or wives of pharaohs. Details of their lives have survived because their tombs contained many statues, paintings, and inscriptions. If the names "Hatshepsut," "Nefertiti," and "Cleopatra" aren't already familiar to you, read on to find out more about these three famous women.

From The Other Half of History: Women in Ancient Egypt by Fiona Macdonald. Text copyright © 1999 by Fiona Macdonald. Reprinted by permission of **The McGraw-Hill Companies.**

herself crowned pharaoh, and became coruler with the young boy. Even after Thutmose III became an adult, Hatshepsut continued to rule Egypt. She was often shown on monuments dressed as a man and performing religious ceremonies normally carried out by male rulers. In writings, she was often referred to as king.

Successful ruler

Hatshepsut's army won many battles, and she sent trading expeditions to the rich kingdom of Punt (present-day Ethiopia). She probably stayed in power until she died. At her death, Thutmose III was crowned king. Many years later, her name was removed from her monuments, probably because people believed it was wrong for a woman to have had a pharaoh's power.

NEFERTITI (1380–1340 B.C.)

Queen Nefertiti[2] was the daughter of a senior palace official and wife of Pharaoh Akhenaten, who ruled from 1352 to 1336 B.C. Nefertiti gave birth to six daughters, but there is no record that she ever had a son. Many carvings and paintings show the royal family as a close-knit group.

Power and influence

Nefertiti moved to live with Pharaoh Akhenaten at his new capital city at El-Amarna. In carvings she is often shown wearing a special crown, and standing by the side of the pharaoh as his equal. In one carving, she is in a war chariot, fighting foreign enemies. Historians think this shows that Nefertiti had great influence over her husband. After twelve years Nefertiti seems to have disappeared from public life. She probably died just two years later. Her place was taken by her eldest daughter, Meritaten.

Scala/Art Resource, NY

▲ Nefertiti.

2. **Nefertiti** (nef′ər•tē′tē).

Glamour and Glitter

Jewelry and makeup were not for women only in ancient Egypt. Tombs of both women *and* men were found to contain stunning necklaces, bracelets, and rings. Golden jewelry was skillfully crafted with inlays of semiprecious stones such as lapis lazuli, carnelian, amethyst, and turquoise. Egyptian men and women also wore eye makeup. They outlined their eyes with a black substance made of lead ore and water, but they didn't just have beauty in mind. They believed that thick eyeliner protected their eyes from sun damage and diseases caused by germs and flies. Women also wore bright green eye shadow made of a crushed green stone called malachite. A gray, glittery eye makeup made of crushed beetles and their shiny shells was also popular!

expeditions (eks′pə•dish′ənz): groups of people making journeys with a definite purpose.

CLEOPATRA VII (ruled 51–30 B.C.)

Cleopatra[3] was a member of a Greek ruling family who had governed Egypt since 305 B.C. At first she coruled with her father (Ptolemy XII) and then with her brother (Ptolemy XIII). After a family quarrel Cleopatra lost power, but regained it with the help of Julius Caesar, the Roman general, who invaded Egypt in 48 B.C. She began to rule with her second brother, Ptolemy XIV.

Defeat and death

In 48 B.C. Cleopatra gave birth to a son and claimed Caesar was his father. She gave orders for her brother to be killed and appointed her baby son as pharaoh. A few years later she married a Roman commander called Mark Antony, having given birth to his children (a twin boy and girl). In 34 B.C. Mark Antony gave Cleopatra the right to rule Egypt on behalf of Rome, but his enemies in Rome disapproved, and declared war. Mark Antony and Cleopatra were defeated in battle. They committed suicide, rather than be taken captive by Roman soldiers.

Priestesses

Egyptian women played an important role in religion, as in many other areas of society. They might be priestesses, musicians, or even wives of gods.

> **Egyptian women played an important role in religion, as in many other areas of society.**

Servants of the gods

The Egyptians saw temples as the homes of the gods. They believed that worshiping in temples was a way of keeping order in the land of Egypt and in the universe. Priests and priestesses were both servants of the gods, and women

---

3. **Cleopatra** (klē′ō·pa′trə).

▲ Cleopatra.

could perform many duties. But priestesses usually held little authority and had to obey orders given by chief priests, who were men. Their most important task was to take care of the temples of the goddesses. (There were rarely priestesses for male gods.) They looked after the goddesses' statues, made offerings, and supervised temple servants and temple estates.

Limited powers

Because women could not read or write, priestesses never became "lector priests" (senior temple staff who read out the prayers at each ceremony from a scroll). By the New Kingdom[4] period, women had fewer duties in the temples. Most priests were men from the top ranks of society who had trained as religious scribes.

The god's wife

As part of their royal duties, many Egyptian royal wives became priestesses. The pharaoh himself was chief priest as well as ruler and army commander. In the Old Kingdom[5] royal priestesses served the goddess Hathor. In later times they honored other goddesses. From the New Kingdom on, royal women, usually the pharaoh's daughter, might also become a wife of the chief male god, Amun. The title "god's wife" was a very important one. A god's wife took part in special ceremonies to bring fertility and prosperity to the kingdom. She also controlled vast estates and had considerable political power. Weak pharaohs relied on the powerful priests of the god Amun, and on the "god's wife," to help them rule.

Music for the gods

The Egyptians believed that music was an important way of communicating with the gods. Hathor, one of the chief female goddesses, was sometimes called Mistress of Music, and women singers, dancers, and instrumentalists played a

---

4. **New Kingdom** (1550–1076 B.C.): the period when Egypt was the world's strongest power.
5. **Old Kingdom** (2658–2150 B.C.): also called the Pyramid Age.

Blowing in the Wind

Ever wonder what an ancient Egyptian orchestra would sound like? It would probably sound kind of familiar because some of the musical instruments we play and hear today were first developed in ancient Egypt. Reed instruments had their origins in the papyrus reeds growing along the Nile River. The Egyptians took small pieces of the reeds and fashioned single-reed instruments, which eventually developed into the clarinet, and double-reed instruments, which evolved into today's oboe. The Egyptians also made flutes out of river reeds. A yard long and a half-inch wide, the reed flute was played vertically, like a recorder.

leading part in many temple ceremonies. While female choirs chanted or sang, women in temple orchestras played a jingling rattle, called a sistrum, tapped tambourines and other percussion instruments, and shook strings of beads. Unlike priestesses, women singers served in the temples of male gods as well as of goddesses. The name "Singer of Amun" was an honorable title, given only to wives of senior scribes and nobles.

Reading Check

1. How was Hatshepsut often portrayed on monuments and in writings?

2. What were some of Hatshepsut's accomplishments during her reign?

3. What evidence do historians have to conclude that Nefertiti was powerful and respected?

4. Who gave Cleopatra the right to rule Egypt on behalf of Rome? What happened because of this decision?

5. What were the duties of priestesses? What roles did women play in temple ceremonies?

MEET THE *Writer*

Fiona Macdonald studied history at Cambridge University and has written numerous books on historical subjects. One of her works, *Keeping Clean, A Very Peculiar History,* won the Times Educational Supplement's Information Book award in 1995.

In ancient times, the lands to the south of Egypt were veiled in mystery. Read on to learn what we now know about the African kingdom of Nubia, or Kush.

from Kush—The Nubian Kingdom

from *Egypt, Kush, Aksum: Northeast Africa*

by KENNY MANN

The construction of the Aswan High Dam[1] in the 1960s caused a flurry of archaeological activity in the region and led to new discoveries about the ancient civilizations of Nubia, or Kush, as it was called. These efforts preserved part of Nubia's history and uncovered much new information.

Interest in Nubia, or Kush, was not new, however. The region has had a hold on the western imagination for centuries. The ancient Greeks and Romans thought that Nubia was one of the greatest civilizations of the world. Although very few Greeks or Romans ever traveled there, they knew that inexhaustible supplies of gold, ebony, ivory, cattle, slaves, ostrich feathers, and panther skins, as well as exotic luxuries such as frankincense[2] and plant oils, came from the mysterious region to the south of Egypt. From the same region came dark-skinned, mercenary[3] warriors whose skill with the bow and arrow was unsurpassed. To Europeans, Nubia was a kingdom of extraordinary wealth and power.

> **You Need to Know...**
> Although ancient Egypt and Nubia (nōō′bē•ə) shared certain traditions, they were not the friendliest of neighbors on the Nile. The two kingdoms were often at war with one another. Nubia extended for a thousand miles along the Nile, and its civilizations lasted five thousand years—longer than those of ancient Egypt, Greece, or Rome. Yet only in the last fifty years have archaeologists and historians begun to discover and appreciate the culture of Nubia, preserved in the remarkable jewelry, pottery, and sculpture it produced.

1. **Aswan High Dam:** dam that Egyptians built at Aswan in the 1960s. The resulting lake flooded many archaeological sites of ancient Nubia.
2. **frankincense** (fraŋk′in•sens′): aromatic tree gum used in perfume and incense.
3. **mercenary** (mʉr′sə•ner′ē): serving only for pay.

Elephants on Parade

Figures and images depicted in artwork often give scientists clues about the plants and animals that flourished in certain areas in ancient times. Ancient Nubian artwork often includes images of ostriches, giraffes, lions, and elephants. Archaeologists believe that lions may have been kept at one temple to represent a lion god, and that elephants were used for ceremonies and in war. In fact, the African elephants that the ancient Romans sometimes used in battle were probably trained by the Nubians.

inaccessible (in'ak•ses'ə•bəl): not able to be accessed or known.

The Greek historian Herodotus, who traveled as far as Aswan, was imaginative in his reports about the kingdom of Kush. He described the Nubians, or Kushites, as the "tallest and handsomest" people he had ever seen. They lived to be 120 years old on a diet of boiled meat and milk, he reported, and they carved their temples from a single stone. Their queen, he said, traveled in a wheeled palace, drawn by 20 elephants.

The Greek historian Herodotus . . . described the Nubians, or Kushites, as the "tallest and handsomest" people he had ever seen.

Other writers of ancient times added further snippets[4] of information about Nubia. Some were pure myth; others were fairly accurate descriptions of the land and people. But it was not until the nineteenth century that Europeans developed enough interest in the region to begin archaeological excavations there. In the 1990s, several major world museums mounted exhibitions of the more recent discoveries in the region. Yet, to the average person, Nubia remains virtually unknown, more remote and inaccessible today than it was in ancient times.

The lack of knowledge about Nubia, or Kush, may certainly be related to its remoteness from Europe. But the region's many different names, and those of its different kingdoms, also made—and still make—its geography and the exact location of its kingdoms confusing.

The ancient Egyptians called the region south of Aswan *Ta-Seti,* meaning "land of the bow," a reference to Nubia's famed archers. From about 2000 B.C., they called it Kush, the name that also appears in the Bible and is widely used by historians today. At one time, Nubia included all of present-day Sudan, Ethiopia, and Somalia. The Greeks and Romans called this region Aethiopia—a Greek word meaning "land of the burned faces" (a reference to the

---

4. **snippets** (snip'its): small bits.

Nubians' dark skin)—and not to be confused with today's nation of Ethiopia, far to the east. Some historians refer to separate Nubian, or Kushite, kingdoms—Napata and Meroë[5]—each centered around its capital city of the same name. Others include the city of Napata and all of Lower Nubia in the Kingdom of Kush and consider Upper Nubia the Kingdom of Meroë. In ancient times, these different names probably referred to different areas of Nubia, depending on the extent of geographical knowledge at the time. The name *Nubia* may be derived from the people known as the Noba, who inhabited the southern areas of the region. It may also stem from the word *nub* which meant "slave" in a local language and was adopted by the Latin-speaking Romans. The term *Nubia* was first applied to the entire region by Europeans in the eighteenth century.

Nubia was a black African kingdom. This may also have slowed European interest in the region. After Nubia became Christianized in the sixth century A.D., there is not a single mention of its kingdoms in European reports until the eighteenth century. The historian David Roberts believes that this neglect is a clear reflection of racial discrimination. Until recently, he says, the western mind found it impossible to believe that Africans could have developed the sophisticated cultures that flourished in Nubia for over 5,000 years. This trend in thinking continued through the early twentieth century. Even the eminent archaeologist George Reisner concluded that the kings whose tombs he excavated in the region must have been descendants of a Libyan—that is, a white—dynasty.

This racial bias was evident from the very first contact of Europeans with Nubia. There is, for example, a record of a Nubian queen's response to an inquiry from Alexander the Great, the Macedonian emperor who conquered Egypt in 332 B.C. Alexander wished to know more about Kush. The queen wrote to him, "Do not despise us for the color of our skin. In our souls we are brighter than the whitest of your people."

---

5. Meroë (mer′ō·ē′).

Made in Meroë

Some art historians believe that the pottery made by the people of ancient Meroë is the finest made anywhere in the Nile Valley. Many beautiful examples have been found in ancient temples and grave sites. The pottery was crafted on a potter's wheel and is exceptionally thin and delicate. It was painted with elaborate designs that were often geometric or floral, or showed figures of humans, animals, and mythological creatures.

---

eminent (em′ə·nənt): prominent; important.

bias (bī′əs): discrimination; prejudice.

gleaned (glēnd): gathered.

dire (dīr): horrible, feared.

▲ Ancient Nubian crown.

Archivo Iconografico, S.A./CORBIS

Most of what is known about ancient Nubia has been gleaned from the reports of other peoples, such as the Egyptians, Assyrians, Greeks, and Romans, who came either to trade or to conquer. Since the Nubians were among Egypt's most dire enemies, the pharaohs often referred to their southern neighbors as "vile" and "wretched" people. They drew images of Nubians on the soles of their sandals and under their footstools, where they could be symbolically crushed. Yet although the Kushite reign in Egypt lasted just over 60 years, the Nubian civilization far outlasted the Egyptian. It continued to flourish for another 1,000 years.

✓ Reading Check

1. What event led archaeologists to discover and preserve information about ancient Nubia? What are two reasons the author proposes for the low level of European knowledge about Nubia?

2. What did the ancient Greeks and Romans think of Nubia? What details did Herodotus report about the Nubians?

3. What were two reasons Egyptians and other people sometimes ventured south into Nubian lands? Name some of the precious items that came from ancient Nubia.

4. What evidence is there of ancient racial discrimination against the Nubians?

MEET THE *Writer*

Kenny Mann (1946–   ) has lived in many places around the world. She grew up in Kenya, then moved to England to study filmmaking. Subsequently, the author lived in Hamburg, Germany, where she worked as a freelance journalist, as a producer of radio shows for teenagers, and as a writer for documentary films. Mann now lives and writes in Sag Harbor, New York.

What if there were no watches, clocks, or calendars in the world? How would you know what time it was and plan for future events? The following excerpt explains how Egyptian astronomy led to developments in timekeeping that were similar to our modern calendar.

from Astronomy and Timekeeping

from *Science in Ancient Egypt*

by GERALDINE WOODS

Photograph by Harry Burton, The Metropolitan Museum of Art

▲ Model of ancient Egyptian boat.

Every ancient Egyptian child knew that the sun god Ra sailed one boat across the sky every day and another through the waters under the earth during the dark hours. The children knew that the stars were also boats which blew through the heavens the same way sailboats blew up and down the Nile. They were aware that the five days of festivals everyone enjoyed each year were a gift from the god Thoth. Thoth had played a dice game with the moon and won some of its light, which he <u>fashioned</u> into five extra days.

Now that we are in the space age, these myths may seem silly. Yet the stories contain a surprising amount of scientific knowledge. The tales of Ra's boat and the stars show that the Egyptians observed the movements of the sun and the <u>constellations</u>. Thoth's game was a fanciful way of explaining the change Egypt made between a calendar based on the moon and one based on the sun.

fashioned (fash′ənd): made or turned into.

constellations (kän′stə∙lā′shənz): groups of stars that have been given definite names.

You Need to Know...

In many ancient cultures, people watched the sky. They observed the natural cycles of the sun, moon, stars, and planets in order to mark dates and times. Egyptian astronomy and timekeeping developed in leaps and bounds because the Egyptians had a system of writing. Over many centuries the early Egyptians kept detailed records of the movements of heavenly objects. They saw patterns and were able to make sophisticated mathematical calculations to predict how celestial bodies would move in the future. In this way they created a reliable way of telling time that affects our lives today.

reckoned (rek'ənd): figured; calculated.

Mad About Measurements

The Egyptians found a way to measure and calculate just about everything that affected their daily lives, from the flooding of the Nile to the measurements needed to build a perfect pyramid. They created precise formulas for measuring distance, length, weight, area, and volume. To do all this measuring, they needed a standard unit of measurement. The standard that the early Egyptians devised to measure length was the distance from a man's elbow to the tip of his middle finger. This unit of measurement was called a cubit and was soon in widespread use throughout the ancient world.

methodical (mə•thäd'i•kəl): using a strict, orderly system or method.

Sirius and the Calendar

The ancient Egyptians' knowledge of astronomy and time started in a very natural way. Like all primitive people, the earliest Egyptians probably first kept time by marking the passage of days on a stick. Later, they probably reckoned time by the most obvious change in their lives—the annual flood of the Nile.

Very soon, however, they turned to the sky. Just about all ancient peoples were stargazers. Without strong artificial light, the nights are darker and the stars show up more clearly. And in a society that has little else for entertainment, the sky can put on the most spectacular show in town!

The brightest object in the night sky, of course, is the moon. The moon's cycles are very short. In only 29 or 30 days the moon grows, becomes full, shrinks, and disappears. Perhaps that is why most ancient people, including the early Egyptians, created a calendar of "moons," or months. Each time a new moon appeared, a new month began. Since this occurs every $29\frac{1}{2}$ days, each month was 29 or 30 days long. Twelve months were counted as one year. Unfortunately, there are only 354 days in this type of year, and the extra days add up quickly. Within a few years, a winter month has turned into a summer month!

The Egyptians solved this problem by switching to a solar, or sun, calendar, which grew out of their observations of the stars. At some point in Egypt's dim past, people began to notice that the stars moved across the sky according to regular patterns. (Of course, it is really the earth that moves, not the stars, but that fact was not discovered until thousands of years later.) The Egyptians, a methodical people, began to keep charts of the stars' movements.

They named constellations after animals they were familiar with, like crocodiles, oxen, and hippos. They also divided the heavenly bodies into three categories. "The Unwearied" were actually planets; they got this name because they never stopped moving. Although they had no telescopes, the Egyptians observed Jupiter, Saturn,

Venus, Mars, and perhaps Mercury. "The Imperishables" were circumpolar stars, those which appeared to revolve around the North Pole and did not set. The Egyptians believed that the Imperishables were located in the Heavenly Fields, where their kings lived an eternal life. The last type, "the Indestructibles," consisted of thirty-six specially chosen stars which eventually gave their names to the Egyptian weeks.

Just about all ancient peoples were stargazers. . . . And in a society that has little else for entertainment, the sky can put on the most spectacular show in town!

Around 3000 B.C., Sirius, the Dog Star, attracted attention because it was brighter than all the other stars. Yet sometimes Sirius vanished. Then it would appear again, just for a few minutes, at dawn. Each day thereafter Sirius would stay in the sky for a longer period of time, until it disappeared again. Soon someone observed that Sirius always returned just before the Nile was ready to overflow its banks.

This knowledge was extremely valuable. All the other methods the Egyptians had tried were fine for recording time. However, Sirius's movements gave them the ability to predict an event. Knowing that the Nile was about to overflow allowed the Egyptians to move their houses and livestock to higher ground and to prepare for the planting season. So the Egyptians based their calendar on Sirius, and calculated a year as the time between one reappearance of the star and another.

This was a lucky choice. Sirius's cycle is $365\frac{1}{4}$ days long—exactly the same amount of time it takes the earth to revolve once around the sun. So the Egyptian calendar followed the seasons correctly, and avoided the traveling months of the moon-based calendar.

▲ Egyptian water clock.

▲ The Egyptian god Thoth.

The Egyptians subdivided their calendar into three seasons: the flooding of the Nile, the planting season, and the dry season. They also created decans, ten-day weeks which were named for the Indestructible star that was <u>prominent</u> in the sky during that period.

The astronomers also decided that three weeks would equal one month—and that created a problem. Twelve months of thirty days each total 360. Five days short! That's where the legend of Thoth comes in. The five extra days that Thoth won from the moon were given as holidays not belonging to any particular month. The year now equaled 365 days. This was still one-fourth of a day short, but it was the best calendar in the ancient world and a major improvement on the moon-based calendar.

✓ Reading Check

1. Who did the Egyptians believe gave them five extra days each year? How were the five days created?

2. How did the ancient Egyptians solve the problem of using a calendar based on the cycles of the moon?

3. What natural event could the ancient Egyptians predict because of their observations of the stars? Why was this ability to predict important?

4. How many days were there between reappearances of Sirius? Why was Sirius important?

5. What were the seasons of the ancient Egyptians?

MEET THE *Writer*

Geraldine Woods (1948–   ) is the author of more than thirty-five books for children. Woods is an English teacher and has served as the director of the independent study program at the Horace Mann School in New York City.

Cross-Curricular ACTIVITIES

■ HEALTH/SCIENCE

Healthy in Life and Death We know that the Egyptians were deeply concerned about the condition of their bodies after death. What about their physical well-being in life? Find out as much as you can about health, diet, and forms of exercise in ancient Egypt. What sports or games did Egyptians play? What did they eat, and how did their diet affect their health? What were some common illnesses and treatments? You might look for ancient Egyptian medical prescriptions, health-related charms, herbal remedies, recipes, and menus for meals. Report your findings to the class.

■ HISTORY/ART

Frieze It Great moments in history have often been immortalized in works of art. One art form commonly used to record history is called a *frieze* (frēz). A frieze is a painted or carved band of images around the top of a building or on a wall or ceiling. You can see friezes on government buildings, in museums, and on monuments. Working in a group, research important events in Nubia's history that could be recorded on a frieze and make a list of your ideas. Then, sketch drafts of your frieze and present them to the class. Explain the events you have represented and your artistic interpretation of them.

■ LANGUAGE ARTS/MUSIC

Ballad of the Boy King King Tutankhamen is far more famous in death than he ever was in life. Although the discovery of his tomb revealed much about ancient Egypt, it created more questions than it answered about Tut himself. For example, we still do not know what happened during his brief reign as pharaoh, or what circumstances surrounded his early death at age 18. Do research to "dig up" as many details as you can about the life of King Tut, and write song lyrics or a poem about him. (You might even try to write a ballad, which is a song that tells a story using rhyme and repetition). Since we don't have all the facts about Tut, feel free to imagine his life and invent details or fictional stories about him to include in your song.

■ HISTORY/DRAMA

Queen of the Silver Screen Quite a few plays and movies have dramatized Cleopatra's life, but the triumphs and tragedies of Queen Hatshepsut have been overlooked. Working with a group, write a short, two-act play dramatizing some events in Hatshepsut's life. Find out more about this powerful Egyptian queen by doing research in libraries or on the Internet. Each member of your little production company might be responsible for one or more of the following tasks: directing, writing, acting, costume design, and set design. Perform your play informally for the class.

■ MATHEMATICS/ART

Do-It-Yourself Pyramid You've read about the complex calculations that went into building the pyramids. Now it's your turn. Do your own calculations to construct a scale model of a pyramid using small blocks that you buy or make from clay or Styrofoam. If necessary, read more about how the Egyptians calculated the slope and dimensions of a pyramid. Be sure to keep a record of your calculations. Also, before you start building, you might want to sketch out a diagram or blueprint of your pyramid.

READ ON: FOR INDEPENDENT READING

■ NONFICTION

Cleopatra by Diane Stanley and Peter Vennema (William Morrow, 1994) describes the life and times of Cleopatra, queen of Egypt, who lived in the first century B.C. and is one of the most famous women in history. This 1995 winner of the ALA Notable Books for Children nonfiction award is accompanied with full-page illustrations.

Pharaohs of Ancient Egypt by Elizabeth Payne (Econo-Clad, 1999) explores archaeological evidence that has shed light on early Egyptian civilization. The author describes the discovery of the Rosetta Stone and goes on to include information about ancient Egyptian religion and the rulers who defined this fascinating era of human history.

Pyramid by David Macaulay (Houghton Mifflin, 1975) describes the step-by-step process of the building of an Egyptian pyramid. Pen-and-ink illustrations accompany this 1976 Boston Globe-Horn Book Honor winner.

The Riddle of the Rosetta Stone by James Cross Giblin (Harper, 1990) tells how the discovery of the Rosetta Stone led to deciphering Egyptian hieroglyphics, which unlocked a great deal of ancient history. This 1991 winner of the ALA Notable Books for Children nonfiction award is illustrated with photos and reproductions of original engravings.

Tales Mummies Tell by Patricia Lauber (Crowell, 1985) explains how a wide variety of mummies can reveal information about ancient civilizations and prehistoric life. This 1986 winner of the ALA Notable Books for Children nonfiction award features many photographs and illustrations.

■ FICTION

Aida by Leontyne Price (Harcourt Brace, 1990) retells the story of Verdi's opera in which the love of the enslaved Ethiopian princess for an Egyptian general leads to tragedy. The author also includes a personal note about the opera and its meaning. This 1991 Coretta Scott King Award winner is accompanied by illustrations.

The Golden Goblet by Eloise Jarvis McGraw (Coward-McCann, 1961) This 1962 Newbery Honor Book tells the mysterious tale of an Egyptian boy who struggles to reveal an awful crime and to reshape his life after his father's death.

His Majesty, Queen Hatshepsut by Dorothy Sharp Carter (Lippincott, 1987) is a fictionalized account of the life of Hatshepshut, the only female pharaoh of ancient Egypt. The book combines history and story-telling and provides a look at a woman who ruled Egypt for over twenty years.

Mara, Daughter of the Nile by Eloise Jarvis McGraw (Econo-Clad, 1999) is the story of Mara, an Egyptian slave girl, who becomes a spy during the reign of Queen Hatshepsut, the "pharaoh queen" of ancient Egypt.

Tales of Ancient Egypt by Roger Lancelyn Green (Penguin Puffin, 1972) is a classic collection of myths, fables, and legends of ancient Egypt.

CHAPTER 4

The People of the Book
The Ancient Hebrews   2000 B.C.–A.D. 70

A Land of Milk and Honey

The Hebrews of Biblical times lived in the Middle East in a strip of land between the ancient empires of Egypt and Mesopotamia. This region was known as Canaan, which would later be called Israel. Although mostly desert land, the Bible called ancient Israel the "land flowing with milk and honey." To the ancient Hebrews, Canaan was also known as the "promised land," a gift directly from God.

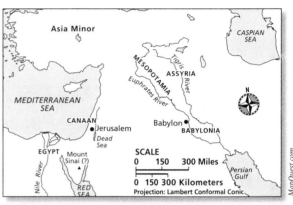

▲ Canaan and the ancient Middle East.

David the Hero and Solomon the Builder

Around the tenth century B.C., the Hebrews chose their first king, Saul. King Saul was followed by King David, a warrior who added more territory to the Hebrew kingdom. He was also a musician who may have written many of the songs in the Bible's book of Psalms. King David was one of the more colorful characters in the Bible. One well-known Bible story tells how David, as a boy, killed an enemy named Goliath by hurling a single stone from his slingshot.

After David's death around 962 B.C., his son Solomon became king. Solomon is remembered as a wise king who started many building projects, the most famous being a new temple in Jerusalem, built to worship God. Solomon's temple stood for four centuries, until the Babylonians destroyed it in 586 B.C.

▲ Solomon's Temple at Jerusalem.

Memorable Quote

"Without the Jews, we would see the world through different eyes, hear with different ears, even feel with different feelings."

—from *The Gifts of the Jews*
by Thomas Cahill

INVESTIGATE: Research the various theories about what happened to the Ten Lost Tribes of Israel. How has the legend of the Lost Tribes been important in Israel's history?

▲ Masada.

SuperStock

VOCABULARY MATTERS

Hebrew is the oldest name for the Jewish people and their language (from *ivri,* "one from across (the Euphrates River)." *Israelite* (iz'rē•ə•līt') is another name for the Jewish people, especially those of Biblical times (from *Israel,* a name adopted by Jacob, Abraham's grandson). *Jew* is a name used since the Romans destroyed the Temple of Jerusalem in A.D. 70 (from *Judah,* a Hebrew tribe). *Israeli* (iz•rā'lē) is the name for a citizen of modern Israel.

The "Lost Tribes"—Where Did They Go?

After the time of David and Solomon, the Hebrew kingdom split in two—into a southern kingdom called Judah and a northern kingdom called Israel. The Assyrians conquered Israel in the eighth century B.C. According to Jewish history, the Assyrians dragged the ten northern tribes of Hebrews off into Assyria and Mesopotamia and resettled the land with people from Mesopotamia. The fate of these northern tribes is lost to history. Some people believe that the "lost tribes" found their way to Ethiopia; others claim that they sailed all the way to the Americas!

Live Free or Die

Judah became a Roman province in A.D. 6 and became known as Judea. The Jews hated Roman rule. In the great revolt of A.D. 66–70, several hundred Jews took refuge near the Dead Sea in a mountain fort named Masada. The Roman army spent many months building a ramp up to the fort, but when the Romans reached the summit, they found hundreds of dead Jews. The Jews had decided to take their own lives rather than submit to the Roman soldiers. Today, the slogan "Masada shall not fall again" can be seen almost everywhere in Israel.

Symbols of Pride and Tragedy

A scroll is often used to symbolize the Hebrew Bible, especially the first five books. These books are called the Torah (tō´rə).

A menorah (mə•nō´rə) is a candlestick with a central upright holder and several curved branches. A seven-branched menorah is used in Jewish services and is also a symbol of Judaism and the modern nation of Israel.

The Magen David, or Shield of David, is another symbol of Judaism and the nation of Israel. The Shield of David, also called the Star of David, is made of two triangles that form a six-pointed star. During the Second World War (1939–1945), German Nazis forced European Jews to wear a yellow Star of David as a badge of shame. The Star of David allowed Nazis to identify Jews easily and, eventually, to murder millions of them.

What makes someone a hero? Maybe heroes are simply those people who are able to overcome hardships when the chips are down. The following short selection from *Women of the Bible* tells the story of Deborah, a Jewish hero who helped save Israel during a dark period in the nation's early history.

Deborah

from *Women of the Bible*

by CAROLE ARMSTRONG

"Awake, awake, Deborah! Awake, awake, utter a song." (Judges 5:12)

Deborah was a great judge[1] of Israel, the only woman ever to have held such a position. Many people flocked to hear her wise words as she delivered her judgments on Mount Ephraim,[2] sitting under a palm tree, the tree of life and a symbol of hope.

At this time, the Israelites were ruled by the Canaanites[3] who were led by a general called Sisera. He was a powerful man and for twenty years he had oppressed the Israelites. Eventually the Israelite leaders came to Deborah in the hope that she could rescue them from their plight. Knowing that she could rely on God's help, Deborah immediately summoned Barak, military commander of the Israelites, and

> ## You Need to Know...
> Before the ancient Hebrews chose kings as rulers, leaders called judges ruled the land. Only one woman, Deborah, served as a judge. Her story is told in the Bible in two chapters of the Book of Judges. One of these chapters is a poem that tells of God sending a storm to help the Israelites defeat the superior forces of an enemy. This chapter—Judges 5—is thought to be one of the oldest passages in the Hebrew Bible. The other chapter—Judges 4—tells the story in prose, or ordinary written language. As you read the following summary of Deborah's story, watch also for the role played by another famous woman—Jael.

oppressed (ə·prest′): treated harshly and unjustly.

plight (plīt): bad or dangerous state or condition.

1. **judge:** in ancient Israel, a leader who settled disputes, spoke in God's name, and served as a military leader.
2. **Mount Ephraim** (ē′frā·im): mountain in central Israel.
3. **Canaanites** (kā′nən·īts′): a people who lived in the land also occupied by the Israelites.

Chariots of Iron

In Deborah's time the Israelites used weapons made mostly of bronze, a mixture of metals that is softer and less durable than iron. Thus, the iron chariots and weapons of the Canaanites gave them superior military power. Since Barak knew about the Canaanites warfare advantage, it is not surprising that he was afraid to fight Sisera.

SuperStock

▲ Deborah served as the only woman judge of ancient Israel. ❓ **What do you think was notable about Deborah, especially given the time period she lived in?**

ordered him to gather together ten thousand men. She reminded him of God's command to lead his people to Mount Tabor[4] and fight Sisera's army. Barak was afraid—Sisera had nine hundred chariots of iron and an army that far outnumbered his. "If thou wilt go with me," he told Deborah, "then I will go." Deborah agreed, for she had God's promise that the Israelites would win: "I will draw unto thee Sisera, with his chariots and his multitude; and I will deliver him into thine hand," she assured Barak, and before long, the Israelites defeated Sisera's army.

Sisera was forced to escape on foot and took <u>refuge</u> in the tent of a friend called Heber. Jael, Heber's wife,

refuge (ref′yo͞oj): safety or shelter.

4. **Mount Tabor** (tā′bər): mountain in northern Israel near Nazareth and the Sea of Galilee.

pretended to welcome the General, but secretly she sympathized with the Israelites. When he fell asleep, she brutally killed him with a blow to his head.

From that day, the Israelites were free from oppression, Deborah composed a beautiful song of triumph and praise to God, as it was with His help that the Israelites had overthrown the Canaanites.

Erich Lessing/Art Resource, NY

▲ The ancient Hebrews were often at war with neighboring cultures. This Mesopotamian relief carving depicts Israelite exiles carrying provisions after their defeat in battle.

✓ Reading Check

1. Why did people flock to Deborah?

2. Who led the superior military forces of the Canaanites? How long had he oppressed the Israelites?

3. Why was Barak afraid to fight the Canaanites?

4. Why was Deborah not afraid to fight the Canaanites?

5. How did the Canaanite general die?

If you were asked to name two people from the Hebrew Bible (known to Christians as the Old Testament), chances are good you'd come up with Abraham and Moses. The stories of these ancient Hebrew leaders are legendary. Abraham is credited as the founder of a new religion, while Moses is known as the great liberator of his people. Read on to find out more about these famous figures of Hebrew history.

Judaism

from *One World, Many Religions*

by MARY POPE OSBORNE

"Hear, O Israel: the Lord our God, the Lord is one." (Deuteronomy 6:4)

The story of Judaism begins with a shepherd named Abraham and his wife, Sarah. They lived almost four thousand years ago in the ancient land of Ur, in what is now Iraq. At that time, the people of Ur worshiped many gods, including gods of fire, water, and the sky.

According to a Jewish legend, Abraham began to wonder which of these gods was the one true God. One day, when the sun was shining, Abraham decided the sun must be God. When the sun went down and the moon rose in the sky, he decided the moon was God. But when the moon vanished the next morning, Abraham decided there must be a power even greater than the sun or the moon—greater than all

You Need to Know...

According to the Bible, Abraham and Sarah were the ancestors of the Hebrews. They came from the land of Ur, in ancient Mesopotamia (today's Iraq), and settled in Canaan. The adventures of Abraham, Sarah, and their family are narrated in Genesis, the first book of the Bible. *Genesis* means "beginnings," and the Hebrew people trace their beginning to Abraham and Sarah.

Several hundred years later, the Hebrews were forced into slavery in Egypt. Moses, a Hebrew raised in the Egyptian court of the pharaoh, eventually stepped in to deliver his people from bondage and led them on a long, long journey back to Canaan, the "promised land."

living things. He thought this great invisible power must be the one true God.

In time, this one true God spoke to Abraham and made a covenant, or agreement, with him. God promised to bless Abraham and Sarah and lead them to a faraway land called Canaan. In return, Abraham promised that he and his family would always be faithful to God.

From then on, Abraham and his descendants believed in only one God, a God who enters every human life in a personal way. This was a stunning new idea—one that made Judaism different from all other religions of the time.

After Abraham and Sarah reached Canaan, their son Isaac had a son named Jacob, who would later be called Israel. As the centuries passed, Abraham's descendants came to be called the Israelites. The Israelites eventually left Canaan because of a shortage of food. About five hundred years after Abraham's death, they were living in Egypt. At first the Egyptians treated them well, but the Israelites grew too numerous, and the Egyptian ruler forced them into slavery.

▲ In this artwork by Dutch artist Gerard Hoet (1648–1733), Abraham is shown leading his family to the land of Canaan.

descendants (dē·sen′dənts): people who trace their families back to a certain ancestor.

stunning (stun′iŋ): striking or remarkable.

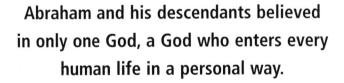

Abraham and his descendants believed in only one God, a God who enters every human life in a personal way.

According to Jewish history, one day God spoke to an Israelite named Moses. God told Moses that he should lead the Israelites out of Egypt and back to the "Promised Land" of Canaan—the land God had promised to Abraham long ago.

Moses went to the Egyptian king and asked him to free the Israelite slaves. When the king said no, God caused ten terrible <u>plagues</u> to happen to the Egyptians, including a hailstorm, an <u>infestation</u> of locusts, and, worst of all, the death of every firstborn son. Finally, the king begged Moses to lead his people away.

The Israelites began to leave Egypt. But the king changed his mind and sent his soldiers after them to bring them back. The soldiers caught up with the Israelites at the Red Sea. The Israelites were trapped—water in front of them, soldiers behind.

Moses climbed up on a rock and prayed to God for help. Then he stretched his hand over the waters, and they parted. The Israelites crossed safely to the other side, and the waters returned, drowning the soldiers. At last, the Israelites were free from slavery. For the next forty years,

St. Peter's Basilica, The Vatican, Rome/SuperStock

▲ In this painting by Italian artist Raphael (1483–1520), Pharaoh's army is swallowed by the waters of the Red Sea. ❓ **What impact do you think such paintings have on believers of the Jewish faith?**

"Who was Moses? He was raised as an Egyptian yet came to the rescue of a Hebrew slave. He could not have spoken Hebrew yet was chosen to lead the Israelites out of Egypt. The Bible suggests that a million or more people followed Moses. Yet there are no Egyptian records of such a mass migration, nor could the desert have supported so many.

Were those who followed Abraham and those who followed Moses four hundred years later perhaps two very different groups of people whom Moses united under his leadership? . . .

Perhaps the ancient soils of the Near East will one day reveal their secrets."

—from *The Ancient Hebrews* by Kenny Mann

they wandered in the desert, learning how to be a free people under the leadership of Moses and God.

During that time, God gave ten laws to Moses to give to the Israelites. These laws, called the Ten Commandments, were carved on stone tablets. They told the Israelites how they should behave in their daily lives.

Moses died before his people reached the Promised Land. But after his death, the Israelites carried the stone tablets bearing the Ten Commandments into Canaan. And there they built a great nation.

The Ten Commandments became the core of Judaism's holy book, which the Jews call the *Tanach*,[1] or Bible. The first five books of the Bible are called the Torah, which means "teaching." Many Jewish people believe that God gave these five books directly to Moses.

The Torah includes some of humanity's greatest stories. It tells us that God created the world in six days, then rested on the seventh. It tells the stories of Adam and Eve in the Garden of Eden; of their son Cain killing his brother, Abel; of Noah and the ark. The Torah tells Jews how they should live their lives, and it tells the history of their people.

---

1. **Tanach** (tä·näkh'): the entire Hebrew or Jewish Bible; the Christian Old Testament.

The Ten Commandments

Thou shalt have no other gods before me.
Thou shalt not make thyself a graven image.
Thou shalt not take the name of the Lord thy God
    in vain.
Remember the Sabbath day, to keep it holy.
Honor thy father and thy mother.
Thou shalt not murder.
Thou shalt not commit adultery.
Thou shalt not steal.
Thou shalt not bear false witness against thy neighbor.
Thou shalt not covet.

✓ Reading Check

1. In God's covenant with Abraham, what did God promise? What did Abraham promise in return?

2. A few centuries after Abraham and Sarah, the Israelites left Canaan and moved to Egypt. Why did they move?

3. Why did the Israelites become unhappy in Egypt?

4. What was carved on the stone tablets God gave Moses?

MEET THE *Writer*

Mary Pope Osborne (1949–   ) has published novels, as well as retellings of myths and fairy tales for young people. Recently, she has focused on picture books, biographies, and nonfiction.

Did you know the Bible seems to contain a little of everything, including stories of war, mystery, and romance? It's not surprising, then, to realize how important the Bible has been through the ages, not only as a religious guide, but also as a source of inspiration for countless creative works.

from The Writings

from *A Treasury of Jewish Literature: From Biblical Times to Today*

by GLORIA GOLDREICH

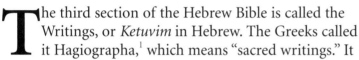

The third section of the Hebrew Bible is called the Writings, or *Ketuvim* in Hebrew. The Greeks called it Hagiographa,[1] which means "sacred writings." It is perhaps the most varied and exciting part of the Bible. It includes many different literary forms, and its content ranges from poetry to history. Its poetic works include the lilting songs of the Book of Psalms, the sad verses of Lamentations, and the passionate love hymns of the Song of Songs. Religious philosophy, popular wisdom, and guidance are contained within the Proverbs, Ecclesiastes,[2] and the Book of Job. The books of Ruth and Esther are known as *megillot*—scrolls—because they were passed on through the

You Need to Know...

The books of the Hebrew Bible were originally written on scrolls. The three main sets of scrolls, or sections, include the Torah, which means "law" or "teaching"; Nevi'im, which means "prophets"; and Ketuvim, which means "writings."

The Torah consists of the first five books of the Bible. These books tell how the Hebrew people developed and give the rules from God that they were required to follow.

The Prophets begins with books that include Jewish history—Joshua, Judges, Samuel, and Kings. This section goes on to present the writings of men such as Amos and Jeremiah, who reveal God's message to the people.

The third section, the Writings, contains many different kinds of literature. At the end of the following selection, you will find examples of some ancient Hebrew poems and proverbs. They come from the Books of Psalms and Proverbs, which appear in the Writings section of the Bible.

---

1. **Hagiographa** (hag′ē•äg′rə•fə).
2. **Ecclesiastes** (e•klē′zē•as′tēz′).

generations in that form. They are moving narratives that tell the stories of great women who molded the destiny of their people in troubled times. The Song of Songs, Lamentations, and Ecclesiastes are also *megillot.* The books of Ezra, Nehemiah, and Chronicles are revealing histories that answer many questions and ask many others.

The Torah, the first section of the Bible, legislates ethical[3] and wise conduct for the nation of Israel. The Prophets, the second section, implores individuals to live moral and just lives. In the Writings, the third section, the Psalms and the Proverbs offer advice on how this can be done.

In the Torah and the Prophets, Israel is addressed by the prophets or by God Himself. In the Book of Psalms, it is Israel and the human heart that speak. The individual psalmist,[4] speaking either for himself or for the Jewish people, expresses sorrow, disappointment, and suffering, as well as gratitude, exaltation, and blessing. The lyric words of the verses convey the inner mood of the individual and give voice to the vast sweep of human emotions. The pathos[5] of sorrow, the thrill of victory, the despair of defeat, and the affirmation of hope all find voice in wondrously linked words, alleged[6] to have been penned by King David, the poet-warrior, "the sweet singer in Israel."

In a more practical vein, Proverbs, said to have been written by David's son Solomon, the wisest of kings, tells us that "a false balance is abomination[7] to the Lord but a just weight is His delight." We clearly see the linkage between truth and holiness.

The Book of Job, a literary masterpiece that the English poet Lord Alfred Tennyson called "the greatest poem of ancient or modern times," poses this

legislates (lej′is•lāts′): brings about by making laws.

implores (im•plôrz′): asks earnestly.

just (just): upright; virtuous.

affirmation (af′ər•mā′shən): act of declaring to be true.

Galleria dell' Accademia, Florence/SuperStock

▲ Michelangelo Buonarroti (1475–1564) is generally thought to be one of the world's greatest artists. His statue of the courageous Biblical hero David stands over fourteen feet tall and is considered a masterpiece.

3. **ethical** (eth′i•kəl): in keeping with standards of proper behavior or actions.
4. **psalmist** (säm′ist): composer of sacred poems or songs.
5. **pathos** (pā′thäs′): quality that arouses tender feelings of pity or sympathy.
6. **alleged** (ə•lejd′): declared to be true without proof.
7. **abomination** (ə•bäm′ə•nā′shən): something very bad or hateful.

basic ethical question: If God is just and merciful, why must the good suffer? Job ultimately affirms his faith and acknowledges the incomprehensible complexity of the universe.

The Book of Ecclesiastes is also known as *Kohelet,* which means "one who addresses an assembly." It is a philosophic work introduced by a philosophic statement: "Vanity of vanities—all is vanity." Just as Job questioned the justice of God, so *Kohelet* questions the relevance[8] of life. Because of its poetic language and its almost contemporary approach, modern writers and thinkers are drawn to *Kohelet* for inspiration and guidance. It was there that Ernest Hemingway found the title for his novel *The Sun Also Rises.* A popular song of the 1960s borrowed the words of the man who spoke before a congregation[9] of ancient Israel: "To everything there is a season, and a time to every purpose under heaven."

© *Dean Conger/CORBIS*

▲ Photo of ancient Torah. This Torah scroll is thought to be more than 3,500 years old, possibly the oldest one in existence.

The works included in the Writings testify to the human being's eternal striving after reason, the quest to understand the world, and the constant battle to live a moral, purposeful, meaningful life.

Perhaps the most beautiful section of this third part of the Bible is the Song of Songs. Said to have been written by Solomon, it is a series of beautiful love poems that celebrate the end of winter and the coming of spring. It is a hymn to renewed strength and soft submission. Although it is, in part, a dialogue between a lover and his beloved, the rabbis interpret it as a recitation[10] of the love of God, the bridegroom, for Israel, the bride. Since Jewish literature is an <u>integral</u> part of Jewish observance, the Song of Songs is read as part of a prayer service in the synagogues on the Sabbath of Passover week.

integral (in'tə·grəl): essential.

8. **relevance** (rel'ə·vəns): importance.
9. **congregation** (kän'grə·gā'shən): people gathered in a group.
10. **recitation** (res'ə·tā'shən): a telling.

Covering the Bases: The Talmud

From how to interpret the Bible to how to deal with a medical problem, the Talmud (täl′mo͝od) probably has something to say. The Talmud is a huge collection of writings that contains ancient Jewish traditions, teachings, and folk tales. Finding an answer to a question might take a while, however: The Talmud consists of over fifteen thousand pages in sixty volumes.

◄ A rabbi—a Jewish spiritual leader—reading the Talmud.

Bettmann/CORBIS

SELECTED PSALMS

Psalm 3

Lord, how the numbers of my enemy have grown!
There are so many who have risen up against me.
Many have said of my soul, "There is no help
for him in God."
But You, O Lord, are a shield to me,
My glory and the reason I lift my head.
I cried to the Lord with my voice
And He heard me from His holy hill.
I lay down and slept,
And I was awakened and the Lord took care of me.
I will not be afraid of ten thousands of people
Even if they surround me.
Arise, O Lord, save me,
O my God, for You have struck all my enemies
upon the cheek,
And have broken the teeth of the ungodly.
Salvation belongs to the Lord:
Your blessing is upon Your people.
Amen.

Psalm 8

O Lord, how great is Your name in all the earth!
For You have set Your glory about the heavens.
Out of the mouths of babes You have sent wisdom
And Your might has stilled the enemy.
When I consider Your heavens,
The work of Your fingers,
The moon and the stars You have created;
What is man that you are aware of him?
And the son of man that you have visited him?
For You have made him a little lower than the angels
And have crowned him with glory and honor.
You made him master of things of your making
And put all things under his feet:
All sheep and oxen, yes, and beasts of the field,
The birds in the air and the fish of the sea.
O Lord, how great is Your name on the earth!

Psalm 23

The Lord is my shepherd, I shall not want.
He makes me lie down in green pastures,
He leads me beside the still waters.
He restores my soul:
He leads me in the paths of righteousness
    for His name's sake.
Yes, though I walk through the valley of the
    shadow of death,
I will fear no evil:
For He is with me.
His rod and His staff they comfort me.
He prepares a table before me in the presence
    of my enemies:
He anoints my head with oil; my cup runs over.
Surely goodness and mercy shall follow me all
    the days of my life:
And I will live in the house of the Lord for ever.

SuperStock

SELECTED PROVERBS

A wise man will hear, and will increase his learning;
And a man of understanding shall look for wise counsel.

Say not to your neighbor, "Go and come again and tomorrow I will give you," when you have it to give today.

The wise shall inherit glory, but shame shall be the portion of fools.

Enter not into the path of the wicked, and go not in the way of evil men. Avoid it, pass not by it, turn from it, and pass away.

The path of the just is like a shining light, the way of the wicked is like darkness; and they know not at what they stumble.

A wise son makes a glad father, but a foolish son is the heaviness of his mother.

He that hides hatred with lying lips, and he that speaks slander is a fool.

The tongue of the just is silver; the heart of the wicked is worth little.

✔ Reading Check

1. Which books in the Writings contain poetry?

2. Which books offer philosophy, wisdom, and guidance?

3. Which books tell the stories of great women?

4. From which book of the Bible did Ernest Hemingway find the title for his novel *The Sun Also Rises*?

5. What is the number of the Psalm that marvels at God's creation of human beings?

The study of ancient literatures involves a little bit of art, a little bit of science, and, sometimes, a lot of mystery. Read on to learn about one of the most important literary "finds" in the history of archaeology.

HISTORY •———
SCIENCE •———
LANGUAGE ARTS •———

The Mystery of Qumran and the Dead Sea Scrolls

from *Muse*

by HERSHEL SHANKS

*O*ne day 50 years ago, a young Bedouin shepherd named edh-Dhib discovered something extraordinary. Thinking that a lost sheep might be hiding in a hillside cave, he threw a rock inside to scare it out. But he didn't hear bleating; he heard the crack of broken pottery. When he and a friend went into the cave, they found some large jars. Inside the jars, wrapped in linen, were seven ancient scrolls that turned out to be almost two thousand years old. Edh-Dhib made his discovery on the northwestern edge of the Dead Sea, about 15 miles—a day's walk—from Jerusalem, and so the scrolls were called the Dead Sea Scrolls.

You Need to Know...

Have you ever heard of the Dead Sea Scrolls, the ancient writings discovered in the 1940s in caves near the Dead Sea? How were the scrolls discovered? Why are they considered to be important? Did people who lived at the village of Qumran (kōōm•rän'), near where they were discovered, write them? What kind of community was ancient Qumran? This selection provides perhaps the best responses that can be given to these questions at this time.

It's an incredible story. Eventually, several caves—numbered 1 through 11—were discovered. The caves held a huge ancient library of over 800 scrolls. Almost all were in <u>tatters</u>; only a few scraps of each scroll could be read. Soon, archaeologists began to excavate a nearby ancient settlement called Qumran. They hoped that they might find clues at Qumran that would

tatters (tat'ərz): rags; shreds.

▲ Caves near the Dead Sea where ancient scrolls were found. ❷ **Why do you think the Dead Sea Scrolls remained undiscovered for so many centuries?**

Erich Lessing/Art Resource, NY

tell them who wrote the scrolls and why. Some caves, like Cave 4, were almost part of Qumran. Others, like Cave 1 (where the scrolls were first discovered), were nearly a mile away.

Why do we care about such old documents? Because the scrolls tell us a lot about the Bible, the origins of Christianity, and early Judaism. They were written between 250 B.C. and A.D. 70, at a time when these religions were developing in important ways. There were many different kinds of scrolls in the caves: biblical books, stories about the end of the world, religious laws, and even a copper scroll that lists places where hidden treasure is supposed to be buried.

But the Dead Sea Scrolls remain mysterious. In fact, we're not even sure how they were found. Was it really edh-Dhib who found them? Several different men—with

---

Why do we care about such old documents? Because the scrolls tell us a lot about the Bible, the origins of Christianity, and early Judaism.

---

several different stories—have claimed to be him. Whose story should we believe? And when scholars try to decide what the scrolls tell us, there is even more disagreement.

Qumran

Though the Dead Sea Scrolls were found near Qumran, we aren't sure whether they have anything to do with the people who lived there. The one thing we *do* know is that Qumran was a Jewish settlement. First of all, it is located in Judea,[1] the ancient homeland of the Jews. Next, archaeologists have found special baths that were used in Jewish rituals. Finally, Jewish names were written on pieces of pottery found at the site.

But what kind of place was Qumran? Who lived there? The most interesting and most likely possibility is that Qumran was some kind of religious settlement where men lived together and shared everything: their belongings, their work, their faith. Qumran is in the middle of the desert and religious people often choose to live away from others so that they can worship and meditate[2] without distractions.

The ruins at Qumran suggest that people lived there communally. There are several large rooms of the kind you'd expect in a religious settlement, sort of like the ones you'd find at a summer camp. One of the large rooms may have been a dining hall. In a small room next to it, archaeologists found hundreds of simple, undecorated plates and bowls. This crude tableware is the kind that would be used by a strict religious group.

distractions (di·strak′shəns): things that draw attention away.

communally (kə·myoon′əl·lē): sharing together as a group.

---

1. **Judea** (joo·dē′ə): southern part of ancient Israel.
2. **meditate** (med′ə·tāt′): think deeply over a period of time; contemplate.

An Ancient Treasure Map?

Perhaps the most puzzling of all the scrolls found in the caves near Qumran is the Copper Scroll. Why? First of all, the Copper Scroll is written in a strange dialect of Hebrew, and the penmanship is not that of a trained scribe. Also, it is inscribed on copper instead of parchment or papyrus. Perhaps most startling, its contents don't resemble *anything* else, except maybe a pirate's treasure map.

What's on the Copper Scroll? A list of sixty-four locations of stacks of valuables. One entry after another goes on like this one: "In the rubble pit of the foundry of Manos, going down to the east 3 cubits up from the bottom, 40 talents of silver." No one knows where to find the places mentioned, but it's clear that the scroll lists parts of a vast store of treasure.

Whose treasure was it? Many scholars think the objects were taken from the treasury in the Temple of Jerusalem to be hidden from the Romans. Were the treasures found and melted down long ago, or do they still lie waiting to be reclaimed? Others believe that the scroll is a work of fiction, an ancient folklore. The only certainty is that the Copper Scroll remains a mystery.

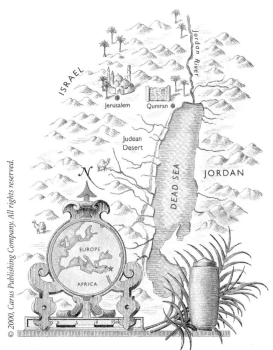

▲ A modern-day map of the area around the Dead Sea.

fortress (fôr'tris): stronghold; fort.

fortified (fôrt'ə•fīd): strengthened against attack by using walls or forts.

But even if Qumran *was* a religious community, what evidence is there to connect the scrolls to the site? First of all, the most important cave where scrolls were found is practically inside the settlement. Second, some scholars have claimed that one of the large rooms was a scriptorium,[3] a room where scribes copied manuscripts.

How do we know writing went on there? Well, two inkwells were found in the room. Does that prove people wrote there? Perhaps, but not a single scrap of scroll was found inside the "scriptorium"—or anywhere else at the site, for that matter. If writing went on at Qumran, shouldn't the archaeologists have found at least *some* scrolls?

The "scriptorium" also contains several strange stone structures that earlier archaeologists thought were benches and desks where scribes sat to work. People believed this theory for a long time. But it was finally shown that if the structures *were* desks, they would have been very uncomfortable. The seats were so low that your knees would always be getting in your way! Nowadays, no one is sure what these "desks" were for.

One scholar claims that Qumran wasn't a religious settlement at all: he thinks it was a military <u>fortress</u>. This is because archaeologists have found some arrowheads and, more importantly, a <u>fortified</u> tower at the site. Forts are often built in isolated areas to watch and protect a country's borders. But Qumran is missing two things most military fortresses had: a single, easy-to-defend entrance and a courtyard for soldiers to practice in. Also, many large farms in the area had towers like the one at Qumran. So perhaps when people built any kind of settlement in the wilderness, they made it easy to defend.

Still other scholars say that Qumran might have been a kind of Dead Sea Hilton hotel, where merchants and

---

3. scriptorium (skrip•tôr'ē•əm).

travelers crossing the Dead Sea on their way to and from Jerusalem could stay and have a meal. Or it could have been some kind of retreat, where people came to purify themselves.

To make things even more complicated, some scholars say it was one thing in one period and something else in another—for example, a fortified farm that later became a religious settlement. What all this comes down to is this: scholars don't know for sure what kind of place Qumran was, and they aren't even sure if it had anything to do with the Dead Sea Scrolls.

The Essenes

There's another part of the mystery that no one has solved. If Qumran *was* the home of religious people, who were they? The most common suggestion is that they were Essenes,[4] a Jewish sect that opposed the powerful priesthood of the Jerusalem Temple. They followed unusually strict laws of purity, lived together in communities, and believed that the end-time was near. Ancient descriptions of the beliefs of Essenes are similar to the rules and beliefs in the Dead Sea Scrolls. But the word Essene never appears in the scrolls. And no synagogue has been found at Qumran. Some scholars suggest that the people of Qumran were a *special* kind of Essene, a little different from those described in the ancient literature. That's a possibility, but still, no one knows for sure.

We know that the Dead Sea Scrolls are one of the most important archaeological discoveries ever made. What they tell us is tremendously important not only to historians and scholars, but also to Jews and Christians who are interested in learning more about the origins of their faiths. But even though the scrolls have been studied

---

4. **Essenes** (es′ēnz).

▲ Fragment of a Dead Sea Scroll.

by scholars for over 50 years, we still have a lot to learn about them, and about Qumran and the Essenes.

Sometimes students—and even scholars—must learn to live with uncertainties and conjectures.[5] But I think that makes the study of ancient history more, not less, interesting and exciting. I hope you agree.

_____

5. **conjectures** (kən·jek′chərz): guesses made from incomplete information.

✔ Reading Check

1. How were the Dead Sea Scrolls found?

2. Why do some scholars think that Qumran was a religious settlement?

3. Why do others think that Qumran was a military fortress?

4. What do still others think that Qumran might have been?

5. Even though much remains to be learned about them, why are the Dead Sea Scrolls important?

MEET THE *Writer*

Hershel Shanks (1930–   ) has spent much of his life studying the ancient Hebrews and helping other people learn about them. He is the founder and editor of two magazines related to Biblical topics, and his books include a guide to Biblical Jerusalem and a study of ancient synagogues.

The Bible has been a bestselling book for ages, but did you know that it's also hit the top of the pop music charts? Psalms and other short excerpts from the Bible have been set to music since ancient times, but more recent tunes have also been made from Bible verses. The following excerpt from Ecclesiastes became a hit in the 1960s and can still be heard on "oldies" radio broadcasts.

PRIMARY SOURCE

LANGUAGE ARTS •

MUSIC •

To Every Thing There Is a Season

Ecclesiastes 3:1–8, *from* the King James Bible

Hulton–Deutsch Collection/CORBIS

▲ This photo of the American folk-rock group The Byrds was taken in 1965, the same year their album *Turn! Turn! Turn!* was released.

1 To every thing there is a season, and a time to every purpose under the heaven:

2 A time to be born, and a time to die; a time to plant, and a time to pluck up that which is planted;

3 A time to kill, and a time to heal; a time to break down, and a time to build up;

4 A time to weep, and a time to laugh; a time to mourn, and a time to dance;

5 A time to cast away stones, and a time to gather stones together; a time to embrace, and a time to refrain from embracing;

6 A time to get, and a time to lose; a time to keep, and a time to cast away;

7 A time to rend,[1] and a time to sew; a time to keep silence, and a time to speak;

8 A time to love, and a time to hate; a time of war, and a time of peace.

> **You Need to Know...**
> The Byrds, a popular folk-rock group of the 1960s, hit the top of the popular music charts with the release of their second album, *Turn! Turn! Turn!* in 1965. The title song, written by Pete Seeger, takes its lyrics from this short Bible passage. Seeger converted the lines from Ecclesiastes to four verses and a haunting refrain: "To everything—turn! turn! turn!—there is a season—turn! turn! turn!—and a time to every purpose under heaven."

---

1. rend: to tear apart.

Seeger and the Sixties

Pete Seeger (1919–   ), the composer of "Turn! Turn! Turn!" was one of the most famous songwriters and folk singers of the 1960s. In songs like "Where Have All the Flowers Gone" and "Little Boxes," Seeger protested war and poked fun at people's concern with status.

© Hulton-Deutsch Collection/CORBIS

▲ Pete Seeger.

✓ Reading Check

1. Which line states the theme of the poem?

2. Which lines use pairs of opposites to illustrate the theme?

MEET THE *Writer*

The writer of Ecclesiastes (*Kohelet* in Hebrew) says he was king of Israel and made wisdom his study. For this reason, it was long believed that King Solomon wrote Ecclesiastes during the tenth century B.C. Clues in the book itself, however, indicate that the writer actually lived some time after the sixth century B.C. Regardless of his or her identity, the author of Ecclesiastes penned some of the best-known passages of the Hebrew Bible.

Cross-Curricular ACTIVITIES

■ ART/GEOGRAPHY

How Did They Get There from There?

Draw a map of the routes of Abraham and Sarah's journey from Mesopotamia to Canaan or the journey of Moses and the Israelites from Egypt to Canaan. (Many Bibles contain a map section.) Then, illustrate your map, showing with words or symbols where key events took place.

■ MUSIC

Singing a Bible Song Psalm 23, "The Lord Is My Shepherd," and Ecclesiastes 3:1–8, "To Every Thing There Is a Season," are two of the most famous passages from the Bible. Find as many different musical versions of Psalm 23 as you can, as well as the Pete Seeger version of Ecclesiastes (made famous by The Byrds as "Turn! Turn! Turn!" and also recorded by other artists). For help, search the Internet or talk to choir directors, music teachers, or music-store clerks. If possible, listen to tapes or CDs of the versions you find. Sing or play your favorite version(s) for the class.

■ HISTORY/SCIENCE

Arms Racing When Deborah's people needed to fight, they faced the superior technology of Sisera's iron chariots. Over the ages, warfare has often spurred inventions—crossbows, armor, cannons, machine guns, and tanks, to name a few. One such twentieth-century invention was radar, which was perfected in the 1940s during World War II. Research the invention of something that was developed for or used in warfare and some of the consequences of its use.

■ HISTORY/SPEECH

You Can Say That Again! In Israel the slogan "Masada shall not fall again!" can be seen almost everywhere. The slogan stands for heroic resistance to any enemy. Think of other places where critical events occurred in history—places like Waterloo, Gettysburg, the Warsaw Ghetto, the Berlin Wall, or Tiananmen Square. Choose one place, and read about the historic event associated with this place. Then, write a slogan that captures the symbolic importance of what happened there. In a brief speech, tell your classmates about the historic event you researched and explain the slogan you wrote.

■ ART/HISTORY

Archaeological Art Locate additional information on Qumran or the Dead Sea Scrolls. Look especially for illustrations of ruins and objects from these places. Then, choose one of these activities: Draw or paint a picture of an item from the archaeological site that interests you, or create a modern treasure scroll.

■ HOME ECONOMICS

Nice Threads Find out about the style of clothing worn in ancient Hebrew times, and design a costume in this style. You may want to create the actual costume for display to your class.

READ ON: FOR INDEPENDENT READING

■ NONFICTION

David: A Biography by Barbara Cohen (Clarion, 1995) is a 1996 winner of the ALA Notable Books for Children nonfiction award. This illustrated biography attempts to depict what King David must have been like. The author draws on a wide variety of records to flesh out a portrait of the legendary Bible hero.

The Dead Sea Scrolls by Ilene Cooper (Morrow, 1997) is a summary of the history of these historic documents and gives readers an understanding of the amazing events that have surrounded the scrolls since their discovery.

Exodus, adapted by Miriam Chaikin (Holiday, 1987), is a retelling of the Hebrew flight from Egypt to Canaan. A map of the probable route of the Israelites' trek through the desert is provided in this picture book.

Israel by Martin and Stephen Hintz (Children's Press, 1999) introduces the nation and people of modern Israel. This book provides a mix of the ancient and the new in today's Israel. A time line of the history of the Hebrew people is included.

Masada by Neil Waldman (Morrow, 1998) is a re-creation of the tragic events of Masada, the site of the Jewish defeat at the hands of the Romans in A.D. 73. The author provides illustrations that complement the text.

Passover Journey: A Seder Companion by Barbara Diamond Goldin (Viking, 1994) follows the story of the Israelites' journey from slavery and explains the traditions and rituals of the Seder (the Jewish feast celebrated on the eve of the first day of Passover). This 1995 winner of the ALA Notable Books for Children nonfiction award includes illustrations.

■ FICTION

The Diamond Tree: Jewish Tales from Around the World by Howard Schwartz and Barbara Rush (Harper Collins, 1991). This collection brings together Jewish stories that span many centuries. The book was named a 1991 Sydney Taylor award winner and a 1992 ALA Notable Books for Children award winner.

Moses and the Angels by Ileene Smith Sobel (Delacorte, 1999) is an illustrated story about the angels who protected Moses throughout his life. Full-color illustrations accompany this mysterious story.

O Jerusalem by Jane Yolen (Blue Sky Press, 1996) celebrates the three-thousand-year anniversary of Jerusalem with poems, narratives, and paintings. The book was named a 1997 ALA Notable Books for Children award winner.

Sefer Ha-Aggadah: The Book of Legends for Young Readers by Seymour Rossel (UAHC Press, 1996). This collection of tales is adapted from *The Book of Legends: Sefer Ha-Aggadah*, the classic tales of exploits of the men and women who were heroes in Jewish lore. Full-color illustrations accompany the text.

While Standing on One Foot by Nina Jaffe (Henry Holt, 1993) is a collection of "puzzle" stories and wisdom tales from the Jewish tradition. This collection includes illustrations.

CHAPTER 5
Early Civilizations in Asia
Ancient India and China 2500 B.C.–A.D. 250

Not Just Another Pretty Face

Although it's not clear exactly when he lived (anywhere from 1,600 to 2,200 years ago), poet and playwright Kalidasa is thought to be one of the greatest of all Indian writers. According to legend, Kalidasa was so handsome that a princess fell in love with him and married him, even though he was a poor, uneducated man.

However, the princess eventually grew ashamed of her husband's ignorance and lack of culture. Legend says that Kalidasa prayed to the Hindu goddess Kali for guidance. She rewarded her loyal namesake (*Kalidasa* means "Kali's slave") with a sudden and amazing gift of wit, which he used to write some of the most beautiful poetry and cleverest plots in Indian literature.

The Granger Collection, New York

▲ Artwork depicting Hindu deities.

What'll They Think of Next?

They invented umbrellas, gunpowder, kites, fireworks, stirrups—even, archaeologists now say, the world's first flush toilet. Is there anything the ancient Chinese *didn't* invent?

The Chinese also invented paper and a way to print on paper. They invented rudders to steer their ships, and compasses (in the shape of fish) to tell them which way to steer. They invented the wheelbarrow—and used it for about 1,300 years—before Europeans finally caught on!

This early seismograph, or earthquake detector, was invented by a royal astronomer of the Han dynasty (an ancient Chinese empire). The tremor of an earthquake caused a rod to fall inside a bronze jar, which in turn caused a ball to drop from the mouth of one of the dragons on the outside of the jar into a bronze toad below. The direction in which the ball fell would tell the general direction of the earthquake.

INVESTIGATE: When did the Chinese invent their system of writing, and how did it change over the centuries? What materials did the Chinese write on before they invented paper?

◀ Early seismograph.

Michael Holford

"What you do not want done to yourself, do not do to others."

—Confucius,
Chinese philosopher

VOCABULARY MATTERS

The word *Hindu* comes from Sanskrit, the ancient language of India. It refers to a follower of Hinduism, one of the main religions of India. *Hindi* is the name of the main language spoken in modern-day India.

© Arvind Garg/CORBIS

▲ Krishna, an important Hindu god, plays a prominent role in the *Bhagavad-Gita*. In this sculpture, he is shown as the divine flute player.

Carry the Twins; Then Divide by Fingers

Imagine having to write your math homework in verse! That's how scientists and mathematicians recorded mathematics in India many centuries ago. They often found other ways to say each number. Instead of *two* they'd write *arms, wings, eyes,* or *twins.* For *ten,* they'd write *fingers,* and for *thirty-two*—can you guess?

Think you could never do math the ancient Indian way? Think again. We constantly use what is possibly one of ancient India's best inventions—the concept of zero. The "invention" of zero made a decimal system possible, where old numbers like 2 can be pushed over to make new numbers like 20, 200, and 2,000,000.

Ancient Chinese Secret

For probably thousands of years, people in China knew how to spin silk from the threads of the silkworm's cocoon. However, silk manufacturing was a closely guarded secret. Chinese merchants could sell silk to foreigners along their trade routes, but telling outsiders how it was made was a crime punishable by death.

Bruce Coleman, Inc.

Wealthy people around the world adored Chinese silk. Some thought it must come from some exotic Asian plant. Others suspected it was the fur of an unknown animal. Pliny, a famous ancient Roman writer, was sure he had the answer: Silk, he wrote, was made from "the hair of the sea-sheep." Baa!

Sacred Inspiration

The *Bhagavad-Gita* (bug´ə·vəd gē´tä), or "Song of the Blessed One," is famous as one of the most sacred texts of the Hindu religion. The *Bhagavad-Gita* is actually only part of what some say is the longest poem in the world—a 100,000-verse epic called the *Mahabharata* (mə·hä´bä´rə·tə).

The *Bhagavad-Gita* focuses on the nature of human relationships to the divine and has played a role in shaping the philosophies of many great writers and leaders.

What causes a civilization to vanish from the face of the earth? Some "lost civilizations," like Atlantis, an island that supposedly sank into the ocean, are most likely ancient legends. Other civilizations that have disappeared are simply mysteries. Read on to find out about a civilization in India that vanished over thirty-five hundred years ago.

Cities of the Indus Valley

from *Weird and Wacky Science: Lost Cities*

by JOYCE GOLDENSTERN

"The attackers left the dead lying where they fell. In one of the houses sprawled thirteen skeletons—men, women, and children—some wearing bracelets, rings, and beads, and two of them with sword cuts on their skulls. . . . Elsewhere again, yet another skeleton was found in a lane. And all these grim relics lay on the highest and latest level of the city, witness to its last moments."[1]

Sir Mortimer Wheeler, a respected scholar of Indus civilization, described the gruesome scene. He was commenting on the end of a great city that flourished in

You Need to Know...

Early civilizations depended on rivers. The very first civilizations grew between the Tigris and Euphrates Rivers in Mesopotamia. Ancient Egypt thrived for thousands of years along the banks of the mighty Nile. Great rivers provided a reliable water supply, and the rich soil along the riverbanks made it possible for people to grow enough food and form permanent settlements. Around the same time the great pyramids were built in Egypt, the people along the Indus River in ancient India built cities and formed a civilization of their own.

It was not until 1921, however, that archaeologists digging at sites near the Indus River rediscovered this ancient civilization. Amazingly, the remains of two large cities, Mohenjo-daro (mō•hen′jō•dä′rō) and Harappa (hə•rä′pə), were excavated. Although the Indus Valley civilizations flourished for over a thousand years, we still know very little about them. What we do know from archaeological evidence is that the people living in Mohenjo-daro and Harappa around 1500 B.C. met a sudden and violent end.

---

1. FROM Sir Mortimer Wheeler, "The Civilization of a Sub-Continent," *The Dawn of Civilization,* ed. Stuart Piggott (New York: McGraw-Hill Book Company, 1961), p. 249.

gruesome (grōō′səm): causing horror or disgust; repulsive.

Borromeo/Art Resource, NY

▲ The excavation site at Mohenjo-daro.

the Indus Valley from 2500 B.C. to about 1500 B.C. This city, Mohenjo-daro, and its sister city, Harappa, first cradled civilization on the Indian subcontinent. The two cities had prospered for nearly a thousand years. Commerce and river trade helped support the two cities, but they drew their greatest wealth from agriculture. Wheat, barley, dates, field peas, and even cotton prospered on the fertile soil of the Indus river valley. Mohenjo-daro lay near the Indus River in what today is Pakistan. Harappa lay about four hundred miles northeast on the Ravi River—a tributary of the mighty Indus.

> ## This city, Mohenjo-daro, and its sister city, Harappa, first cradled civilization on the Indian subcontinent.

Accomplished Artisans
The wealth from agriculture supported many crafts. Toolmakers crafted chisels, axes, knives, and other tools from bronze and copper. Potters used wheels to throw pots, and then painted them with red ocher.[2] Weavers wove cotton into garments. Some artisans must have even known how to create statues using molds. Among the ruins, archaeologists found a statue of a pert and pretty dancer cast in bronze.

The inhabitants had had leisure time. They threw dice and played board games. They made toys for their children: little birds and tiny carts with wheels—miniatures of real ox carts that adults used for plowing. The people of these river cities evidently had a strong sense of ownership: Archaeologists found hundreds of seals, used

---

2. ocher (ō′kər): variety of clay, usually reddish brown or yellow, used as a pigment in paints.

for marking belongings, and decorated with a sunken pattern of an animal—elephants, rhinoceroses, antelopes, crocodiles, even unicorns. Most impressively, though, inscriptions marked each seal. Perhaps the inscriptions were personal names. No one knows for sure, because no one has been able to decipher them. Nonetheless, the inscriptions show that the people of the Indus valley had developed writing. About 1500 B.C., Aryans[3] invaded the Indian subcontinent, and everything started to change.

Fort Destroyers

Until the 1920s, no one in modern times knew about the people of Mohenjo-daro and Harappa. Both cities lay buried and forgotten. It was thought that the warrior Aryans were the first to bring civilization to the Indus Valley. The Aryans, it was thought, had found wandering tribes when they arrived. Yet some scholars wondered: In the Aryan saga *Rig-Veda*,[4] there were references to forts. Indra, chief god of the Aryans, was called *Purmamdara*, which means "fort destroyer." One passage described Indra destroying ninety forts; in another passage, Indra "rends forts as age consumes a garment."[5] Scholars wondered whether this meant that the conquering Aryans had found a settled civilization, rather than a nomadic people.

Excavation

In the 1920s, the Indian Archaeological Survey excavated many sites in the Indus Valley. It was during these excavations that archaeologists unearthed the cities: first Harappa, and then Mohenjo-daro.

Harappa, a city about three miles in circumference, stood on a huge mound. Its most remarkable structure, a citadel[6] about 460 yards long and 215 yards wide, rose

---

3. **Aryans:** Indo-European tribe of nomadic warriors.
4. ***Rig-Veda***: a long collection of hymns and scriptures of the Aryans, including poetry and historical tales. Later Indian religion and philosophy comes from the Vedas. The *Rig-Veda* is considered a sacred Hindu text and is often recited at weddings and funerals.
5. FROM *Rig-Veda* quoted in *The Horizon Book of Lost Worlds*, ed. Marshall B. Davidson (New York: American Heritage Publishing Company, 1962), p. 210.
6. **citadel:** fortress or stronghold.

Everything Old Is New Again

Even though the cities of the Indus Valley were destroyed over 3,500 years ago, their influence is still seen in modern India. Houses are still built around courtyards, and drains still empty into the streets outside the courtyard walls.

Other features of ancient Indian cities are found in nearly all modern cities. Grids of streets, with residential blocks intersected by broad avenues and narrower side streets, were modeled in Mohenjo-daro. In addition, various conveniences, such as private water supplies, bathrooms with toilets, and city drainage and sanitation systems, were evident in ancient Indian cities.

---

decipher (dē·sī′fər): to interpret the meaning of something.

circumference (sər·kum′fər·əns): distance bounding an area of a circle or an area suggesting a circle.

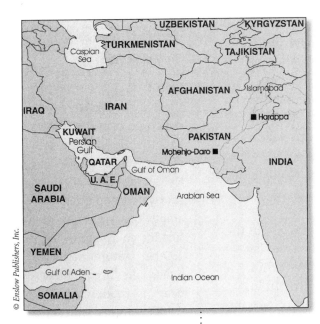

▲ Map showing present-day location of the ancient cities of Mohenjo-daro and Harappa.

© Enslow Publishers, Inc.

anthropologists (an′thrō·päl′ə·jists): scientists who study human origins, including physical and cultural development.

ecology (ē·käl′ə·jē): pattern of relationships between living things and their surroundings.

high above the city. Bastions[7] projected above the fort, a mighty baked-brick wall surrounded it, and gates prevented enemies from entering. To the north of the fort stood huge granaries.[8] Straight streets ran in a perfect grid. On the streets, modest but spacious houses once stood. They contained bathrooms and latrines. The city had excellent sewer and drainage systems.

Mohenjo-daro, just like its sister city, boasted a towering citadel and huge granaries. The plan of the city followed a design similar to that of Harappa. Sewers and drainage systems were evident. Most impressive was a huge public bath, made watertight with baked bricks. Archaeologists found these structures in even better condition than those at Harappa. The mystery of the forts mentioned in the *Rig-Veda* had evidently been solved.

A Lesson of Ecology

The skeletons described by Wheeler testify to many raids on the cities, but scholars do not hold the Aryans completely responsible for the decline of the ancient civilization. Many other factors may have caused its fall. Some anthropologists who specialize in environmental issues speculate that the ecology of the region may have been a factor. The rivers had been a source of wealth for the inhabitants, offering trade routes and soil fertile from flooding. But the rivers could also have contributed to problems.

Some theorize that the inhabitants may have destroyed the forests surrounding the rivers. The Indus and Ravi valley people used huge quantities of baked bricks in their structures. Some anthropologists reason that the inhabitants kept cutting down trees for fuel to bake the bricks. For

---

7. **bastions:** projecting parts of a fortification.
8. **granaries:** buildings for storing and protecting grain.

about a thousand years, structures continually had to be mended and rebuilt. Old cities crumbled, and new ones were built on top of them. As trees were cut down, the bare hills no longer absorbed the water from heavy rains. The rainwater could rush down the hills to the swelling river, and even high dikes might fail. As the people struggled with floods, their resources and energy may have dwindled. When Aryan invaders challenged them, the weakened inhabitants could not defend their magnificent forts.

✓ Reading Check

1. Where was Mohenjo-daro? How do we know that the last people who lived there died violently?

2. What factors were responsible for the flourishing of the Indus Valley civilizations?

3. The author says that archaeologists found hundreds of seals in the ancient cities of the Indus Valley. What was their purpose? What do the inscriptions on the seals tell us about the people of the Indus Valley?

4. Who was Indra? The author says that Indra was also called *Purmamdara*. What does this name mean?

5. The author says that most likely the invading Aryans were one of the causes for the fall of the Indus Valley civilizations. What were other factors that led to the decline of the civilizations before the Aryans invaded?

MEET THE *Writer*

Joyce Goldenstern (1948–   ) is a writer of wide interests, including history, science, and architecture. She has written several books for children and has also published works of fiction and nonfiction for adult readers.

Unexpected events can sometimes completely change the course of someone's life. Ashoka, an Indian emperor who ruled in the third century B.C., started his reign in the bloodthirsty tradition of violent conquests. However, life experiences dramatically changed his views of how to rule. Read on to find out more about Ashoka's story.

A Vow to Conquer by Dhamma

from *Calliope*

by JEAN ELLIOTT JOHNSON

ethical (eth′i•kəl): in keeping with moral standards and values.

diverse (də•vʉrs′): made up of various people or things.

You Need to Know...

Ashoka (ə•shō′kə) was the third and greatest of the Mauryan emperors of India. Like his father and grandfather before him, Ashoka began his reign by conquering new territories, slaughtering many people in the process.

Then, a few things happened that completely changed the way Ashoka would rule for the rest of his life. First, Ashoka personally accompanied his soldiers as they waged war. The death and destruction his troops left in their wake sickened the emperor. Ashoka then became a devout Buddhist and vowed to turn away from using violence and fear to conquer people. Instead, he decided to use some of the basic ideas of Buddhism to unite people. An ancient stone pillar explains that Ashoka felt remorse for the "slaughter, death, and deportation of people" and that he resolved "to follow Righteousness, to love Righteousness, to give instruction in Righteousness." Because of this change, many people consider Ashoka one of the greatest—and wisest—rulers who ever lived.

After the Kalinga campaign[1] and his conversion to Buddhism, Ashoka changed his approach to ruling. He became one of the first leaders in history to add an <u>ethical</u> and moral dimension to governing. Instead of using his army to take control of new territory, Ashoka wanted conquests to result from righteousness and virtue.

Ashoka was greatly influenced by Buddhism, but he was careful to keep his own personal religious beliefs separate from his duties as leader of a <u>diverse</u> empire. Rather than try to convert[2]

1. **Kalinga campaign:** Ashoka's war against the tribes of Kalinga (present-day Orissa).
2. **convert:** to cause (someone) to change to a new belief or religion.

Indians to what he believed, he respected the many differences among his subjects and urged each person to be tolerant.

The centerpiece of Ashoka's new public policy was *dhamma,* a Buddhist term that he adapted and defined in his own way. The concept of *dhamma* was close to the Hindu idea of *dharma,* which means "that which supports or upholds" the universe. *Dharma* refers to the way things or people ought to behave. Each part of the universe has its *dharma*—its attributes or appropriate way to act. The sun shines and the moon reflects. Rivers flow, snakes bite, cows give milk, and wheat seeds grow into wheat. *Dharma* also applies to human beings: Teachers teach and students learn. Parents set the rules and children obey. If everyone and everything tries to carry out its role, the universe will function harmoniously.

▲ Relief carving from Buddhist *stupa* in Nepal. Ashoka built a number of *stupas,* or religious structures honoring the Buddha.

[Ashoka] became one of the first leaders in history to add an ethical and moral dimension to governing.

When early Buddhists spoke of *dhamma,* they meant the Buddha's teachings. These included being <u>compassionate</u> toward all living things, including animals and plants, and trying not to hurt anything any more than was necessary. Buddhist *dhamma* also encouraged people to avoid stealing, to speak the truth, not to gossip, not to envy others, and to do work that did not harm others.

compassionate (kəm·pash′ən·it): feeling or showing sympathy for the sorrow or suffering of others.

Three Great Men, One Principle

Emperor Ashoka, Mohandas K. Gandhi (the great leader of Indian independence), and American civil rights leader Dr. Martin Luther King, Jr., all shared a common belief. Each of these men promoted change through nonviolent means and rejected force as a tool to accomplish his goals. Ashoka rejected violence after seeing the results of his army's victory at Kalinga. Gandhi used a campaign of nonviolence (he called it "nonviolent resistance") that led to India's independence from Great Britain in 1947. In the 1950s and 1960s, Dr. Martin Luther King, Jr., followed Gandhi and Ashoka by choosing nonviolent means to demand an end to racial oppression in the United States.

---

principles (prin′sə•pəlz): rules of conduct.

prosperous (präs′pər•əs): successful.

Ashoka defined *dhamma* as the:

> . . . *non-slaughter of animals for sacrificial purposes. Non-violence toward human beings, proper attention to kinsmen,*[3] *welfare of mother and father, welfare of the aged and many other kinds of moral behavior.*

(Rock Edict IV)

Ashoka believed that anyone, whether Jain,[4] Buddhist, a follower of Brahmanism (the most common religion in India at the time), or a holy man faithful to some other religious system could practice *dhamma* as he defined it. He also hoped that if everyone followed *dhamma*, his diverse kingdom would be united, and everyone would be content.

Ashoka sent Officers of Righteousness throughout the empire. Their mission was to spread the idea of *dhamma*, thereby ensuring that all Ashoka's subjects were being treated well and that people were judged fairly and punished appropriately for crimes. Ashoka also ordered hospitals built for human beings and for animals, and he supervised the growing of medical herbs. He urged his subjects to make pilgrimages[5] instead of hunting, and he had roads constructed, resthouses built, trees planted, and wells dug to aid travelers. Ashoka urged his subjects to bring their concerns to him at any time of the day or night. Many of these activities were based on good Buddhist <u>principles</u>, but Ashoka made them general principles for everyone.

Ashoka wanted to be an ideal ruler called a *chakravartin*, the king who "turned" (*vartin*) the "wheel" (*chakra*) of righteousness and moral authority. According to Indian mythology, a *chakravartin* had ruled the world during the mythical golden age. This was an ancient time when poverty, ill-will, violence, and wrongdoing did not exist because the king's purity ensured a peaceful and <u>prosperous</u> existence. Ashoka consciously tried to present

3. **kinsmen:** relatives.
4. **Jain:** Jainism is a religion of India that resembles Buddhism. A Jain believes in the importance of every living thing and follows a simple lifestyle.
5. **pilgrimages:** journeys to shrines or sacred places.

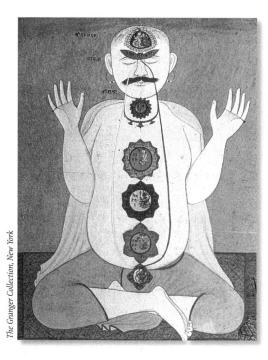

◄ This illustration depicts a Hindu version of major *chakras* in the body.

? **What reasons might explain why Buddhism and Hinduism share some similar beliefs?**

The Granger Collection, New York

himself as a *chakravartin* in order to establish his connection with past traditions. He claimed a great wheel had appeared to him in the sky, signifying that he was a *chakravartin.*

Ashoka protected and supported monasteries, universities, and scholars that promoted *dhamma,* and even sent Buddhist missionaries to other parts of Asia. Yet, of all his policies, perhaps the most significant are those that encouraged people of all religions to follow their beliefs and to avoid praising their own faith while insulting someone else's. He stated:

> *One should honor another man's sect [beliefs], for by so doing one increases the influence of one's own sect and benefits that of another man; while by doing otherwise one diminishes the influence of one's own sect and harms another man's.*

(Edict XII)

Certainly, Ashoka's rule by *dhamma* was very different from rule by force. As a result, for many, Ashoka is one of the greatest rulers who ever lived.

1. Most rulers before and after Ashoka used force to control their people and to add more territory to their empires. How was Ashoka's reign different from that of other rulers?

2. What religion influenced Ashoka's behavior? What were some of the practices early followers of this religion taught?

3. What did Ashoka hope to achieve if everyone followed *dhamma*?

4. What were some of the concrete things that Ashoka did to put his ethical principles into action?

5. Why did Ashoka try to present himself as an ideal ruler, or *chakravartin?*

MEET THE *Writer*

Jean Elliott Johnson taught history for many years at Friends Seminary in New York City. She has also worked in Asia, developing instructional materials for students, and has written various nonfiction works on Asia and a world history textbook for secondary students.

Siddhartha Gautama, the founder of one of the great world religions, Buddhism, began his life as the son of an Indian prince. What caused this man to leave the comfort of his father's palace to wander in poverty, searching for the meaning of life? Read on to find out more about the Buddha's life and teachings.

Siddhartha Gautama: The Buddha

from *Buddhism*

by JOHN SNELLING

History tells us that Siddhartha Gautama was born the son of a king in northern India about 2,500 years ago. As you can imagine, his early life was one of luxury and <u>privilege</u>. He lived in fantastic palaces, enjoying the best food, clothing, and entertainments. This good life, however, was not enough for Gautama; he wanted to know what the rest of the world was like. So he began to go off in his chariot to visit the village near his palace. He saw poor people, sick people, and even dead bodies being carried off to be cremated.[1]

These discoveries so horrified Gautama that he could enjoy palace life no longer. He longed to find out whether there was a way of ending suffering.

privilege (priv′ə·lij): special favor.

You Need to Know...

Buddhism is one of the major religions of the world, with hundreds of millions of followers. The founder, Siddhartha Gautama (sid·där′tə gou′tə·mə), lived from about 563 to 483 B.C. At this time, Brahman priests had gained a great deal of power, causing some people to rebel and search for other spiritual paths. Among these new religions was Buddhism. It began when Gautama rejected his privileged life as the son of a prince.

One day, after years of searching for answers to life's meaning, Gautama sat down to rest and think under a tree. After several hours of deep thought, Gautama felt that he understood the essential truths of life. He then became the Buddha—the "Awakened One." Gautama spent the rest of his life teaching others his message. After his death, Buddhist ideas spread gradually across Asia. Buddhism has also gained growing acceptance in the Western world.

---

1. **cremated** (krē′māt′id): burned to ashes.

▲ The Great Buddha at Kamakura, Japan.

The Quest

Determined to answer this question, he slipped out of his palace one night, leaving his wife and young baby behind, and took the road to the next kingdom. As soon as he had crossed the frontier[2] river, he took off his gorgeous silk robe and put on one of patched and faded orange cloth. He cut off all his fine, jet-black hair and gave his rings and ornaments[3] to the servant who had come to the frontier with him. Then, carrying nothing but a simple begging bowl into which kind people could if they wished put food for him, he said goodbye to his servant and set off in search of an answer to his great question. He was no longer Prince Siddhartha, but just a penniless holy man.

[Gautama] longed to find out whether there was a way of ending suffering.

In India there have always been people who have given up everything in order to go off into lonely places and search for truth. Gautama in his day sought out the most famous of them and begged them to teach him all that they knew. He studied very hard under them and also performed various exercises, rather like yoga[4] exercises, which were supposed to help him see the truth. It is said that he lived in terrifying forests, burning in the heat of the midday sun and freezing at night, and that he slept on beds of thorns. He also starved himself until his body became so weak and thin that if he touched his stomach, he could feel his backbone poking through from the other side.

---

2. **frontier:** boundary or border.
3. **ornaments:** objects used to decorate.
4. **yoga** (yō′gə): a Hindu system of meditation that involves specific body positions and controlled breathing.

He did not, however, find an answer to his basic question. Moreover, he realized that if he went on treating his body as he had been, he wouldn't live much longer. He therefore took a little food to give him strength, whereupon the other holy men who had been his friends promptly declared that "Gautama has taken to the luxurious life" and left him.

Enlightenment

Alone and <u>forsaken</u> now, Gautama realized that he had to carry on his <u>quest</u> by himself. He came to a place nowadays called Budh Gaya, where he found a huge bo tree.[5] Making himself a cushion of grass beneath the tree, he determined to sit there until he found an answer to his question.

forsaken (fər·sā′kən): cast aside; abandoned.

quest (kwest): search or pursuit, usually of knowledge or some important goal or object.

Now, instead of looking outside himself, Gautama lowered his eyelids and began to look within. He saw thoughts, feelings, memories, sensations, desires, fears, and much else besides. As he watched them, he began to see how these powerful forces, working together, created the idea of the person Gautama—the person he himself identified as "I."

When he looked more closely, however, where was this Gautama, the "I"? He could certainly trace shifting, unstable patterns of feeling and thought, but no fixed and unchanging soul or self. In fact there was nothing—but not an empty, meaningless nothing. It was indeed a powerful reality, something that was in everything.

This reality was not subject to change, nor could it be rocked by the emotions. As it had never been born into the world, it could not die, so Gautama called it "the deathless," or *nirvana,* a relaxed state of being in which there was no grasping after anything. Most of all, it could not be affected by suffering, so it was precisely what Gautama had set out to find.

▲ The lotus flower is a symbol of Buddhism.

Legend has it that Siddhartha's final understanding, or "enlightenment," came after the night of the full moon of May. As dawn broke, he looked up and saw the morning

---

5. bo tree: type of fig tree.

star rising. At that moment he saw the truth for himself. He was Gautama no more, but the *Buddha,* or "Awakened One."

Turning the Wheel of *Dharma*

reluctant (ri·luk'tənt): hesitant.

At first the Buddha was <u>reluctant</u> to tell other people about his great discovery. He thought that they wouldn't want to know. But then he was persuaded that there were some who had "just a little dust in their eyes." These people might, with a little assistance, be helped to see the truth.

He therefore went to Isipatana (modern Sarnath, near Benares in northern India), where he delivered a sermon to a small crowd in the deer park there. As the Buddha's teaching is called the *Dharma* and is often symbolized by an eight-spoked wheel, this first sermon is celebrated as the occasion upon which he "first turned the wheel of the *Dharma.*"

This was the beginning of a great forty-five-year period during which the Buddha walked the dusty roads of northern India, spreading his message among the people. He taught without caring about which class, race, or sex his listeners belonged to. Some of his followers were householders: people with jobs and homes. Others, however, were prepared to give up everything like that in order to devote themselves entirely to listening to the Buddha's teaching and putting it into practice. These people eventually became known as the *sangha,* the community of Buddhist monks and nuns. From the start, they were supported entirely by

▼ Mandala.

Silvio Fiore/SuperStock

Buddhist Art: Mandalas

Ever since the Buddha lived, people have been creating art-work representing him and his teachings. A form of Buddhist art that is especially important in Nepal, Tibet, and Bhutan is the mandala. Mandalas are colorful geometric designs that represent the ideal world. They are often used for meditation.

Before Buddhist monks may construct a mandala, they must be trained in how to draw the figures that make up a mandala and taught what the various figures and colors represent. This training period can take years. Using grains of colored sand, monks often work together carefully assembling the design. Mandalas are viewed as not only an art form but also an act of worship since the mandala represents the enlightened spirit of the Buddha. After painstakingly creating a complex mandala design, Tibetan monks will destroy the mandala to express the temporary nature of all visible forms.

laypeople.[6] They just wandered from place to place, accepting gifts of food and drink from the people. Later, monasteries[7] were built in which they could live together as a community for at least part of the year.

Parinirvana

The Buddha was a very remarkable person, but he was not a god or a superman of any sort. He was a human being with the same problems and limitations as the rest of us. He therefore had to die at some stage.

His death took place in a small town in northern India called Kushinagara, apparently as the result of some kind of food poisoning. His last message to his followers was: "Impermanent[8] are all <u>compounded</u> things. Strive on

compounded (käm·pound'id): made up of various elements; complex.

---

6. **laypeople:** persons who are not ministers or members of the clergy.
7. **monasteries:** living quarters for persons bound by religious vows.
8. **impermanent:** temporary.

SIDELIGHT

A parable is a simple story that illustrates a lesson. Like the founders of other religions and philosophies, the Buddha often used parables to share ideas with others. The moral of the parable is stated at the end.

The Burning House

"Once there was a man who had many children. While he was away one day, his house caught fire with the children still inside. Smoke and flames encircled the house when he returned. 'Run out the door!' he cried. But the children did not realize that they were in danger and continued to play.

"Suddenly the father thought of a way to lure them outside. 'I have new toys for you to play with!' he shouted. 'A deer cart, a goat cart, and an ox cart. Who wants to ride in them first?' A moment later, the children ran safely through the door.

"The world is like a burning house. People are trapped inside, unaware of the flames of petty, worldly desires that threaten to destroy them. I am like the father who spoke to his children in a way they understood, to lead them to safety. And so I speak to you, to show you the path to enlightenment."

—from *Buddha* by Demi

Borromeo/Art Resource, NY

▲ Detail of ancient wall painting depicting the Buddha on a lotus flower.

mindfully." He then passed into what Buddhists call his *parinirvana*. His first *nirvana* at Budh Gaya had been a kind of death to self; his *parinirvana*, then, involved something more—death of the body as well. What actually became of the Buddha after the death of his body is a great mystery. It is something that is beyond the mind of any ordinary man to know and of words to tell.

✓ Reading Check

1. What facts do we know about the Buddha's birth and early life?

2. Why did the Buddha decide to leave his family and his privileged life?

3. In what ways did the Buddha first seek the answer to human suffering? What was the result?

4. How did the Buddha reach enlightenment? What did he do after becoming enlightened?

5. What is the teaching of the Buddha called, and how is it often symbolized?

MEET THE *Writer*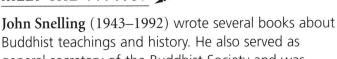

John Snelling (1943–1992) wrote several books about Buddhist teachings and history. He also served as general secretary of the Buddhist Society and was editor of the Society's journal, *The Middle Way*.

Two of the greatest figures in all of Chinese history are Confucius and Lao-tzu. Although these two men viewed themselves as humble messengers, their teachings laid the foundations for Confucianism and Taoism, two of the most influential Chinese traditions.

Confucianism and Taoism

from *One World, Many Religions*

by MARY POPE OSBORNE

"I AM A TRANSMITTER
AND NOT A CREATOR.
I BELIEVE IN AND HAVE
A PASSION FOR THE
ANCIENTS."

—THE ANALECTS[1] OF
CONFUCIUS: VII.I

Confucianism is based on the ideas of a humble Chinese scholar named Confucius. When the Buddha was teaching in India 2,500 years ago, Confucius was teaching in China. The son of a military officer, Confucius studied music, poetry, and the writing of China's ancient sages, or wise men.

For centuries, the sages had taught the Chinese people how to live a good life. But in Confucius's time, leaders had forgotten the teachings of

You Need to Know...

The great Chinese philosopher Confucius (kən•fyoo′shəs) was born around 551 B.C. during a stormy period in Chinese history. The turbulent times led Confucius to study the wisdom of ancient Chinese philosophers. By his twenties, Confucius was tutoring many students and disciples in the traditional teachings. Eventually, Confucius sought to apply his teachings by serving in public office. Unfortunately, his political career was a failure. Only after his death did Confucius become famous and earn the title, "The First Teacher."

The founder of Taoism is known as Lao-tzu (lou′dzu′), or "Old Master." Almost nothing is known about him, not even his given name, yet Lao-tzu's thoughts about the Tao (dou), or "the way," have been very influential in China and around the world. Taoism focuses on connecting with the natural world.

Together with Buddhism, Taoism and Confucianism have coexisted in China for thousands of years. Although some of the beliefs of these three spiritual paths conflict, there is an old Chinese saying that "the Three Faiths are One."

---

1. **Analects:** group of literary works or excerpts.

the past. Society had fallen into chaos, and greed and violence had taken over.

Afraid that China's great civilization might be destroyed forever, Confucius began traveling around his country, teaching the wisdom of the sages.

Confucius taught the old traditions, which were based on goodness and truth. He said that government leaders should stop being so selfish and should start caring for their people the way a loving father cares for his family. He said that people should start respecting their leaders, their parents, and their ancestors; and that rich and poor children alike should get a good education.

Confucius also taught the ancient Chinese belief that everything in the universe is a combination of two forces called yin and yang. Yin is all that is cold, dark, moonlike, and mysterious. Yang is the opposite of yin—everything that is bright, warm, sunlike, and clear. All growth and change come from a combination of these two forces.

▲ Confucius.

Confucius also said that all people should be <u>courteous</u> and kind to one another. One of his best-known sayings is: "Never do to others what you would not like them to do to you." Most major religions teach a version of this saying, which is sometimes called the golden rule.

Confucius thought of his teachings as a guide to wisdom and good behavior rather than as a religion. But after his death, temples were built to honor him, and Confucianism became the official religion of China. Applicants for government jobs had to study the books of Confucianism, and rulers <u>relied</u> on Confucian scholars for help and advice.

Confucius believed his duty was only to remind people of the teachings of the ancient sages. But he brought new meaning to the wisdom of the past. For more than two thousand years, many Chinese have considered him the wisest sage of all. A plaque in a Confucian temple in Taiwan, the main island of the Republic of China, calls Confucius "the great teacher of 10,000 generations."

For more than two thousand years, many Chinese have considered [Confucius] the wisest sage of all.

Taoism began with a man named Lao-tzu, who lived during the time of Confucius. Not much is known about Lao-tzu, whose name means "Old Master." Legend says that when he was a very old man, he grew tired of war and violence and decided to leave China. He drove an ox cart to the border of the country. But a guard there recognized the wise thinker and wouldn't let him pass until he wrote down all his wisdom.

The Old Master quickly wrote his teaching in a short book that later came to be called the *Tao Te Ching*. For many centuries, the *Tao Te Ching* was one of the most important books in China.

The Yin and Yang

One of the most important ideas in Confucianism is the concept of yin and yang. You have probably seen this symbol for the yin and yang, sometimes described as two fish encircling one another. The white half represents yang, and the dark half represents yin. However, the eyes of the fish illustrate the idea that each force contains the seed of the other. Everyone and everything contains a mixture of both the yin and yang. In addition, all conditions that one might experience—health, misfortune, pleasure—may change into their opposites.

---

courteous (kʉrt′ē·əs): polite and considerate.

relied (ri·līd′): depended on; trusted.

infinite (in'fə•nit): having no limits; vast.

The teaching of the *Tao Te Ching* concerns a mysterious force in the universe called the Tao. The word *Tao* means "the way," or "the road." The Tao is the <u>infinite</u> source of all life, and it is impossible to truly name. The more you try to name it, the more it escapes you. The Tao is often described as a flowing stream. Just as you cannot hold flowing water in your hands, you cannot grasp the Tao.

humble (hum'bəl): modest.

Taoism teaches that in order to live in harmony with the Tao, you should try to live a quiet and simple life close to nature. You should be <u>humble</u> and compassionate. You should do your work without seeking fame or fortune.

Like Confucius, Lao-tzu wasn't interested in creating a religion. But over time, his teachings were combined with Chinese folk religions—the ancient customs and religious practices of ordinary people. Taoism began to include beliefs in gods and goddesses, dragons and musicians, spells and charms. The ancient Chinese religion of ancestor veneration, or respect, also became increasingly important in Taoism.

© Bettmann/CORBIS

▲ Lao-tzu riding a sacred cow.

Folk tradition teaches that the ancestors connect the world of the living to the world of the gods. If people honor their ancestors, the spirits of the ancestors will protect them. During the Chinese New Year celebration, the most important Chinese religious holiday of the year, families gather to feast and honor their ancestors.

After the Chinese Communists took over China in 1949, they discouraged the people of mainland China from following their traditional religions. But in Taiwan, Hong Kong, and other parts of the world, including the United States, many Chinese people still practice a combination of Confucianism, Taoism, folk religion, and Buddhism.

revere (ri•vir'): to feel deep respect toward; to worship.

Each religion offers something different. Families might <u>revere</u> the wise Confucius and study his teachings. At the same time, they might keep a shrine[2] to worship a Taoist god, a shrine to honor the Buddha, and a special place to honor their ancestors. For Chinese people, all these ways of worship unite to form one spiritual world.

---

2. shrine: place of prayer or meditation.

1. The author says that Confucius studied the writings of the sages. Who were the sages? Why did Confucius begin teaching the wisdom of the sages?

2. What connection did Confucius make between government leaders and the family?

3. The Christian religion teaches "do unto others as you would have them do unto you." Which saying of Confucius parallels this?

4. How is the *Tao* usually translated? What does Taoism say about how people should live if they want to live in harmony with the Tao?

5. What does Chinese folk tradition teach about the ancestors?

MEET THE *Writer*

Mary Pope Osborne (1949–   ) and her family lived on different Army posts until they settled in North Carolina when she was fifteen. Osborne captured that experience in her first novel, *Run, Run as Fast as You Can*—the story of a girl whose family retires from the military and settles in the South. In addition to realistic fiction, the author has published retellings of myths and fairy tales for young people. Recently, she has focused on picture books, biographies, and nonfiction.

The Great Wall of China is as high as a three-story building and wide enough for several horses to travel across side by side. Stretching for well over a thousand miles, the Great Wall has become a symbol of the vast size and long history of China.

from The Great Wall of China

from *Walls: Defenses Throughout History*

by JAMES CROSS GIBLIN

When Hadrian's Wall[1] was new, another wall already stretched across a vast country on the other side of the world. This rampart[2] is the longest structure ever built. It contains enough building materials to circle the entire globe at the equator with a wall eight feet high and three feet thick. It is the only man-made structure on earth that can be seen with the naked eye from the moon. It is the Great Wall of China.

The Great Wall extends across northern and central China from the Yellow Sea in the east to a point deep in central Asia. There are different estimates of its overall length. Those who count only its distance east

You Need to Know...

The ancient Chinese considered the outside world a hostile place. The Great Wall is a testament to this belief. In the third century B.C., the emperor Shih Huang-ti (shir•hwäŋ•dē) ordered the Great Wall to be built in order to prevent invasions from the north (and possibly as a lasting monument of his own greatness).

Of course, the wall has survived much longer than Emperor Shih's rule, which lasted only eleven years. Today, sections of the wall stand as reminders of the labor and skill of ordinary Chinese people—hundreds of thousands of whom may have died from overwork and exhaustion while building the wall.

---

1. **Hadrian's Wall:** ancient Roman wall about seventy-five miles long, built across northern England by the Roman emperor Hadrian in A.D. 122–128.
2. **rampart** (ram'pärt'): protective wall.

to west say it is approximately sixteen hundred miles long. Others claim that, with all of its loops and offshoots included, the wall is more than thirty-six hundred miles long. If straightened, they say, it would cross the United States from New York City to San Francisco, and there would be enough left over to wind back to Salt Lake City.

Construction of the wall spread over almost two thousand years, from 400 B.C., when the first sections were erected, until the 1600s A.D., when it was rebuilt and extended. But most of the wall was built in the ten years between 224 and 214 B.C. by Emperor Shih Huang-ti.

> **If straightened, they say, [the Great Wall] would cross the United States from New York City to San Francisco, and there would be enough left over to wind back to Salt Lake City.**

▲ Section of the Great Wall of China. ❓ **What do you think this structure says about the society that built it?**

© Wolfgang Kaehler/CORBIS

ruthless (rōōth′lis): showing no mercy; cruel.

embarked (em·bärkd′): set forth; began.

ambitious (am·bish′əs): requiring great skill or effort for success.

priority (prī·ôr′ə·tē): something that is first in importance or order.

Shih was the first ruler to unify the scattered city states of China into a single nation. He accomplished this by a ruthless use of force. Like Adolf Hitler in the twentieth century, Shih ordered the burning of books he disagreed with, especially the writings of the philosopher Confucius. When some scholars continued to teach from these books, Shih had the scholars buried alive as an example to others who might think of disobeying him.

So that people and goods could travel easily from one part of China to another, Shih embarked on a vast road- and canal-building program. And to protect his new nation from northern invaders, Shih launched his most ambitious project—the linking of many smaller, older walls into one great defensive wall.

Such a wall was badly needed. For years the Tartars and other nomadic tribes had swept across the loosely defended border and attacked Chinese living in settled communities. The nomads looted Chinese homes, shops, and temples, burned the settlements to the ground, killed most of the men and children, and carried off some of the women as slaves.

The nomads laid siege to larger cities, too. Sometimes the inhabitants managed to hold out for a few weeks behind their city's walls. But unless an army garrison[3] came to relieve them, the city dwellers were usually forced by hunger and disease to surrender. Then the looting, burning, and killing began all over again.

To prevent such terrible raids and bring hope to Chinese living on the border, Emperor Shih made construction of the Great Wall his first priority. He assigned an army of three hundred thousand men under one of his best generals, Meng Tien, to work on the project. Local laborers were recruited to assist the soldiers. Among them were thousands of women, who were hired to weave tents and help to carry loads.

Some of the hardest jobs were given to prisoners who were sent to the construction sites under armed guard. Besides common criminals, these prisoners included many

---

3. garrison: troops stationed at a fort or military post.

people who had been captured in war or arrested for political reasons.

Historians estimate that all told more than a million people worked on the Great Wall. They labored from dawn to dusk, in freezing winter blizzards and blinding summer sandstorms. Clay for bricks was carried in baskets at the ends of shoulder poles. Building stones often had to be transported for long distances on crude sledges[4] or wagons. In mountainous areas, the stones were sometimes raised into position by teams of specially trained goats.

Most of the workers suffered under harsh living conditions. Food rations frequently ran short and wells dried up. Flimsy tents offered little protection from blazing summer heat or sub-zero winter temperatures. Another problem was surprise attacks by nomadic enemy tribes. Often the soldiers in General Meng's army had to stop work in order to protect the other laborers.

----

4. **sledges:** sleds mounted on low runners, pulled by work animals, and used to carry heavy loads across ice, snow, or rough ground.

SIDELIGHT

"Stories have been told about the Great Wall ever since it was built. Some Chinese thought that, as it twisted its way across the mountainous country of the north, it looked like a dragon. The image of a dragon was one that the Chinese were very fond of, and it turns up frequently in Chinese art and literature often symbolizing the emperor.

Another story tells how the Great Wall came to be built. Emperor Shih, it says, was a magician who created a flying horse. In one night he rode this wonderful animal right across China, and as he went, he mapped out the course the wall should take.

In another legend Emperor Shih is supposed to have owned a magic whip which he used to cut a way through the Daqing mountains in order to alter the course of the Yellow River so that the Wall could be built."

—from *Mysterious Places: The Magical East* by Philip Wilkinson and Michael Pollard

Protection or Prison?

Although the Great Wall was built to keep invaders out, the heavily guarded structure may have served more than one purpose. Emperor Shih was a cruel dictator, and the wall may have also served to prevent his unhappy subjects from leaving the country to seek greater freedom elsewhere.

▲ Shih Huang-ti, China's first emperor.

As a result of all this, according to some Chinese historians, more than four hundred thousand men and women died while working on the wall. That was almost half the total work force. Many of the dead were buried within the wall, causing some people to call it "the longest cemetery in the world." . . .

At last, after more than ten years, the Great Wall was completed. Its thirty-five-hundred-mile route ran across plains and deserts, bridged ravines and rivers, and climbed over mountains as high as six thousand feet above sea level.

The wall was generally twenty-five feet wide at the base, slanting to seventeen feet at the top. It was between twenty-five and thirty feet high. In eastern China, where rocks were plentiful, the sides were faced with large stones or granite boulders, and the top was paved with bricks. The interior was composed of small stones and earth, cemented with a mortar so hard that nails couldn't be driven into it.

Five-foot-high stone parapets[5] rose on both sides of the wall's flat top. The parapets had openings at regular intervals through which arrows could be shot at attackers. The top itself served as a road, wide enough for eight people to walk abreast, or two horse-drawn chariots to pass each other. . . .

For centuries the Great Wall protected northern China against small-scale attacks. But gradually the number of troops manning it was reduced, and large sections fell into ruin. In 1211 A.D. it proved no barrier to the Mongol[6] leader Genghis Khan. He and his horse soldiers broke through the wall's defenses and conquered much of China.

The Mongols were driven out of China in the late 1300s and the wall was rebuilt. Frontier defense forces patrolled its fortifications from Manchuria in the east to Kansu in the west, and kept China largely free of Mongol raiders.

---

5. parapets (par′ə•pets′): earth or stone walls built by soldiers as a defense.
6. Mongol (män′gəl): native of Mongolia, a region in East Central Asia.

As the military threat from the north lessened, much of the wall was abandoned again. People living nearby started chipping away at it and removing stones to use in building houses and temples. Over time, long stretches of the wall—especially those made of earth—simply crumbled into dust. Other sections remained intact, however. During the war with Japan in the 1930s, Chinese soldiers marched to the northern front along the ancient brick road atop the wall.

After the Chinese Communists took power in 1949, several sections of the wall were restored once more—not as a military fortification[7] but as a historical monument. Today the Communists point to the wall with pride, saying that "it embodies the wisdom and blood and sweat of the Chinese working people." The restored section north of Peking has become a major tourist attraction, visited each year by thousands of people from all over the world.

It takes two hours to reach this restored section by train or bus. Suddenly, craggy mountains loom into view above the plain, and then the wall itself appears, curving over and around the mountains like a giant stone snake.

From the parking lot, steep inclines lead up to watchtowers at both ends of the restored section. It's a hard climb, but the view from the towers is worth the effort. Gazing out at the wall as it winds away across the mountains, one can't help but be amazed at the simple fact that it's there.

Besides its appeal as a tourist attraction, the wall is being used in other ways today. Scientists study it to learn the effects of earthquakes that occurred in the past. Archaeologists dig in and around it in search of tools and other objects from the time when it was built.

And previously unknown sections are still being discovered. In 1983 archaeologists unearthed a sixty-two-mile segment, thus adding to the already incredible length of the Great Wall of China—truly one of the wonders of the world.

restored (ri·stôrd′): brought back to a former condition.

---

7. fortification (fôrt′ə·fi·kā′shən): structure used for defense.

1. Some people say the Great Wall is sixteen hundred miles long, and others say it is thirty-six hundred miles long. What accounts for this large difference?

2. The first Chinese emperor, Shih Huang-ti, began linking smaller walls together to create the Great Wall. What kind of ruler was the first emperor? Support your answer with examples.

3. All together, about how many people worked on the Great Wall? What were their living conditions and working conditions?

4. When the author of this selection visited the restored section of wall near Peking (Beijing), to what did he compare the sight of the wall in the distance?

5. Besides being a tourist attraction, what purpose does the Great Wall serve today?

MEET THE *Writer*

James Cross Giblin (1933–   ) was an editor of children's books for many years and has written many award-winning books for young readers, including *Walls: Defenses Throughout History*, from which "The Great Wall of China" was taken.

An army of soldiers has guarded a Chinese emperor for more than two thousand years! The author of the following article records her thoughts upon viewing these life-size clay figures, whose discovery was one of the most amazing archaeological finds of the twentieth century.

March of the Terra-Cotta Soldiers

from *Archaeology's Dig*

by VICTORIA C. NESNICK

The moment I stepped inside the massive tomb of Emperor Shihuangdi[1] in central China, I felt as though I was facing a humongous firing squad. My body shook as I imagined one of the emperor's generals shouting, "Ready, Aim, Fire!" before a storm of arrows pierced the air on their way to my body.

But then I remembered that these soldiers that seemed so terrifyingly real were made of terra cotta, a baked clay also used through the centuries to make pottery. Secretly buried for 2,200 years until it was found in 1974, the awesome army of artifacts is part of the burial complex of Qin Shihuangdi, who was China's first emperor (221–206 B.C.). As I looked at this amazing site filled with lifelike soldiers and horses, I could understand

massive (mas'iv): huge.

You Need to Know...

The Egyptian pharaohs weren't the only ancient people to build huge tombs, complete with all the things they would need for a comfortable afterlife. Around 200 B.C., China's first emperor built vast burial chambers for himself. He filled them with thousands of life-size clay soldiers, probably in the belief that he would continue to be a powerful man in the afterlife.

The emperor's tomb lay hidden for more than two thousand years under a huge hill that stood over fifteen stories tall. In 1974, while digging a well, some farmers unearthed several of the clay soldiers. The ancient burial site had been discovered. Eventually, thousands of clay soldiers were recovered from the earth. Now, many visitors to China make a point of seeing this amazing collection of clay figures.

1. **Shihuangdi** (shir•hwän•dē): also spelled Shih Huang-ti.

▲ These terra-cotta soldiers have been guarding Shihuangdi's tomb for over two thousand years.

❷ What might these statues reveal about Emperor Shihuangdi's beliefs about death?

SuperStock

why it has been called "The Greatest Archaeological Find of Our Time" and "The Eighth Wonder of the World."

Just 25 years ago, these tremendous troops were a company of crumbled clay. Ever since they were accidentally found in the tomb at the foot of Mount Li, east of the city of Xi'an,[2] archaeologists in China have been putting the pieces together as if they were working on a huge three-dimensional jigsaw puzzle. Think connecting 1,000 pieces of pictured cardboard is tough? Try putting together little bits of more than 7,000 life-size warriors and horses.

"If on a given day we find one piece that fits, that's a lucky day," says Song Yun, a member of the team that's been mending the broken soldiers for more than 20 years.

How Were They Found?

The soldiers were accidentally discovered when a group of local farmers was digging a well during a drought. One of the shovels pulled up the head of a clay warrior. "We all thought he was a ghost who drank all the water meant for the crops," recalls Yang Jungeng. Yang and his fellow farmers thought they had unleashed an evil spirit that would

---

2. **Xi'an** (shē'än').

cause a terrible catastrophe. But when they found more sculpted warriors, they called in experts to investigate. Once excavations began, the site stretched to the size of four football fields.

"We couldn't believe what we found," says Yuan Zhongyi, the first archaeologist at the site. The first pit contained about 6,000 statues that formed the infantry of Shihuangdi's terra-cotta army. Many had been beheaded and smashed by ancient warlords who also set the pit on fire, causing the roof to collapse, which destroyed more statues.

In 1976, archaeologists discovered a second pit, containing 1,400 foot soldiers, cavalry, and the remains of 90 war chariots. (Soldiers and senior officers were sculpted in different styles.) A third pit held the military headquarters, where 68 officers, four horses, and one chariot were stationed. A fourth pit, excavated in 1977, was empty. Many scholars believe the emperor died before it was completed.

Why Were They Made?

Shihuangdi didn't build his terra-cotta army simply because he wanted to play with very large toy soldiers. Some scholars say he built it to protect his tomb and

catastrophe (kə·tas′trə·fē): a widespread misfortune or disaster.

Potion of Death?

The Chinese have an extremely long medical tradition. Over thousands of years they learned how to make many potent herbal remedies from plants. Emperor Shihuangdi seems to have had a personal interest in Chinese medical knowledge—he hoped to find a potion that would allow him to live forever. In his quest for eternal life, the emperor drank many mixtures of herbs and chemicals. Instead of extending his life, however, these mixtures may have slowly poisoned him. He died around 210 B.C., probably in his late forties.

© John P. Stevens/Ancient Art & Architecture Collection Ltd.

▲ Clay soldiers and horses from Emperor Shihuangdi's burial complex.

escort him into the afterlife. Others say the emperor wanted the army as a memorial to celebrate his military victories. Whatever the reason, it took more than 700,000 people, working for 40 years, to build the emperor's burial complex. Archaeologists believe that since all the warriors' faces are different, the sculptors must have come from many different places throughout Shihuangdi's empire.

Many of the emperor's loyal workers, however, were not rewarded for their hard work. Hundreds of nearby gravesites contained skeletons of tomb builders, ministers, and nobles. According to the *Shiji*, an ancient Chinese history book, anyone who knew about the burial complex was locked in and buried alive so they could not reveal its secret location.

[A]nyone who knew about the burial complex was locked in and buried alive so they could not reveal its secret location.

To make the tube-shaped bodies of the huge statues, the sculptors looped together coils of wet clay. Heads and hands were cast from molds. Then an outer layer of clay was applied and individual details sculpted. The moist statues were placed in low-temperature kilns[3] to dry. Then they were fired at high temperatures for several days, until they actually glowed red-hot. Modern artisans are copying such methods to learn more about the sculpting techniques used during the emperor's time. They are also creating reproductions for display purposes and selling replicas as souvenirs to tourists to help raise money for the conservation effort.

Some of the smallest pieces provide the largest clues. From tiny paint chips, archaeologists have determined that the warriors were originally painted in 13 different colors. The paint was made from vegetable dyes and minerals mixed with binders such as animal blood or egg

souvenirs (soo′və•nirz′): things kept as reminders of the past.

---

3. kilns (kilz *or* kilnz): ovens used to bake pottery.

white. But fire, floods, time, and recent exposure to air erased most of the ancient hues.[4]

The Last Puzzle Piece?

The biggest puzzle of all may be Shihuangdi's tomb, located under Mount Li. If it hasn't been looted, the tomb is expected to contain all the possessions the emperor wanted to have in his afterlife. Sima Qian, the author of the *Shiji*, wrote in about 100 B.C. that Shihuangdi's tomb is "filled with models of palaces, precious stones, and rarities." The walls and roof are said to be made of copper and studded with diamonds and pearls to represent the heavenly sky. Miniature silver and gold ducks and geese float along quicksilver (mercury) streams and lakes. The landscape is adorned with foliage and trees made of precious jade.

Some people doubt the accuracy of Sima Qian, but Robert Murowchick, an expert on East Asian archaeology, says, "Sima Qian is one of the best historians. The things he wrote, that we've been able to check, have all turned out very much as he described them."

Although China's archaeologists are anxious to open Shihuangdi's tomb, there is a chance they may find an empty pit. If they do find one huge treasure chest, they will be faced with an enormous conservation job.

"The Chinese have learned from excavating other tombs that items like silk and paper will disintegrate in a matter of days once exposed to air," says Murowchick. "They realize the importance of not opening the emperor's tomb until they are ready to take care of the things inside it." Lack of money may also delay excavations. "It might take between five and 10 years before the problems surrounding the tomb will be solved," says Murowchick.

Then, of course, there are the booby traps to worry about. Booby traps? The *Shiji* warns about crossbows that are mechanically triggered at the tomb's entrance "so that any thief breaking in would be shot." Sounds like this excavation may be a job for Indiana Jones.

---

4. hues (hyo͞oz): shades of color.

conservation (kän′sər·vā′shən): careful use and protection; preservation.

disintegrate (dis·in′tə·grāt′): to break apart into small pieces; to crumble.

▲ Pottery warrior from Qin Shihuangdi's eternal "army."

✓ Reading Check

1. Who were the first modern people to see the ancient terra-cotta soldiers? What did they think they had discovered?

2. How many statues were in the first pit to be excavated? What did archaeologists find in the second pit?

3. Name some of the reasons scholars think Qin Shihuangdi had all these soldiers made. According to the *Shiji,* what happened to the sculptors and other people who worked on the emperor's tomb?

4. Archaeologists have not yet opened the tomb of Qin Shihuangdi. If they do, what might be in it, according to the ancient historian Sima Qian?

5. What have the Chinese learned about tomb items from excavating other tombs? What other concerns may delay excavating Qin Shihuangdi's tomb?

MEET THE *Writer*

Victoria C. Nesnick (1945–   ) was an elementary school teacher for many years and has written numerous works of nonfiction for young readers. She is also the founder of The Kids Hall of Fame, an organization that spotlights both contemporary and historic achievements of young people.

Cross-Curricular ACTIVITIES

■ SCIENCE/HISTORY

Made in China The ancient Chinese made a number of scientific innovations. Research some of the technological, scientific, or medical contributions of the ancient Chinese by using the Internet or other research tools. Then, make a list of important discoveries or advancements made by this ancient culture, including the approximate dates of each innovation, and discuss your findings with your classmates. If you wish, make a visual time line of Chinese inventions.

■ HISTORY/GEOGRAPHY

Map It Out The cities of the Indus Valley were perhaps the first to be modeled on a grid plan, with streets running parallel and perpendicular to each other. Research Mohenjo-daro and Harappa further, and find photographs of the excavations. Use these photos to draw your own map of these ancient cities. Include on your grid the positions of homes, granaries, public baths, and any other structures or important sites.

■ LANGUAGE ARTS

Sum It Up An epitaph is a tribute to someone, generally written on his or her tombstone. Epitaphs tend to be short because there's not much space on a tombstone. Re-read the selections about the Great Wall and the terra-cotta soldiers to gather more information about the first emperor of China, Shihuangdi. Then, do further research on the Internet and in the library. When you think you have a good idea about the life and accomplishments of Emperor Shihuangdi, write an epitaph that summarizes his life.

■ HISTORY/ART

Cartoon Characters In India you can find comic-book versions of history, many featuring the life of Ashoka. Think about comic books you have read. How do the pictures and words work together to tell a story? Imagine that you have been hired to turn the story of Ashoka's life into a comic book. Focus on one key event in his life. Then, draw your cartoon pictures and write speech bubbles to reveal the characters' thoughts and words.

■ LANGUAGE ARTS

Three of a Kind Ashoka, Mohandas K. Gandhi, and Dr. Martin Luther King, Jr., were great leaders. Write an essay comparing and contrasting the three men. To get started, you may want to think about these questions.

- What did the three leaders each want for their people?
- What obstacles stood in their way?
- How did they overcome their obstacles?
- What were key aspects of their philosophies?

■ DRAMA/MUSIC

Scenes from a Life Choose two scenes from either the life of Confucius or the life of the Buddha. Work with a partner or in small groups to rewrite the scenes as scripts. Then, find music that accompanies the scripts you have written. Perform your work for the class.

READ ON: FOR INDEPENDENT READING

■ NONFICTION

Ancient Cities of the Indus Valley Civilization by Jonathan Mark Kenoyer (Oxford University Press, 1998) presents archaeological information on Indus Valley civilizations. The book contains numerous maps and illustrations.

Eyewitness: Ancient China by Arthur Cotterell (Knopf, 1994) explores the highlights of three thousand years of Chinese history, from the earliest dynasty to the twentieth century, and includes a mixture of full-color photographs and illustrations.

The Great Wall of China by Leonard Everett Fisher (Aladdin, 1995) gives a pictorial history of the Great Wall. Black-and-white illustrations accompany the story of the construction of this remarkable wall. A map and history of the Great Wall are included.

India, Now and Through Time by Catherine Galbraith (Houghton, 1980) introduces the history and culture of India from ancient times to the twentieth century.

Science in Ancient China by George Beshore (Franklin Watts, 1998) explores the many achievements of the ancient Chinese in science, medicine, astronomy, and math.

■ FICTION

Journey of Meng: A Chinese Legend by Doreen Rappaport (Dial, 1991) is an ancient Chinese legend of love and courage that takes place during the construction of the Great Wall. Meng's husband is taken away and forced to help build the Great Wall. In the end, Meng tricks the cruel emperor, Qin Shi Huangdi, in order to honor her husband.

Lon Po Po: A Red-Riding Hood Story from China by Ed Young (Philomel Books, 1989) is a retelling of the classic and familiar tale in a Chinese setting. In this version the wolf disguises himself as the grandmother of three children. Illustrations accompany this 1990 Caldecott Medal winner.

Savitri: A Tale of Ancient India by Aaron Shepard (Whitman, 1992) is a retelling of a tale from the *Mahabharata*, one of the great epics of ancient India. The story focuses on the wise princess Savitri, who outwits the Lord of Death to regain her husband's life. Ink-and-watercolor illustrations accompany the text.

Seasons of Splendour: Tales, Myths and Legends of India by Madhur Jaffrey (Atheneum, 1985) is a collection of ancient Indian stories that includes illustrations.

Shiva's Fire by Suzanne Fisher Staples (Farrar Straus & Giroux, 2000) blends history and legend in the tale of a young girl with exceptional dancing talents. The book was a 2000 Parents' Choice Gold award winner.

CHAPTER 6

The Classical World
Ancient Greece and Rome   1000 B.C.–A.D. 350

Why They're Classics

When you think of a "classic," what comes to mind? Whether it's a fine automobile or a book beloved by generations, a "classic" has timeless appeal.

In the Western world, the "classical period" is the time of the ancient Greeks and Romans. The ancient Greeks gave us new ideas about government and public entertainment. They also left us enduring traditions such as the Olympic Games, great art and architecture, and the teachings of some of the best minds of all time, including Socrates, Plato, Aristotle, and many others.

▲ The ancient Greeks produced great plays which were staged in open-air theaters.

The ancient Romans gave us legal systems, building and road technologies, our calendar, military strategies, and centralized government. They also advanced the notion of planned cities and public squares. In addition, the Romans, like the Greeks, left us recorded histories and literary masterpieces. All in all, the contributions made by these two ancient cultures continue to influence the Western world in countless ways.

INVESTIGATE: Why did people in the ancient world say "All roads lead to Rome"?

. . . And Stay Out!

The Greeks of ancient Athens had a great idea—instead of bowing to whatever king or emperor took over, they got together and elected their own leaders. They called it democracy, or rule by the people.

What happened if a leader they elected was a bad choice? No problem. Once a year, each citizen could take a bit of broken pottery called an *ostrakon* and scratch on it

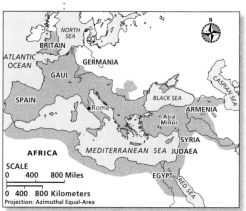

▲ The Roman Empire around A.D. 117.

The Classical World **165**

▲ The Pantheon, a temple begun in 27 B.C. to honor all the gods, still stands in Rome.

Memorable Quote

"To the glory that was Greece, and the grandeur that was Rome."

—from "To Helen"
by Edgar Allan Poe

VOCABULARY MATTERS

Mediterranean (med'ə•tə•rā'nē•ən) comes from the Latin words *medi*, or "middle," and *terra*, or "earth." The Roman Empire surrounded the great sea that separates Europe from Africa. To the Romans, it was a sea "in the middle of the earth." The Mediterranean Sea, in the heart of the Roman Empire, was important to the area's commerce and travel.

the name of a politician he disliked. If enough people voted against an unpopular politician, he was banished not only from office, but from Athens—*ostracized* (shut out) for ten years.

Making Up for Lost Time

Before the reign of Julius Caesar, the Roman calendar was based on the phases of the moon. However, this calendar was confusing, at best. The Roman year had 355 days, with an extra 22 or 23 days thrown in every few years. In order to create a standard calendar, Julius Caesar gave Sosigenes, an Egyptian astronomer, the job of fixing this problem in 48 B.C. Sosigenes created a calendar with 365 days in each year. In order to align the calendar with the sun, the year 46 B.C. had to have 445 days! The Romans called this year *annus confusionis,* or "the year of confusion." Sosigenes' solar calendar, called the *Julian* calendar to honor Julius Caesar, was still not perfect—by the Middle Ages, it was off by 10 days. It was eventually adjusted by Pope Gregory XIII in 1582. The Gregorian calendar, which we still use today, was the result.

A Shared Mythology

The ancient Greeks saw their gods and goddesses as being much like human beings—but far more powerful. The gods and goddesses fought with each other, got married, had children, and felt emotions like love and greed. Cities held great festivals and built huge temples to honor the gods and keep them happy.

The motto of Roman religion might have been "the more, the merrier," since the ancient Romans worshipped hundreds of gods. When the Romans conquered new lands, they often added local deities to their worship. Many Roman gods were originally Greek. In Roman mythology, Zeus, the king of the Greek gods, became Jupiter. His daughter Athena, the goddess of wisdom, was renamed Minerva. The hunter Artemis became Diana, warlike Ares became Mars, and so on, down to Eros, who the Romans called Cupid.

You probably know how popular the Olympic Games are around the world today, but did you know that the Games started almost three thousand years ago in ancient Greece? Read on to find out more about the ancient Olympics.

from The Ancient Olympics

from The Olympic Games

by THEODORE KNIGHT

It is impossible to say precisely when the Olympic festival began. We know that it was very early in Greek history because it is mentioned in some of the writings of the earliest <u>anonymous</u> Greek poets. Several popular Greek legends describe the first Olympic competition. The most popular one tells of a famous chariot race held near Olympus between a king named Œnamaus[1] and a prince named Pelops. Œnamaus, according to legend, had a beautiful daughter named Hippodamia. Œnamaus promised her in marriage to the first man who could find her and then escape in a chariot with her father in pursuit. Thirteen young men tried and were defeated. Œnamaus put each one to death. Then came Pelops's turn. The race got underway

anonymous (ə•nän′ə•məs): not known by name.

You Need to Know...

The Olympic Games began in ancient Greece and were held to honor the gods, especially Zeus, the king of the gods. Warfare ceased during the Games so that athletes could safely travel to attend them. The Games were held at a sacred site—in a valley in western Greece at a place called Olympia. The Olympic Games brought together people throughout the Greek world. For athletes, victory in Olympic events was the ultimate achievement.

The "Olympic Village" of ancient Greece grew into a great complex. A vast temple that held a forty-foot-tall statue of Zeus was built there. The sculptor, a man named Phidias, carved the form of Zeus from ivory, wood, and stone and seated him on a throne made of cedar wood. The statue wore a golden robe, and the throne was decorated with precious gems. The complex also included a huge hippodrome—an arena big enough for chariot races. The giant gymnasium came complete with steam baths and practice areas. The huge stadium could seat fifty thousand fans.

---

1. Œnamaus (ē•nä•mā′əs)

▲ "The Discus Thrower" represents the Greek ideals of athletic and physical perfection.

initiating (i·nish′ē·āt′iŋ): starting; beginning.

barred (bärd): kept out; banned.

spectators (spek′tāt′ərz): onlookers.

but ended abruptly when the axle on the king's chariot mysteriously broke. Pelops, according to the legend, had cut the axle. The king broke his neck and died. Pelops married Hippodamia and declared himself king. He ordered a great feast day to celebrate his victory and give thanks to Zeus, thus initiating the first Olympic festival.

The earliest written record of the Olympic festival concerns a man named Coroebus. Coroebus apparently won a footrace of about 200 yards (180 meters) at the Olympic festival in 776 B.C. and was rewarded with a wreath of olive branches. Archaeological excavations have uncovered the remains of a temple and other buildings at the Olympic site that date back several centuries before this race. Nevertheless, historians view Coroebus's victory as the start of the ancient Olympics. From 776 B.C. to A.D. 393, when the Games ended, 293 Olympic festivals were held. . . .

Olympic Participants

Originally, athletic competition at the Olympic festival was limited to male Greek citizens; foreigners, slaves, and women were barred from competition. Every athlete had to take the Olympic oath, swearing that he had trained for ten months before the Games and that he had done nothing to offend the gods. Athletes who competed in the ancient Olympics were not just average citizens. They had to be wealthy enough to travel to and from the Games and to pay their living expenses while they trained. In the early days of the Games, the only reward was a wreath. Winning athletes, however, were expected to provide huge banquets to celebrate their victories. This meant that competition in the ancient Olympics was mostly for members of the wealthy, ruling class, since only they had enough time and money to take part.

For many centuries, women were barred not only as competitors but also as spectators. The penalty for breaking this rule was death. Even so, some women still tried to watch the Games, even if it meant donning[2] a disguise.

2. **donning:** putting on; dressing in.

One story tells how the mother of a young runner named Pisidorus did just that. When the young man's father died while training him, the mother took over the training and then attended the race disguised as a man. When Pisidorus won the race, the mother's cries of joy were so loud she was discovered. She was not put to death, however. To this day, no one knows why.

As time progressed, Olympic rules changed. By the time of the 128th Olympics, women were allowed to compete in as well as watch the Games. In that year, according to ancient written records, the winner of the chariot race was a woman named Belisiche, from the country of Macedonia, or what is now parts of Greece, Bulgaria, and Yugoslavia.

Earliest Events Thrill Spectators

For many decades (at least up to the time of Coroebus's victory in 776 B.C.) it appears that the festival's athletic competition was confined to a few footraces. As the years passed, more and more races and other athletic events were added, but no records exist to tell us when particular events were added. We do know that footraces, chariot races, wrestling, boxing, and a brutal sport called the *pancratium* were among the early Olympic sports. Pancratium combined boxing, wrestling, biting, kicking, gouging, and strangling. Men were often permanently injured or killed in this event. The *pentathlon*, which combined five sports, was also an early popular event. In the pentathlon, contestants threw a flat wooden and metal plate called a discus and a light spear called a javelin. They also wrestled and competed in the long jump and the sprint.

Robert Gill; Papilio/CORBIS

▲ Olympia, the site of the ancient Games, was named for Mount Olympus (shown above), the highest peak in Greece. The ancient Greeks believed that the gods lived at the top of Mount Olympus rather than in a remote heaven. ❓ **What might this belief tell us about how the early Greeks viewed their gods?**

confined (kən·fīnd'): restricted.

▲ Ancient Olympic events, such as chariot racing, were very popular.

hostilities (häs·til′ə·tēz): warfare.

Records indicate that the wrestling, boxing, and pancratium competitions drew especially huge and enthusiastic crowds. The high level of interest probably stemmed from the strong <u>hostilities</u> between cities and tribes. Because a truce[3] was in effect during the Games, these events offered a chance for athletes from hostile cities to do physical battle with one another. No matter how great their passion for conflict, however, the Greeks' high regard for physical beauty was greater. When it came time to erect statues honoring new Olympic champions, it was the smoothly muscled pentathlon athletes who were honored rather than the bulky wrestlers or the wiry runners.

Chariot races, too, thrilled Olympic spectators. The most important chariot race was the *quadrigae*[4]—a race for light, two-wheeled chariots pulled by four horses. The distance of the race course was twelve laps around two columns at opposite ends of the hippodrome—about ten thousand meters, or six miles. Often as many as forty teams entered the race, and accidents were common on the crowded track. Once, in a race of forty chariots, only one man finished. Everyone else had been injured or killed.

---

3. truce: temporary halt in fighting by agreement on both sides.
4. quadrigae (kwä·drī′gē).

Other Ancient Events

Three footraces were especially popular. The *dolichos*[5] was a race of twenty-four lengths of the stadium field. The runners ran around two columns, with much shoving and pushing and many injuries. A shorter, similar race, the *diaulos*,[6] was only two stadium lengths. The *stade* was a sprint for one stadium length, or about 883 meters. In addition, foot-soldiers dressed in full armor and carrying their swords and shields ran in a special race.

When the ancient Games were at their peak, they comprised five days of pageants, parades, feasts, and religious rituals as well as the athletic events. Sacrifices were offered daily to all the gods. The athletes themselves offered prayers at the altars of various gods and placed sacrifices and gifts before the statues of previous Olympic victors. City-states tried to outdo each other by presenting the largest and most magnificent sacrifices and gifts. Nothing, however, equaled the spectacle of the third day of the festival when one hundred cattle were ritually slaughtered at once and then burned on a special altar.

Much went on at the Games also that was not directly connected with either religion or sports. Tribal chiefs, magistrates,[7] kings, and consuls from all over the Greek world used the time of truce at the festival to conduct discussions and to negotiate treaties. Merchants and traders gathered to sell their wares[8] and make trade agreements. Jugglers, musicians, magicians, poets, and fortune-tellers all performed for the crowds.

Olympic Decline

The history of the ancient Olympic Games parallels the history of ancient Greece. Over the centuries, as Greece grew to be the most powerful nation in the civilized world, the Olympics grew also in size and importance. When the Roman Empire conquered Greece around 100 B.C., however, Roman culture and beliefs replaced the

pageants (paj′ənts): colorful shows or entertainments.

spectacle (spek′tə·kəl): dramatic public display.

negotiate (ni·gō′shē·āt′): to bargain with others in hope of reaching agreement.

---

5. **dolichos** (däl·ē·kôs′).
6. **diaulos** (dē′ô·lôs).
7. **magistrates:** government officials with power to enforce laws.
8. **wares:** items for sale.

The Games Return

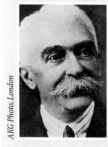

AKG Photo, London

Frenchman Baron Pierre de Coubertin (1863–1937) is the person most responsible for reviving the Olympic Games. Because of his vigorous efforts, the first modern Games were finally held in Athens, Greece, in 1896. Since then, the Games have been held at different cities around the world every four years (except during World War I and World War II). The modern Games include several track-and-field events like those of the ancient Olympics, as well as many newer sports like water polo and the luge (a Winter Olympics event).

Coubertin's efforts to restart the Olympic Games proved to be wildly successful. After his death, Coubertin's heart was buried near the ruins of the ancient Olympia.

bribery (brīb′ər·ē): giving money to someone to do something illegal.

Greek way of life, and the Olympics went into a decline that lasted for several centuries. For the Romans, war and trade were more important than philosophy, religion, or athletics. The Olympic festival lost most of its original significance as a celebration of patriotism and religion. Contestants had once competed to honor the gods and win their blessings; now they wanted to win for themselves. They began to demand prizes and money for competing. With money rather than spiritual rewards at stake, cheating and bribery increased among the athletes and officials. The Games themselves became a brutal form of entertainment. There were battles between animals, battles between men and animals, and combat-to-the-death between gladiators. Real athletic competition faded away. When the Roman emperor Nero built himself a great palace at Olympia and then entered Olympic events as a competitor, all sense of true competition died. Defeating the emperor was a dangerous thing to do because, as the supreme monarch of the empire, he was considered all-powerful. So Nero was always victorious. Following several centuries as a form of public entertainment that had little to do with the Olympics' religious beginnings, a religious change came to the Roman world. This change ironically signaled the end of the Olympics. In A.D. 393, with the spread of Christianity, the Roman emperor Theodosius I declared an end to all pagan[9] rituals including the Olympics.

---

9. pagan: of or relating to the practice of a form of worship of various religions that came before Christianity.

In later years, the temples and altars at Olympia were destroyed by invading barbarian[10] tribes. Then, in A.D. 426, Emperor Theodosius II ordered the walls surrounding the Olympic fields completely pulled down. About a century later, several earthquakes completed the ruin of the historical site. The Alpheus River flooded the original Olympic meadow. All signs of the ancient Olympic Games had been completely erased. After well over twelve hundred years, the festival at Olympia had ended. There would be no Olympic Games for more than fifteen hundred years.

Wolfgang Kaehler/CORBIS

▲ Zeus, the king of the gods. The ancient Olympics were held in his honor.

---

10. **barbarian:** crude, uncivilized, or backward. In ancient Greece, all foreigners were considered to be barbarians.

✓ Reading Check

1. Who was originally allowed to compete in the Olympic games? Why did an athlete need to be rich in order to compete?

2. At which set of Games were women finally allowed to compete? How well did they do?

3. When the ancient Games were at their peak, what kinds of events filled the five days of the festival?

4. How did the Olympic Games change after the Romans conquered the Greeks?

5. Who declared an end to the ancient Olympic Games? Why?

MEET THE *Writer*

Theodore Knight (1946–   ) has written about world cultures, the Olympic Games, art education, study skills, and pioneer women. He has also managed a bookstore and worked as an editor and college teacher. "I'm constantly trying to combine my knowledge and background with my interests," he says. He enjoys writing for young people because he gets to learn about all sorts of interesting subjects.

Spartan soldiers were trained to obey orders, ignore pain, and fight to the death. The result was a fearsome army that terrorized ancient Greece for more than two hundred years. Read on to find out how the harsh discipline of its army influenced all of Spartan society.

The Spartan Way
from *Junior Scholastic*

by SEAN PRICE

Visitors to ancient Sparta often heard the story about the boy and the fox cub. A Spartan boy, the story goes, stole a pet fox cub and hid it under his cloak. When the boy was caught, he calmly denied every-thing—even though the fox had bitten and scratched him terribly. The boy showed no pain, but soon slumped over dead from his wounds.

deceit (dē·sēt′): misleading by telling lies.

You Need to Know...

Sparta's desire for a strong army had a great deal to do with its relationship with neighboring Messenia. Conquering Messenia gave Sparta control over a large area of fertile land. The Spartans demanded half the food grown by the people of Messenia. Resenting this treatment, the Messenians rebelled. During the decades of fierce fighting that followed, Sparta became increasingly concerned with military training. This focus on the military made Sparta even more dependent on the food grown in Messenia. That, in turn, pressured Sparta to further increase the strength of its military—to become, in effect, a society of soldiers.

Most visitors who heard the story thought that the boy's behavior was strange. To Spartans, though, the boy represented the qualities that they held dear: strength, deceit of an enemy, and fearlessness about death.

For more than 200 years, Sparta was the most power-ful city-state[1] in ancient Greece. Sparta's power came from its tough, professional army. Brutal training and discipline made Sparta's army one of the most-feared fighting forces ever.

_____

1. **city-state:** an independent city, plus its surrounding territory.

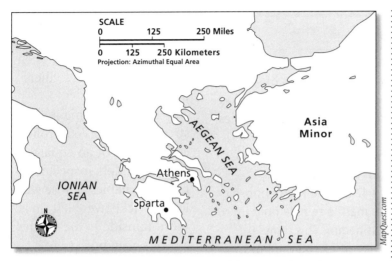

▲ Athens and Sparta were the two most powerful city-states in ancient Greece.

Deadly Rivals

Sparta waged[2] one of history's most famous feuds with its rival, Athens. Both city-states left legacies[3] that still shape the modern world.

Athens was the birthplace of democracy, where all full citizens could vote on city matters. In Athens, great artists and thinkers built the foundations of Western culture.

Sparta, on the other hand, was a secretive place run by an oligarchy[4] of rich families. Sparta has been admired over the centuries by people who value order and discipline over everything else.

Spartans kept few written records and left few ruins for historians to study. Almost everything we know is second-hand, from enemies or visitors. But we do know that Sparta dominated ancient Greece from about 600 B.C. to 371 B.C. leaving an unforgettable mark on history.

dominated (däm′ə•nāt′id): controlled; ruled over.

Growing Up In Sparta

According to legend, a great lawgiver named Lycurgus created the rules and customs that made Sparta so powerful.

---

2. **waged:** carried on.
3. **legacies** (leg′ə•sēz): things handed down to future generations.
4. **oligarchy** (äl′i•gär′kē): government in which the ruling power is in the hands of a few people.

Athens and the Golden Age

SuperStock

Unlike the harsh and severe Spartans, the citizens of Athens had an eye for art and literature. In the fifth and fourth centuries B.C., Athens was the center of Greek culture. This period is known as the Golden Age.

In 447 B.C. the Parthenon, a white marble temple built in honor of the goddess Athena, was begun. This temple, whose ruins still stand in Athens, is considered the finest example of Greek architecture. Athens was also known for its delicate and realistic sculpture, as well as for its philosophers, including the great Socrates and his student Plato. In addition, Athens produced some of the Western world's greatest literature, including drama, poetry, and histories.

endure (en·door′): to put up with quietly.

provisions (prǝ·vizh′ǝnz): food and other supplies.

About 10 percent of Spartan men were full citizens known as equals. Their job was to serve as soldiers in Sparta's army.

Sparta's government and strong traditions controlled every aspect of an equal's life. City elders inspected all newborn babies. Those who looked sickly were left on a mountainside to die. At the age of seven, boys were taken from their families to begin military training.

New trainees were put into packs, which were run by older boys. Trainees were taught to obey orders and endure pain. They were whipped for making the slightest mistake, and were expected to show no sign of suffering. Boys always went barefoot and wore only a cloak, even in winter.

While boys in Athens were given lengthy educations, Spartan boys were taught only the basics of reading and writing. Their trainers gave them barely enough food to live on, encouraging them to fend for themselves.

"The boys also steal whatever provisions they can, thereby learning how to pounce skillfully upon those who are asleep or keeping guard carelessly," wrote one historian who lived in ancient times. "[But] a boy is beaten and goes hungry if he is caught."

Woman Power

Men became full citizens at the age of 30. Only then could they vote, or hold public office.

All Spartan men ate their meals at army mess halls, not with their families. Spartans looked down on any form of luxury, and their food was deliberately bad-tasting.

One visitor remarked that after eating the Spartans' food, he understood why they were so willing to die in battle.

One visitor remarked that after eating the Spartans' food, he understood why they were so willing to die in battle.

While the main job of Spartan men was to be soldiers, the main job of Spartan women was to have children. Spartans believed that physically fit women had strong babies. So Spartan girls were just as athletic as the boys. They learned to wrestle, throw javelins,[5] and exercise daily.

Despite their overbearing government, Spartan women were more free than other women in ancient Greece. In Athens, for instance, girls and married women were supposed to stay in their homes. They went outside only for special occasions, such as religious festivals and funerals.

overbearing (ō'vər·ber'iŋ): arrogant or domineering.

Spartan women could not wear jewelry, perfume, or nice clothes. Even so, they had far fewer restrictions than other Greek women. Spartan women could own land, run their own households, and do business.

Such power was shocking to Greek men from other city-states. One time, a visitor kidded a Spartan woman, saying, "You Spartan women are the only ones who can rule men." She replied, "This is because we are the only ones who give birth to men."

No Work Allowed

Spartan men were not permitted to do any manual labor outside of their jobs as soldiers. But Sparta was not always at war.

© Vanni Archive/CORBIS

▲ This statue of Leonidas, a Spartan king who lived during the 400s B.C., stands atop a monument honoring his bravery.

---

5. **javelins** (jav'linz): light spears.

Spartan Chokehold

Given their many differences, it's not a complete surprise that Sparta and Athens were bitter enemies. The Peloponnesian War, named after the Greek peninsula of Peloponnesus, began in 431 B.C. when a treaty between the two Greek powers was broken. The war lasted for twenty-seven years. By 405 B.C. Sparta, sensing victory, set up a blockade to prevent food from being imported into Athens. Facing starvation, Athens finally surrendered for good the following year.

So, on an average day, Spartan men had plenty of free time.

"Except when they were [fighting battles]" one historian wrote, "all their time was taken up by choral[6] dances, festivals, feasts, hunting expeditions, physical exercise, and conversation."

That free time was made possible by two groups of conquered peoples: perioeci[7] and helots.

Perioeci, or neighbors, were allowed to be free, but had no rights. They lived in their own towns and were usually treated well. Some even grew rich as craftsmen or traders.

Helots were slaves who were owned by Sparta's government. All Greek city-states relied on slavery. Democratic Athens had the largest slave population in ancient Greece. But no Greeks treated their slaves more cruelly than the Spartans did.

The helots' main job was to work the farms owned by Spartan citizens. Helots outnumbered citizens by as many as 10 to 1, so Spartans constantly feared a slave revolt.

To keep a revolt from breaking out, teenage boys patrolled country roads. They killed any helot they saw traveling at night. They also killed helots who seemed more intelligent or looked stronger than the others.

Despite these and other efforts, helots did revolt several times. Some of the revolts lasted years, but all of them were put down. Helots despised the Spartans so much, said one visitor, that "they would eat [a Spartan] raw."

A Dreadful Sight

Sparta's army and loyal soldiers made it a powerful city-state. Some opposing armies crumbled at the very sight of Spartan soldiers marching toward them.

All Greeks knew that a Spartan equal was expected to fight to the death. One Spartan mother supposedly told her son to return from battle "with your shield or on it." In other words, come back victorious—or dead.

---

6. **choral** (kôr′əl): of or including a group of singers, in this case a dance that features the singing of a choir.
7. **perioeci** (per•ə•ē′sī).

Sparta conquered Athens in the Peloponnesian War (431 to 404 B.C.). Athens lost that war in 404 B.C., and never regained its former glory.

Sparta remained the leader of ancient Greece. But that dominance lasted only until 371 B.C., when the city-state of Thebes crushed Sparta's mighty army for good.

Sparta's Collapse

Without its army, Sparta's power collapsed. By the time the Romans took over in 146 B.C., Sparta had become a tourist attraction. Visitors went there to watch little boys who could be whipped without showing pain.

Sparta's government was admired among ancient Greeks. People still admire Sparta today, and several U.S. towns are named after it. But the ancient historian Xenophon pointed out that most admirers of Sparta go only so far.

Reading Check

1. What qualities did Spartans hold dear?

2. How did the education of boys differ in Sparta and Athens?

3. What did Spartan men do during their free time?

4. Why were Spartans so afraid of a slave revolt?

5. What had become of Sparta by the time the Romans had taken over?

Ron Sheridan/Ancient Art & Architecture Collection Ltd.

▲ This bronze statue of a Spartan soldier dates from the sixth century B.C.

LINKING PAST AND PRESENT

Alexander the Great left a trail of death and destruction as he built his vast empire. However, he also left some positive marks on the culture and society of Asia and India. In the following excerpts based on a television documentary series and its companion book, British historian Michael Wood provides glimpses into the "real" Alexander as he retraces the famous conqueror's journeys.

from In the Footsteps of Alexander the Great

based on the Maryland Public Television series

by MICHAEL WOOD

Ever since I started in television, I have wanted to tell the story of Alexander the Great. Every conceivable template[1] of human destiny is put on this man. I never quite cracked the split in his personality.

He was chivalrous,[2] even generous, to his enemies. He was <u>vindictive</u>, and he killed thousands, maybe millions. In a drunken argument, he even killed a friend who had saved his life years before.

Walking in his footsteps, I drew Alexander the Great's portrait from written history and local tales. I saw an extraordinarily gifted man

vindictive (vin·dik′tiv): desiring revenge.

You Need to Know...

As a teenager, Alexander the Great earned the respect of his father's soldiers by leading them to victory on the battlefield. When his father was assassinated in 336 B.C., Alexander became king of Macedonia. He immediately set out on a long-planned invasion of Asia, taking with him surveyors, engineers, and architects. Along the way, he established more than seventy cities. With each new triumph, Alexander became more convinced that he was a god. It is said that he wanted to rule the entire world, but toward the end of his life he seemed more interested in exploring than conquering. At the age of thirty-three, Alexander became ill and died. Without the force of his personality behind it, his empire slowly dissolved.

1. **template:** mold or pattern used as a guide for reproducing something.
2. **chivalrous** (shiv′əl·rəs): courteous; gallant.

who could lead his men through the toughest of circumstances. I also saw a man who let no resistance go unpunished.

Throughout our trip we saw Alexander's legacy. On one level, Alexander brought death to the people of Asia. On the banks of the Ganges,[3] Indian historian A.K. Narain told me that following Alexander was "going in the footsteps of violence."

On another level, Alexander's crusade unleashed tremendous social and cultural energy. After Alexander, Greek culture flourished in east Asia and India. Three great world religions rose in the Hellenistic culture of the Near East. Alexander's legend appeared in art and story all over the ancient world.

In Taxila, Pakistani archaeologist Ahmed Dani said of the merging Greek culture on the Indian subcontinent, "There was destruction and loss of life, to be sure, but great things occurred which advanced the history of humanity."

Our eyewitnesses along the journey helped us bring Alexander the Great's story to life. It is a story that exists forever in the telling.

▲ Alexander the Great was only twenty when he became king of Macedonia. Over the next thirteen years, he created the largest empire the world had known.

The Journey

By the time he was 30, Alexander III of Macedon had created an empire the likes of which the world has seldom seen. Stretching from the Balkan Mountains to the Indus River, it brought most of the known world under the command of this young and <u>dynamic</u> leader. But, just who was this enigmatic[4] man?

Was he the person we know as Alexander the Great, a political visionary on a heroic search for glory . . . the folk hero of Jewish tradition . . . the "perfect knight" of medieval Europe . . . Superman as a real life hero?

Or was he Dhul Qarnain, The Two-Horned One of the Koran . . . "murderous and <u>melancholy</u> mad," as one

dynamic (dī·nam′ik): strong and energetic.

melancholy (mel′ən·käl′ē): sad; gloomy.

3. **Ganges** (gan′jēz): river in northern India.
4. **enigmatic** (en′ig·mat′ik): puzzling; difficult to understand.

contemporary remembered him . . . a despised tyrant capable of the worst kind of crimes? I soon realized that the only way I could uncover the true story of Alexander was to actually experience his journey myself.

Following in Alexander's footsteps took my film crew and me to sixteen countries and through four war zones. We traveled over 20,000 miles—on everything from foot, camels, and horses to helicopters, boats, and Jeeps. We slept under the stars in places where mothers still tell their children, "Go to bed or Alexander will get you."

Across the Great Sand Sea

On the edge of the Great Sand Sea, the oasis at Siwa is a feast for the senses. Shaded by luxurious date palms even during the hottest part of the day, the area is full of gardens and trees bearing olives, lemons, figs, and pomegranates. You can imagine our reluctance to leave such a paradise, especially when the trip back was through the relentless desert that supposedly gobbled up an entire Persian army centuries ago.

But leave we must. The question remained: by which route? Most historians assume Alexander went back to the Nile the way he came, but Arrian[5] says otherwise. There were two other choices Alexander might have made: an old caravan route that went along the Qattara Depression to Memphis,[6] or another that went due east to the Bahariya Oasis, then northeast to Memphis. Following my hunch, we chose the latter.

The twelve-hour trek that followed was a true test of our wills. Driven by gusting winds, razor-sharp sand crystals threatened to cut our vehicles' tires. The sand and the sky merged together into a giant white blur. Our drinking water became boiling hot. Our jeep broke down, costing us precious time and further taxing our resources and spirits. We were engulfed with an uncanny sense of isolation.

But when we reached the oasis, I felt vindicated. Alexander must surely have come this way. The very first

vindicated (vin′də•kāt′id): cleared of blame or suspicion; justified.

5. **Arrian:** ancient Greek historian who wrote about Alexander's campaigns.
6. **Memphis:** ancient city in northern Egypt, on the Nile River.

known temple to Alexander as Pharaoh and another small chapel in his honor have been discovered near the oasis. Surely these must mark what must have been a momentous route for Alexander.

This wasn't the first time that I'd felt that walking in Alexander's footsteps was more than just merely tracing a path through history—and it wouldn't be the last. . . .

Alexander the Despot

Visiting Samarkand[7] today, it is easy to see why Alexander would be attracted to this place. Even in his times, it was a bustling and pleasant city, an oasis on the legendary Silk Route, nestled on the edge of the Kyzyl Kum desert. But its great domes and brilliant turquoise tiles give lie to the brutality it witnessed at the hands of Alexander.

It was the end of the summer when Alexander brought his troop back to Samarkand after five months of hard

---

7. **Samarkand:** city in eastern Uzbekistan, in central Asia.

SIDELIGHT

"My father gave me life, but it was Aristotle who taught me how to live," Alexander once said about his unique education. Aristotle, a student of the well-known philosopher Plato, was one of the world's greatest thinkers. From his observations of sea life on the Greek island of Lesbos, he concluded that we learn what is "real" through our senses. For three years, Aristotle tutored the young prince in grammar, literature, and politics. Alexander never forgot his teacher and, years later, he sent him specimens of the new plants and animals he discovered as he led his troops across Asia. When news of Alexander's death reached Greece, loyal Greeks who wished to be free of Macedonian domination turned against Aristotle because of his close relationship with their former overlord. Saddened by the actions of his fellow Greeks, Aristotle retired to a secluded village outside Athens, where he died a few months later."

—"Alexander's Tutor" by Susanne Hicks and Duane Damon from *Calliope* (December 1998)

Culver Pictures Inc./SuperStock

battle. There, he decided to appoint Cleitus as satrap of Bactria.[8]

Cleitus had known Alexander since he was an infant; his sister had been the child's nurse. He had served in the army under Alexander's father, and had been at Alexander's side throughout the long years of his conquest. In fact, Cleitus had once saved his commander's life in one of their first encounters with the Persians. So, it seemed fitting that a man of such loyalty be rewarded.

There was a party. As usual, everyone there had drunk a great deal. Alexander started raving, claiming credit for the battles his father won. Cleitus listened until he had heard enough. "All your glory is due to your father," he finally said. Alexander met his words with a sharp thrust of his javelin. Cleitus lay dying in a pool of blood. Seeing what he had done, Alexander tried to kill himself, but, instead, collapsed in a drunken mass of tears.

Later, his men excused him. As king, he was the embodiment of justice, wasn't he? Whatever he did had to be right simply because he did it.

Even now, the logic astounds.

Great Alexander Lives and Rules

Why and how Alexander chose the route for his men to return to their homeland will never be known. He led them straight through one of the most inhospitable places on earth, the Makran Desert. Even today, it remains a seemingly endless stretch of long serrated[9] ridges between tracts of barren gravel and sand. Was it punishment for their refusal to go onward? Now that he had conquered the known world, did he need to conquer nature as well?

Questions like these crowded my mind as we followed his route. At Pasni, we joined a camel train going straight through the desert. For most of the first day, we trudged along the coast of the Arabian Sea with not even the

---

8. Cleitus . . . Bactria: Cleitus, one of Alexander's commanders, was appointed as satrap (an ancient Persian word for "governor") of Bactria, an ancient country in what is now northeastern Afghanistan.

9. serrated (serʹātʹid): jagged, like the cutting edge of a saw.

slightest hint of shade, and then on to the high dunes, where the sand sucked our feet back at every step.

The next day we came through a ferocious salt-desert of ridges and peaks that eerily resembled a lunar landscape more than anything else. Salt flats, broken ranges of hills, wildly eroded ridges dusted with a white powder all presented themselves as we inched onward in the unbearable heat.

We had enough water to keep us going, but not enough to make us forget the complete incongruity[10] of a thirsty Alexander draining a helmetful of the precious liquid into the sand, refusing to drink when his men could not.

When Alexander reached the summit of the Khawack Pass, he must have been astonished to discover that he had not yet encountered the end of the earth. I was astonished we did not find it here in the complete desolation of the Makran desert.

AKG Photo, London

▲ Detail of mosaic from Pompeii showing Alexander the Great in battle.

eroded (ē·rōd′id): worn or eaten away.

---

10. **incongruity** (in′kän·grōō′i·tē): something that is unsuitable or doesn't make sense.

✓ Reading Check

1. How does the author describe Alexander?

2. What was discovered near the Bahariya Oasis? Why did this make the writer happy?

3. Who was Cleitus? What did he say that made Alexander angry enough to kill him?

4. Why did Alexander pour a helmetful of water into the desert sand?

5. What does the author think Alexander must have felt when he reached the summit of the Khawack Pass?

MEET THE *Writer*

Michael Wood is a historian, author, and television writer. He worked as a journalist before moving on to write and narrate more than sixty television documentaries. Wood lives in London.

Have you heard the saying "Curiosity killed the cat"? Fortunately, at least for humans, curiosity can also lead to a new understanding about the world around us. Read on to find out how the curiosity of the ancient Greeks led to important discoveries in science that forever changed the way we live in our world.

Science in a Hellenistic World

from *Calliope*

by LOUISE CHIPLEY SLAVICEK

The Hellenistic[1] period was a time of remarkable scientific achievement. During the 300 years following Alexander's[2] death, great advances were made in the areas of mathematics, physics, astronomy, and medicine. The most famous Hellenistic mathematicians were Euclid[3] and Archimedes.[4] Euclid created a brilliant system for studying geometry. For more than 2,000 years his book, titled *Elements*, would remain the most important geometry text in the world. Archimedes used mathematical reasoning to solve physical problems, such as explaining how levers and pulleys work. He demonstrated his theory by single-handedly maneuvering a fully-loaded ship into the shore with pulleys!

You Need to Know...

The ancient Greeks didn't have calculators, microscopes, computers, or the other math and science tools that we take for granted today. Yet, by observing nature and thinking about what they saw, the Greeks were able to establish the foundations of many modern sciences. The early Greeks made key discoveries in the fields of mathematics, physics, astronomy, and medicine. As you read the selection, think about how much of what you study today was first discovered by the Greeks.

maneuvering (mə·noo'vər·in): skillfully moving, managing, or manipulating.

1. **Hellenistic** (hel'ən·is'tik): period between the death of Alexander the Great and Rome's conquest of Egypt (323–30 B.C.).
2. **Alexander:** Alexander the Great (356–323 B.C.).
3. **Euclid** (yoo'klid).
4. **Archimedes** (är'kə·mē'dēz').

When King Hieron II of Syracuse (in Sicily) asked him to find out whether a crown was pure gold without melting it down, Archimedes was puzzled. Then one day, as he was bathing, he noticed that the lower he sank into the water, the more water spilled out of the tub. He suddenly realized that he could test the crown by placing it and a chunk of pure gold of the same weight into water-filled containers. If the crown and the gold caused different amounts of water to overflow the containers, he would know that the crown was not solid gold. Tradition says that Archimedes was so delighted by his discovery that he jumped out of the tub and dashed to the palace naked, shouting, "*Eureka!*"[5] ("I have found it!"). As a result of his experiment with the king's crown, Archimedes developed a major new physical law. His "law of buoyancy" explained why objects appear to lose weight in water and other liquids.

The achievements of Hellenistic astronomers rivaled those of the Hellenistic mathematicians. Aristarchos of Samos was the first astronomer to question the belief that a motionless earth was the center of the universe. His observations of the heavens led him to a startling

CORBIS

▲ Archimedes.

buoyancy (boi'ən•sē): ability of something to float.

___

5. **Eureka** (yo͞o•rē'kə).

The Price of Fame

Bettmann/CORBIS

Hypatia (ca. A.D. 370–415) was a gifted scholar who lived in Alexandria, Egypt, during the post-Hellenistic period. She was a leading thinker of a type of philosophy called Neoplatonism and attracted large numbers of students to her lectures on scientific and classical topics. Hypatia also wrote books about mathematics and astronomy and invented scientific instruments.

In A.D. 415, Hypatia was attacked and killed by a mob. It's not clear why Hypatia was murdered, but she may have gotten caught in a political or religious struggle. Although she was brutally killed, Hypatia's fame as a leading scientist, mathematician, and philosopher of her time endures.

▲ Hellenistic thinkers added to the knowledge of various sciences. This painting presents a rather idealized image of Hellenistic achievements in astronomy.

comprehensive (käm′prē·hen′siv): of wide scope; complete.

anatomy (ə·nat′ə·mē): science dealing with the structure of the body.

conclusion: The earth revolved around a motionless sun. Aristarchos also correctly proposed that day and night are caused by the earth rotating on its axis. Another great astronomer was Hipparchos, who compiled the first-known comprehensive chart of the stars. His findings shaped the study of astronomy for centuries.

A final area in which Hellenistic scientists excelled was medical research. Herophilos, a Greek physician who lived in Alexandria, has been called the father of scientific anatomy. Using dissected human bodies as study tools, he accurately described the structure of the brain and other organs, and corrected the old idea that arteries carried air, not blood. Erasistratos, another Greek physician based in Alexandria, carried out groundbreaking research on the circulatory[6] system and rejected the popular belief that all disease resulted from an imbalance of bodily fluids known as "humors."

---

6. **circulatory** (sʉr′kyo͞o·lə·tôr′ē): having to do with movement of blood through the body.

Why did the Hellenistic world produce such an impressive record of scientific achievement? One reason was the close contact between Greeks and non-Greeks that followed Alexander's conquests. For centuries, Babylonians had kept careful records of the stars. When Babylon was brought within the Greek sphere,[7] these records became available to Greek astronomers like Hipparchos, who used them extensively.

As for developments in the field of medicine, Egypt was as important to these as Babylon was to astronomy. The fact that Herophilos and Erasistratos chose to live in Alexandria was of enormous significance for their anatomical research, because in Alexandria human dissection was permitted. In Greece, such dissection was strictly forbidden because of religious beliefs concerning the burial of the dead.

The extraordinary achievements of the Hellenistic scientists were also tied to an increase in royal support for science. Hellenistic rulers competed with one another as

---

7. sphere (sfir): here, range or scope.

SIDELIGHT

"About 325 years before Christ was born, Pytheas, a scientist and astronomer from the Greek colony of Masilla, set sail to explore the Atlantic Ocean. He was looking for the 'Tin Islands,' a source of tin for Mediterranean civilizations. He found the tin mines of southern Britain but didn't stop there.

He continued north, seeking a land called 'Thule' by the Britons. He didn't turn around until he found a land surrounded by a 'sea of ice.' It was perhaps Norway or even Iceland. On his way home, he sailed around the British Isles, likely the first person ever to do so.

Although Pytheas traveled for six long years and sailed more than 7,000 miles—correctly figuring latitudes with a device he invented—the people of Masilla didn't believe his stories of icy seas and long northern days. Things just weren't like that on the warm Mediterranean! He was branded a liar, and it wasn't until much later that people realized he was probably telling the truth about his travels."

—"Pytheas Finds an Icy Thule" by Kent Bushart from *Boys' Life* (November 1999)

innovative (in·ə·vā′tiv): new and different.

patrons of scientists. The Ptolemies[8] who ruled Egypt after Alexander were particularly generous in their support of science. Through direct financial assistance and through the library and museum Ptolemy I founded in Alexandria, the Ptolemies promoted the work of many leading scientists, including Euclid, Herophilos, and Erasistratos.

After the death of Cleopatra VII, the last Ptolemy to rule Egypt, in 30 B.C., many of the scientific ideas of this period were put aside and nearly forgotten for centuries.

By the A.D. 1000s, Muslim scholars in the Middle East were reevaluating the innovative ideas of the Hellenistic scientists. In time, Muslims carried these ideas to Europe, where they contributed to the great scientific advances that began in the 1500s.

8. **Ptolemies** (tăl′ə·mēz): family of rulers descended from Ptolemy I, one of Alexander's generals.

✔ Reading Check

1. Name one great Greek mathematician who worked in geometry, and one who developed a new physical law.

2. Who were two great astronomers of the Hellenistic world?

3. Name two old ideas or beliefs about the human body that were rejected by Hellenistic physicians.

4. How did the conquests of Alexander make advances in science possible?

5. How did royal patrons help science in Hellenistic Greece to advance?

Hannibal, a general from the powerful city-state of Carthage, set out to destroy Rome. His secret weapon? The ancient equivalent of the modern tank—the war elephant.

MAGAZINE ARTICLE

HISTORY •

Doing the Impossible: Hannibal Crosses the Alps

from *Calliope*

by GLENNA DUNNING

AKG Photo, London

▲ Hannibal.

translated (trans'lāt'id): led to or resulted in.

ally (al'ī): partner, especially in a formal agreement or alliance.

Throughout history, the element of surprise has been the key to success for many military leaders. Doing what the enemy considered impossible often translated into victory for a daring commander, and made legends of great generals such as Hannibal.

A sworn enemy of Rome, Hannibal had eagerly forced the start of the Second Punic War[1] by attacking Rome's ally in Spain, the city of Saguntum. Having taken the city after a siege of eight months, Hannibal began preparations to attack Rome itself. Since the Roman navy controlled the Mediterranean Sea, the only safe way for him to approach Italy was by an overland route. This meant crossing the Alps, the greatest mountain barrier in Europe. While the Romans dismissed all thoughts of a Carthaginian invasion, especially from the north, Hannibal was gathering information about Alpine terrain.[2] The 1,500-mile journey from Spain to

You Need to Know...

Over two thousand years ago, Hannibal set off from Carthage, a powerful city-state in North Africa, to conquer Rome. The obvious route from Carthage to Rome was to sail north and east across the Mediterranean Sea, and then to continue overland through Italy to Rome. This route was closed to Hannibal, however, so he decided to catch Rome and its defenders by surprise through their "back door" to the north. In order to do this, he had to march his army in a huge 1,500-mile circle through the treacherous mountains of Spain and Gaul (present-day France).

1. **Second Punic War:** The Punic Wars were fought between Carthage (founded by the Phoenicians) and Rome in the third and second centuries B.C. *Punic* comes from *punicus*, the Latin adjective for "Phoenician."
2. **terrain** (tə·rān'): area of land, in this case the mountains Hannibal planned to cross.

Elephants in Battle: Pros and Cons

Armies in Asia had used war elephants long before Hannibal's legendary journey. The elephants' size and speed terrified armies, who were crushed in their path. Sometimes armies built towers on the elephants' backs so that archers and javelin throwers could be placed there. From this position high above the battlefield, archers had a great advantage over enemies on the ground.

There was one great drawback in using elephants in battle, though. When wounded, the enormous creatures could panic and become a danger to their own side as well as to the enemy's.

---

chronicles (krän'i•kəlz): records of events as they happened in time; histories.

replenished (ri•plen'isht): provided with a new supply; restocked.

Italy would take him five months and become one of the greatest feats ever accomplished in military history.

To accompany his army and record its achievements, Hannibal hired a few Greek "war correspondents." Years later, the Roman historians Polybius and Livy used these chronicles as references for the passages they wrote about Hannibal's life and career. Hannibal's army consisted of approximately 90,000 infantry and 12,000 cavalry[3]—all seasoned[4] African and Spanish soldiers. Hannibal also planned to bring 37 war elephants. He was not the first general to use elephants in battle. Many others had done the same, including the Indian rajah[5] Porus in his battle against Alexander the Great. Elephants were highly prized as weapons because their appearance and noise often frightened the enemy, and they were dangerous when they charged.

In the spring of 218 B.C., Hannibal's army left Spain. At first, the pace was relatively brisk—more than ten miles a day. It slowed, however, as they crossed the Pyrenees, the mountain range between Spain and Gaul (present-day France). Not all Gallic people were friendly to their cause, and Hannibal fought and won several minor skirmishes[6] with hostile Gallic tribes. When Hannibal reached the Rhone River, he ordered his troops to collect all available boats and rafts and prepare them to ferry the army across the river. The horses easily swam the short distance. The elephants, on the other hand, had to be coaxed onto large rafts, and many of them panicked and overturned the rafts. Fortunately for Hannibal, the river was shallow and the elephants, lifting their trunks above water to breathe, walked along the river bottom until they reached the opposite shore.

By the time the army reached the Alps, they had been marching for four months. While the troops rested and replenished their supplies, a few friendly Gauls approached Hannibal and offered to guide his army through the Alps.

---

3. **cavalry** (kav'əl•rē): soldiers trained to fight on horseback.
4. **seasoned:** experienced.
5. **rajah** (rä'jə): prince, chief, or ruler in India.
6. **skirmishes:** brief conflicts between small groups.

Winter was coming and snow was beginning to fall in the mountain passes. With little time to waste, Hannibal and his army began the difficult climb.

Slowly and carefully, they inched their way along the steep and narrow passes that allowed only two or three soldiers to walk abreast of each other. Above them, the rock walls of the Alps stretched skyward for thousands of feet. Since marching in regular formation was impossible, the troops and animals had to forego all thoughts of attack and rearrange themselves into a column that was more than five miles long. The paths that had been hacked out of sheer rock faces were extremely slippery. As a result, many men and animals lost their footing and fell to their deaths in the gorges[7] below. It was bitterly cold. The animals, especially the elephants, could not find enough vegetation to eat. Even worse, hostile Gauls positioned themselves in the higher passes and sent rocks and boulders crashing down on the Carthaginians as they struggled forward.

In an effort to curb[8] troop and animal losses, Hannibal advanced his cavalry to the head of the marching column and placed the heavily armed infantry[9] at the rear, so that the soldiers might protect the pack animals and supplies. He also sent a few lightly armed soldiers ahead of the main troops. Accompanied by a few elephants, these men were to act as scouts, clearing the way and securing the next pass.

AKG Photo, London

▲ Crossing the Alps into Italy proved to be very difficult for Hannibal's army.

---

7. **gorges** (gôrj′iz): narrow, deep gullies or valleys.
8. **curb:** to control or restrain.
9. **infantry** (in′fən·trē): soldiers trained to fight on foot.

The Legend of Elissa

Legend says that a Phoenician noblewoman named Elissa founded Carthage when an African chief told her that she could take all of his land that she could fit within the hide of a bull. Elissa cleverly sliced a bull's hide into thin strips and used them to encircle the land she wanted. There she built Carthage, known as the "jewel of the Mediterranean."

Later, Elissa fell in love with Aeneas, the founder of Rome. They lived happily in Carthage for a while, but one night Aeneas abandoned her and returned to Rome. Bitterly, Elissa prayed for eternal war between Carthage and Rome—and then took her own life. Hannibal was said to be the champion who set out to avenge Elissa's death.

allegiance (ə·lē′jens): loyalty.

Finally, 15 days after beginning their ascent, the Carthaginians reached the Col de la Traversette summit at an elevation of about 10,000 feet. In the distance stretched the plains of northern Italy, a sight that gave new confidence to the exhausted men. Even though he had lost half his troops and many of his elephants, Hannibal's crossing was a victory against impossible odds.

Even though he had lost half his troops and many of his elephants, Hannibal's crossing was a victory against impossible odds.

Some local tribes agreed and pledged their allegiance to the daring general from Carthage. After replenishing their supplies, Hannibal and his troops continued their advance against Rome. The Romans, meanwhile, found the news of Hannibal's crossing impossible to believe. Their main armies had sailed for Africa and Spain where they planned to oppose the Carthaginians and Hannibal. Realizing that defeat was now a distinct possibility, the Roman Senate recalled its troops and ordered them north. Rome's future would depend on the outcome of this historic encounter.

What Happened Next?

For sixteen years, Hannibal's army fought the Roman forces but was eventually defeated. Hannibal escaped surrendering to Rome only by taking his own life.

For many Romans, merely conquering Carthage wasn't enough. They wanted to crush the city. In 149 B.C., Rome again declared war on Carthage. When the city was defeated three years later, the Romans torched it and then dismantled Carthage stone by stone. Finally, the Romans plowed salt into the ground so that crops could not be grown and the city would remain in ruins. The phrase "Carthaginian solution" is still used today to refer to the total destruction of an enemy.

1. How did Hannibal's crossing of the Alps use the element of surprise?

2. Hannibal and his elephants crossed the Alps over two thousand years ago. How do we know so much about him?

3. What happened to the elephants when Hannibal's army crossed the Rhone River?

4. Identify at least three dangers or difficulties that Hannibal and his army faced while crossing the Alps.

5. Where had the Romans originally planned to oppose Hannibal and the Carthaginians?

MEET THE *Writer*

Glenna Dunning, like Hannibal, has traveled over the Alps. However, her journey was made several years ago by car and without elephants. Dunning has written several other magazine articles.

With its gladiators, wild animals, and thousands of scream-ing, bloodthirsty fans, the Roman Colosseum was quite a sight some two thousand years ago. Read on to find out how the Romans built this amazing structure—and how time is slowly tearing it down.

from Stadium of Life and Death

from *National Geographic World*

by JERRY DUNN

majestic (mə•jes′tik): impressive; grand.

feat (fēt): achievement.

A majestic sight to this day, the Roman Colosseum was an amazing feat of building by people who lived some 2,000 years ago. Construction took only eight years. Gangs of slaves helped the master crafts-men. Other than hoists, or human-powered elevators, they had no large machines to help them work. The structure stood more than 150 feet high and stretched 620 feet long. It enclosed an arena about as long as a modern football field. The Romans built the strong stone walls with open arches. Solid stone walls

You Need to Know...

In A.D. 80 the Roman emperor Titus officially opened the Colosseum with one hundred days of games. Unlike today's sporting events, however, these games were literally matters of life and death. A day at the Colosseum often began with a staged fight between gladiators using wooden weapons. Then, trumpets were sounded, the gladiators traded their wooden props for real weapons, and blood began to flow. Other events held at the Colosseum included fights between gladiators and animals, and even "pretend" naval battles.

collapsed (kə•lapsd′): fell down or caved in.

efficiently (e•fish′ənt•lē): in a manner that does not waste time, energy, money, or materials.

would have collapsed under their own weight.

Designers planned the stadium to handle crowds efficiently. The Colosseum held 50,000 spectators. How did they move such a large number of people in and out of the arena? Each spectator received a ticket or token, numbered to show which of the 80 entrances to use and which seat to take. The whole crowd could be seated with-in ten minutes of arriving.

▲ The Colosseum in Rome today. ❷ **How do the Colosseum's design and original purpose continue to influence us?**

Inside, the emperor, his friends, and priestesses known as the Vestal Virgins[1] sat in ringside seats. In <u>sloping</u> tiers[2] of marble seats above them sat important citizens, then middle-class men, then slaves and foreigners. A fourth zone in the high upper reaches of the stadium was for women and very poor people.

sloping (slōp'iŋ): slanting upward or downward.

Beneath the stadium floor the builders created a series of chambers to confine prisoners and cages to hold wild animals.

The Colosseum was much too big for a wooden roof. So how did the Roman builders shelter the audience from the baking sun? They constructed a *velarium*, or canvas awning,[3] which they stretched across a system of ropes attached to long poles around the top of the Colosseum.

---

1. **Vestal Virgins:** priestesses of the Roman goddess Vesta, the goddess of the hearth.
2. **tiers** (tirz): rows of seats.
3. **awning:** a rooflike covering.

▲ Other large stone structures that remain standing from Roman times include aqueducts. A channel, cut into the top of the aqueducts, carried fresh water from distant springs to Roman cities.

SuperStock

Beneath the stadium floor the builders created a series of chambers to confine prisoners and cages to hold wild animals. Hoists lifted the cages to a level where the animals could enter the arena up a ramp.

Since gladiator days, the Colosseum has been damaged by earthquakes. Much of its stone was carried away during the 14th century. Today traffic rattles the stadium, while air pollution blackens it and eats away the stone. Efforts are underway to restore the monument. It's a good thing: An old saying warns that "when the Colosseum falls, also ends Rome; and when Rome falls, the world will end."

✔ Reading Check

1. Why did the Romans include arches in the stone walls of the Colosseum?

2. Who sat in the ringside seats during events at the Colosseum? Who sat in the seats farthest from the action?

3. How did the builders protect the crowd from the sun?

4. How long did it take to build the Colosseum? Who did most of the work?

5. How many people could attend an event at the Colosseum? How long did it take to seat the crowd?

MEET THE *Writer*

Jerry Dunn is a regular contributor to many national magazines. He lives in Ojai, California, and is the author of five books.

What was it really like to be a gladiator in ancient Rome? How did these men and women become gladiators? Did they all die in the arena? Read on for the answers to these questions.

Who Were the Gladiators?

from *Gladiator*

by RICHARD WATKINS

Bettmann/CORBIS

▲ The fate of a gladiator was sometimes determined by the will of the audience.

conquest (kän'kwest'): act of conquering and acquiring territory.

auctioned (ôk'shənd): sold to the highest bidder.

O f the thousands of men who ended up in the arena, the vast majority were either prisoners of war, criminals, or slaves. As the Roman Empire grew through constant wars of <u>conquest</u>, soldiers of the defeated armies found themselves on the way to Rome, roped neck to neck with their arms tied behind their backs. Among them were Samnites, Thracians, and Gauls from territories conquered early in Rome's history, followed by Britons, Germans, Moors, and Africans, captives from virtually every land that became part of the empire. These human trains were whipped and beaten as they marched, or were packed into the dark and dirty holds[1] of cargo ships bound for Rome. Captives ended up in Rome's slave markets to be <u>auctioned</u> off. Many of the biggest and strongest were bought for the gladiator schools to be trained for combat in the arena.

> ## You Need to Know...
> In ancient Rome, thousands of men and a few women (known as gladiators) were forced to fight and die in staged battles that were wildly popular with a large portion of the Roman population. In fact, the Colosseum was built especially to provide a place where large crowds could be entertained by violence and death. These spectators often held the life or death of the gladiator in their hands—perhaps literally. Legend says that a "thumbs down" signal from the crowd doomed a gladiator to death. Cheers for a brave gladiator spared his or her life—at least until the next fight.

---

1. holds: compartments where cargo is stored.

AKG Photo, London

▲ Detail of mosaic from a Roman villa showing gladiator contest (ca. A.D. 2nd century).

Criminals were another major source of gladiators. Originally, those convicted of murder, robbery, arson[2], or sacrilege[3] were sent to the arena to be killed by an executioner with a sword (*damnati ad gladium*) or thrown to the beasts (*damnati ad bestius*), in the belief that this would act as a deterrent for would-be criminals. As the games grew in popularity and entertainment became more important than deterrence, more criminals were sentenced to train in gladiator schools (*damnati in ludum*). The amount of instruction they received varied. In general, a sentence to the schools meant three years of training and combat in the arena followed by two years teaching in the schools (anyone who survived three years as a gladiator made an excellent teacher). Some of these convicted criminals turned gladiators learned their new profession well and became heroes of the arena, winning fame, fortune, and, possibly, freedom from further combat. Occasionally, though, large-scale shows demanded so many gladiators that any criminal, regardless of his crime, could find himself holding a sword and fighting for his life with little or no instruction whatsoever.

Ordinary slaves were the other major source of gladiators. Owners could dispose of their slaves any way they wanted, just like other property. A slave who tried to run away or was accused of theft or simply bored his master could be sent to the arena. It wasn't until the second century A.D. that owners were prohibited from sending a slave into the arena without just cause.[4]

Obviously, prisoners of war, criminals, and slaves had no choice but to fight, so it is incredible to think that there were men who actually volunteered to be gladiators. At the height of the Roman Empire, more than half of all gladiators were in this deadly profession by their own

---

2. arson: crime of setting fire to someone's property.
3. sacrilege (sak'rə•lij'): disrespectful act toward a sacred person, place, or thing.
4. just cause: good or fair reason.

Archivo Iconografica, S.A./CORBIS

▲ This detail from a Roman mosaic shows a gladiator battling a leopard.

choice. Most were simply poor and desperate, and the life of a gladiator, however short, offered regular meals and the dream of glory.

Champion gladiators who showed exceptional skill and bravery in the arena were sometimes presented with a wooden baton, the *rudius*, that awarded the champion honorable retirement from further combat. Many continued to fight, even after winning the *rudius*, knowing they could command a high price to enter the arena again, this

---

Champion gladiators who showed exceptional skill and bravery in the arena were sometimes presented with a wooden baton, the *rudius*, that awarded the champion honorable retirement from further combat.

---

time as a volunteer. The great Syrian gladiator Flamma (the Flame) earned four *rudi*, only to keep on fighting. The emperor Tiberius offered one thousand pieces of gold per performance to entice retired gladiators back to the arena. Many accepted, not only for the money, but to hear again the roar of the crowd and experience the thrill of combat.

Animals in the Arena

Gladiators were not the only fighters in the arena. Lions, tigers, elephants, bears, and bulls were just a few types of animals forced to fight each other or to fight humans. When the Colosseum opened in A.D. 80, over nine thousand animals were killed in the first one hundred days.

Special gladiators called *bestiarii* were trained to fight wild animals. Because of the high demand for wild animals for the arenas, the population of these animals decreased in the Roman provinces. In fact, it is claimed that the elephant disappeared from North Africa and that the lion in Mesopotamia (present-day Iraq) eventually became extinct.

Bettmann/CORBIS

▲ This well-known painting, ***Pollice Verso*** (Thumbs Down) by Jean-Léon Gérôme (1824–1904), depicts a triumphant gladiator looking into the crowd to determine his victim's fate.

Occasionally a nobleman would dare to be a gladiator. An appearance by one of these wealthy thrill-seekers would send the audience into a frenzy. To see an aristocrat[5] fighting among the slaves and criminals thrilled the mob of *plebeians*, or common people, in the stands. The demand for them was so great at times that some emperors, Augustus and Tiberius in particular, tried to stop them, but there were always some noblemen ready to risk their lives in the arena. Sometimes, though, these privileged gladiators could fight without fearing for their lives. Their status would entitle them to special consideration, allowing them to fight not to the death, but only as a special exhibition between the regular fights. As popular as these blue-blooded gladiators were with the mob at the amphitheater, they were an embarrassment to their peers[6] in the upper class.

The lure of the arena was so strong that even some emperors played at being gladiators, among them Caligula and Hadrian. The emperor Commodus did more than play. He claimed to have fought more than one thousand fights and paid himself one million *sesterces* for each. By comparison, a laborer in Rome might earn one thousand *sesterces* a year.

Because every level of Roman society had representatives in the arena, emperors and slaves, senators and criminals, it is not surprising that women also appeared as

exhibition (ek′sə•bish′ən): display; public showing.

---

5. **aristocrat** (ə•ris′tə•krat′): person of high rank, birth, or title.
6. **peers:** persons of equal rank or ability.

gladiators. They were considered a novelty,[7] but a carving found in Halicarnassus in Asia Minor (what is now Turkey) shows a pair, one appropriately called Amazon,[8] fighting with the same equipment and, apparently, the same intensity as men. The carving says they were honorably discharged. In one way, these women gladiators succeeded where men failed; they managed to offend Roman sensibilities enough to be banned in A.D. 200.

---

7. **novelty:** something new or different.
8. **Amazon:** in Greek legend, member of a race of female warriors.

✔ Reading Check

1. What types of people were the majority of gladiators?

2. How were gladiators trained?

3. The author says that the gladiators had excellent teachers. What reason does he give for this statement?

4. What was the *rudius*, and why would a gladiator want to win one?

5. Who volunteered to become gladiators, and why did they volunteer?

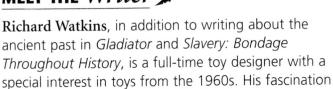

MEET THE *Writer*

Richard Watkins, in addition to writing about the ancient past in *Gladiator* and *Slavery: Bondage Throughout History*, is a full-time toy designer with a special interest in toys from the 1960s. His fascination with gladiators began early. He was only twelve when his parents returned from a trip to Italy, bringing him a book with stories and pictures of ancient Rome.

Netmen and Swordsmen

Roman spectators soon tired of simple bloodshed, demanding more exciting entertainment. They got it by creating an event in which two gladiators were forced to fight with different weapons—a man with a net and a trident (three-pronged spear) fighting a man with a sword, for example. The netman struggled to entangle his opponent in his web and stab him with the trident, while the swordsman fought to cut his way out of the net and kill the netman. Other popular weapons included spears and daggers. Each type of gladiator wore a different costume, often eye-catching but offering little protection.

It started with a handful of believers talking to people about the teachings of a man named Jesus from Nazareth. Today, Christianity is a major worldwide religion. The following article describes how Christianity, despite intense persecutions, or oppression, spread from a group of Jewish believers to include people from all races and backgrounds.

The Spread of Christianity

from *Calliope*

by PAMELA PALMER

From a small core of just a few followers, Christianity spread rapidly. Most early Christians were ordinary folks without high position or training, and few were born into Christian families. Each had made a personal choice to accept the new religion. They lived and worshipped simply, eating together and remembering Jesus Christ. But the power of their message overcame obstacles, and believers soon numbered in the thousands.

The earliest believers were Jews. However, as more and more non-Jews joined the faith, members of this group began to be called "people of the way" to differentiate[1] them from the Jews. Later, they were called "Christians." They learned about their faith from the Apostles[2] and prayed and shared their

You Need to Know...

Being a Christian was dangerous in the early days of the religion. The Roman Empire persecuted Christians because they would not make sacrifices to the Roman gods. A crop failure or a defeat in battle was often blamed on the followers of Jesus because it was thought that they had angered the Roman gods by not worshipping them. At the height of the persecution, being a Christian was considered a crime punishable by death. The only way to escape a death sentence was to reject Christianity and make a sacrifice to the gods of Rome. That was something many of the early Christians refused to do.

---

1. **differentiate** (dif′ər·en′shē·āt′): to recognize a difference; to distinguish.
2. **Apostles:** Christian missionaries, especially those from the original group of twelve disciples and Paul of Tarsus, a Roman convert to Christianity.

possessions with one another. As the number of Christians continued to grow, many rejected the traditional belief that the end of the world was <u>imminent</u>. They encouraged their religious community to develop and establish definite rites and rituals.

The Apostles and evangelists (preachers of the Gospels[3]) were the first missionaries as they traveled to lands beyond Jerusalem. Pilgrims to Jerusalem, especially those who heard the sermon preached by the Apostle Peter on the day of Pentecost,[4] also spread the message of Christianity when they returned home to their own countries. Just northwest of Jerusalem, in Lydda, Peter healed the <u>invalid</u> Aeneas, and at Joppa, he brought Dorcas back to life. Miracles such as these attracted many followers, which gave the Church increasing <u>diversity</u>.

The Apostles and their disciples provided the first Church structure, but it soon was obvious that more was needed. On one occasion, some Greek-speaking Christians felt that the widows in their community were not receiving a fair portion of the food and funds being distributed by the local churches. To resolve the situation, seven Church officials called deacons were appointed to handle the distribution of Church goods. These seven then acted as missionaries, spreading the word of Christianity to other communities. Church elders were their spiritual counterparts. The leading elder, called a bishop, helped other elders supervise Church discipline and teaching.

The letters of the missionary Paul to early churches throughout the Mediterranean area present an excellent picture of Christian life and also show that both strong commitment and squabbles[5] were common. Letters credited to Paul stress that each community needed moral leaders who were strong both religiously and personally in order to resolve issues and thus safeguard the Church. While most problems were solved at

imminent (im′ə·nənt): about to happen.

invalid (in′və·lid): very sick person.

diversity (də·vʉr′sə·tē): variety.

© Ronald Sheridan/Ancient Art & Architecture Collection Ltd.

▲ Gustave Doré illustration of St. Peter in the house of Cornelius.

---

3. **Gospels:** the first four books of the New Testament that record the life of Christ.
4. **Pentecost** (pen′tə·kôst′): a Jewish festival coming 50 days after Passover; also a Christian festival coming on the seventh Sunday after Easter.
5. **squabbles** (skwäb′əlz): petty quarrels; arguments.

San Giovanni In Fonte, Napoli, Italy/Mauro Magliani/SuperStock

▲ Early Christian mosaic depicting Jesus Christ.

converts (kän′vʉrts′): people who change from one religion to another.

decreed (dē·krēd′): established by command.

precedent (pres′ə·dənt): example to be followed.

authoritative (ə·thôr′ə·tāt′iv): official.

heritage (her′ə·tij): beliefs or traditions handed down from the past.

the local level, some required the attention of the entire Christian community.

By A.D. 49, differences of opinion made the first Church council necessary. Called the Jerusalem Council, it was held after Paul's first journey. Those attending made decisions that greatly shaped Christianity. First, they decreed that Gentile[6] converts were not required to follow Jewish law to become Christian. This new rule helped attract large numbers to the Church. Second, they decreed that believing in salvation by faith was more important than just observing rituals. While the council did not solve all issues, its open discussion in seeking spiritual answers to problems set a precedent.

At the start of the second century, a set of definite beliefs and a workable Church structure held together Christians separated by distance, language, and time. Central to the faith was the belief in God as Trinity of persons: Father, son Jesus Christ, and the Holy Spirit, all sharing in the same divine substance of God.

The Old Testament and a growing body of literature later known as the New Testament were the authoritative guides, showing how to find salvation and live as Christians. Early Christians were familiar with the Old Testament, which was part of their Jewish heritage. It, and memories of Jesus' teachings, were their scripture. Throughout the first century, New Testament writings appeared. In the process, trouble arose.

Marcion, a Christian from Asia Minor who traveled to Rome about A.D. 140, rejected much of the Apostolic writings because they were rooted in Jewish belief. Marcion decided to write his own version of Christian history and teachings. He kept the Gospel written by Luke, and some of Paul's letters, but he rewrote them to please himself.

Marcion's refusal to accept Apostolic authority was one of several heresies[7] the Church faced. Other threats came

---

6. Gentile (jen′tīl′): a person who is not Jewish.
7. heresies (her′ə·sēz): beliefs that are rejected by Church leaders.

from envious religious groups and government officials. Yet, despite the problems, the Church gained strength. Its members continued working to further the faith, and they followed the sacred rituals, including baptism, the Eucharist,[8] and the forgiveness of sins.

Admission to the church was through baptism. The purpose of being baptized was to be identified with the death and resurrection of Jesus—dying to sin and rising to a new life. The early rituals accompanying baptism varied. For decades, Easter Eve was the time when new Christians were baptized. At first, baptism involved simple immersion[9] in water or pouring water over the new Christian's head. By the third century A.D., candidates for baptism were required to take two or three years of instruction and then spend several days fasting before their actual baptism. Such rules made it that only adults, both men and women, were eligible for baptism.

Another important ritual was the Eucharist, also called the Lord's Supper, or Communion. The Eucharist commemorated Jesus's taking unleavened[10] bread and wine at his last supper with the Apostles and declaring them to be his body and blood, given to make salvation possible. Before the second century, the Eucharist was taken informally, at meals. Gradually, Church officials regulated it as a formal ceremony. On Sunday mornings, when members of a Christian community gathered together, those who had been baptized shared the bread and wine of the sacred meal. Unbaptized persons attending the service were not eligible to receive Communion. Neither were those who had not followed the teachings of the Church. Only those who had been forgiven for their sins could share in Communion and be accepted as true members of the faith.

Common to all Christian communities was the emphasis on living a strictly moral life and on observing a set worship service. In his first letter to the members of the

On Common Ground

The first followers of Jesus were Jews who believed that he was the Christ—the Jewish messiah. They believed that the Hebrew scriptures foretold the coming of a leader who would deliver the Jewish people into freedom. Jesus's disciples believed that he fulfilled these ancient prophecies, but many Jews did not. The resulting split formed the Christian church. As the early Christians collected the writings of the Apostles to form the New Testament, they came to call the Hebrew Scriptures the Old Testament. Together, the two testaments make up the Christian Bible.

envious (en′vē·əs): jealous.

commemorated (kə·mem′ə·rāt′id): marked or celebrated the memory of.

---

8. **Eucharist** (yōō′kə·rist)
9. **immersion** (i·mʉr′zhən): the act of dipping completely under water.
10. **unleavened** (un·lev′ənd): made without yeast, in this case referring to a flat bread.

From Victims to Victors

The beliefs of the early Christians angered many Romans, who thought the Christians defied the Roman gods. At times, Christians were cruelly persecuted, sometimes to the point of death. However, in A.D. 312, Constantine, a general in the Roman army, fought another general for the right to become emperor. According to legend, before the battle Constantine saw a vision of a burning cross in the sky with the words, "In this sign, conquer." Constantine won the battle and issued the Edict of Milan in A.D. 313. The Edict made Christianity an accepted religion. In A.D. 392, Christianity became the official religion of the Roman Empire.

▲ Constantine.

AKG Photo, London

Church in Corinth, Paul described how members attending a service each should have a responsibility. One could lead a hymn, share a revelation,[11] or deliver a lesson or an interpretation. Paul believed that the purpose of these communal services should be to help each Church member become a better person spiritually and morally. In these early years, most services were held in private homes, usually those belonging to wealthier members of the community. For the early Christians, the idea of church was not a building or a place of worship. Rather, it meant people gathering together to worship and honor Jesus Christ.

———————————

11. revelation (rev′ə•lā′shən): communication of a divine truth.

Reading Check

1. What kinds of people were most early Christians?

2. What types of leaders did Paul believe the Church needed?

3. What important decisions were made by the Jerusalem Council in A.D. 49?

4. What was the purpose of being baptized?

5. What did all Christian communities have in common?

When the people of Pompeii felt the ground shake, they thought it was just another earthquake. They were used to mild earthquakes. What they got instead was a rain of fire and ash that completely buried the city. In just under a day, the eruption of the nearby volcano Mount Vesuvius wiped Pompeii off the map—but preserved it for the ages.

NONFICTION BOOK

SCIENCE •

HISTORY •

from *The Buried City of Pompeii*

by SHELLEY TANAKA

Vesuvius[1] erupted on August 24, A.D. 79. Pompeii had been experiencing earth tremors[2] for a few days, and many people still remembered an earthquake that had damaged much of the city seventeen years before. But they did not realize that they were living in the lap of a deadly volcano.

At about 1 P.M., the mountain roared, and her <u>summit</u> cracked open. A huge column of pumice[3] and ash shot up into the air like a rocket. When the column reached the height of 12 miles (20 kilometers), it spread out like a fountain. Ash and pumice began to fall to the ground.

In horror, the people of Pompeii had to decide whether to flee or stay. Most chose to run, and soon the gates were clogged with humans and pack animals trying to push their way out

summit (sum'it): highest point or top.

> ## You Need to Know...
>
> In A.D. 79, Pompeii (päm•pā') was a busy port city of between 10,000 and 20,000 people. Merchants of Pompeii exported goods all over the Roman Empire. City life was centered in the Forum, a large, rectangular area surrounded by stone columns. Inside the Forum were a marketplace, temples, government offices, and the headquarters of the city's wool industry. The city also contained many fine homes and villas.
>
> We know a great deal about ancient Pompeii because so much of it has been preserved beneath a thick layer of volcanic rock and ash. In fact, much knowledge about everyday life in the Roman Empire has been gained by studying the buried city of Pompeii.

1. **Vesuvius** (və•sōō'vē•əs)
2. **tremors** (trem'ərz): tremblings or shakings of the ground from an earthquake.
3. **pumice** (pum'is): volcanic rock.

▲ Photo of present-day Pompeii. **?** **From a historical viewpoint, what is "fortunate" about the eruption at Pompeii?**

suffocated (suf′ə•kāt′id): smothered or choked.

earnest (ur′nist): in a serious manner or with sincere effort.

of the city. Others hid in their homes, hoping that by some miracle, the rain of fire would soon stop.

But it didn't. With every passing hour, another 6 inches (15 centimeters) of pumice covered Pompeii. By late afternoon, the sky was almost black. Roofs caved in. Walls collapsed as earth tremors rocked the city.

At midnight, the column of ash and pumice finally collapsed back to earth. That's when superhot rock and gas spewed up out of the volcano and began to flow down the mountain, smothering and burning up the countryside.

The avalanche[4] reached the walls of Pompeii at 5:30 the next morning. The people who remained in the city died from the extreme heat, or they were suffocated as they breathed in the hot ash. Within three hours, the city was completely buried.

After the eruption, many people returned to their homes, but Pompeii lay under a sea of pumice and ash. Some got shovels and tried to uncover the bodies of their loved ones. Some searched for their strongboxes and money. Others dug down to the majestic temples and public buildings, hoping to find valuable statues or building materials. Several of these diggers were buried when the ground caved in on top of them.

Eventually, though, the survivors drifted away. And after many years, the slopes of Vesuvius were again covered with green forests and meadows.

But centuries later, people still remembered stories about an ancient buried city. And in 1748, they began to dig down to the city in earnest. At first the work was sloppy and disorganized. Treasure hunters ripped out priceless statues and artwork. Coins and vases were carted away.

---

4. **avalanche** (av′ə•lanch′): the falling of a large mass of snow, ice, rock, or other material down a mountainside.

For 1,500 years, Pompeii had been buried under a thick blanket of pumice and ash. This material had protected the city beautifully from the air and rain. But as soon as the buildings were uncovered, they began to crumble. The brilliant paintings on the walls began to fade.

In 1860, Giuseppe Fiorelli was put in charge of the excavation. Fiorelli was an archaeologist, and he knew that the town should be uncovered in an organized and scientific way. He made detailed maps and carefully recorded each new find. He began to restore the buildings and art, instead of hauling away the most valuable pieces and leaving the rest to rot.

Over the years, the excavations continued, making Pompeii one of the oldest and most studied archaeological sites in the world. Then, between 1927 and 1932, an archaeologist named Amedeo Maiuri discovered one of the finest houses in the city, the House of the Menander. Here diggers found the remains of a grand residence that was undergoing major renovations. *Amphoras*[5] full of plaster were found in the courtyard. Farm implements[6] hung on the wall of the steward's[7] apartment. In the cellar were two chests full of gold and silver coins, jewelry, and 118 beautiful silver dishes.

The diggers also found bodies. The skeleton of a dog lay in a corner of the stable yard. Several bodies were found in the hallway outside the slaves' quarters. And in the corner of a small room in the steward's apartment, a man lay on a narrow bed. He had a leather purse full of money and a seal that identified him as Eros, steward of one of the most important families in Pompeii. Nearby was the skeleton of a young girl. On the ground beside her were pieces of a tiny bronze ring engraved with a picture of a winged horse.

Scala/Art Resource, NY

▲ Volcanic ash covered many of the victims of the eruption at Pompeii and left outlines of their bodies. Archaeologists discovered that liquid plaster poured into the imprint of the ash outlines created plaster casts of the bodies.

archaeologist (är′kē·äl′ə·jist): a person trained in scientific study of earlier peoples, mainly done by digging up and examining remains of cultures.

renovations (ren′ə·vā′shənz): repairs.

5. **amphoras** (am′fə·rəz): two-handled jars patterned after those of ancient Greece.
6. **implements** (im′plə·mənts): tools.
7. **steward:** a person in charge of another's property.

Eyewitness to Disaster

When Vesuvius began erupting, a Roman naval commander, Pliny the Elder, was stationed across the Bay of Naples at Misenum. Moved by a plea for help— and eager to get a closer look at the strange cloud rising in the distance—Pliny and a crew sailed toward the smoldering mountain. They arrived to a scene of panic. Pliny tried to calm the frightened crowds, but eventually he collapsed and died, smothered by the ash like so many others. Although he perished, first-hand reports from those who had been with Pliny made their way to his nephew, Pliny the Younger, who wrote two letters about these events to the Roman historian Tacitus. The letters present a vivid picture of the tragedy at Pompeii.

Did the skeletons in the hallway belong to servants or workmen who were in the house when the eruption occurred? Was the little girl the daughter of the steward? Had they stayed in the house to protect the treasure? Or had they for some reason been unable to run? No one knows for sure.

The skeletons cannot tell us their story. But Pompeii can still teach us a great deal about what life was like almost two thousand years ago. Every object, every building gives us a glimpse into this long-ago world.

✓ Reading Check

1. What did the people of Pompeii do when Vesuvius first began erupting?

2. When did people start making a sincere effort to dig up Pompeii? Describe the quality of their work.

3. What happened to the buildings when they were uncovered after 1,500 years? What happened to the paintings on the walls?

4. How did Giuseppe Fiorelli organize the excavation of Pompeii?

5. What was the House of Menander? What did diggers find there?

MEET THE *Writer*

Shelley Tanaka is an award-winning writer and editor of books for young people. She lives in Ontario, Canada.

Cross-Curricular ACTIVITIES

■ HEALTH/VISUAL ART

Classic Good Looks Plays and other writings from the Classical Age tell us a lot about the clothing and grooming habits of ancient Greeks and Romans. Women and men wore various fashions and favored assorted hairstyles and beauty treatments.

Do some additional research in the library or on the Internet on ancient Greek or Roman clothing (materials, colors, styles) and accessories (jewelry, hair adornments, etc.); grooming aids (at home and at public baths); or beauty treatments. Then, prepare drawings or a short talk for your class.

■ LANGUAGE ARTS

Gladiators of Yesterday and Today Various spectator sports, such as rodeos, as well as professional wrestling and boxing, can be seen as descendants of the gladiator fights in the Roman Colosseum. Of course, there are also many differences between these present-day sports and ancient gladiator fights.

Choose a popular spectator sport of today and write a comparison-contrast essay explaining how it is similar to and different from the gladiator entertainments of ancient Rome.

To get started, think about these topics

- Costumes
- Training and discipline
- Danger level
- Popularity and entertainment value

You may want to illustrate your essay with drawings of the present-day sport and of the ancient gladiators.

■ GEOGRAPHY/HISTORY

Covering Ground In the days before planes, trains, or automobiles, Alexander, Hannibal, and their armies traveled thousands of miles. Draw or trace a map that includes the places mentioned in either "Doing the Impossible: Hannibal Crosses the Alps" (page 191) or "*from* In the Footsteps of Alexander the Great" (page 180). Then, do more research on either leader's journey and add additional details to your map. You might show the route of either leader and include important mountain ranges and rivers on your map. You might also wish to include illustrations with your map.

■ HISTORY/SPEECH

Let's Hear the Pros and Cons What do you think of the Spartan way of life? Jot down your ideas about what it would be like to live in a society that most valued discipline, strength, and military might.

Form two teams and choose a panel of three judges. Have one team be pro-Spartan and the other anti-Spartan. Each team will receive an equal length of time to present its views of Spartan life and to give reasons supporting those views. Focus your debate more clearly by arguing specific questions. For example:

- Should any Spartan values be part of our educational system today?
- Are any Spartan values dangerous? Which ones are useful?
- Is it better to have life decisions made by the state or the individual?

After the teams have presented their opinions, the judges should decide which team made the stronger presentation, and why.

READ ON: FOR INDEPENDENT READING

■ NONFICTION

Ancient Greece by Anne Pearson (Dorling Kindersley, 1992) and *Ancient Rome* by Simon James (Dorling Kindersley, 2000). Both titles are surveys of the cultures, cover topics from science to the Olympics, and are packed with color photos and illustrations.

City: A Story of Roman Planning and Construction by David Macaulay (Houghton Mifflin, 1974). How do you make a city from scratch? Artist and award-winning writer David Macaulay builds an imaginary Roman city from the ground up, from the first survey of the site (including an examination of a rabbit's liver!) to the completion of a twenty-thousand-seat public stadium. The text is accompanied by color photos and illustrations.

The Greek News by Anton Powell and Philip Steele, editors (Candlewick Press, 1996). Read all about it in this newspaper-style history book. Various features include a travel writer from Athens who sneers at the strange customs of the Spartans, and a social columnist who offers advice on attending a grand feast.

Science in Ancient Greece by Kathlyn Gay (Franklin Watts, 1999). This survey of scientific discoveries in classical Greece includes illustrations and maps. Learn how the work of such Greek greats as Hippocrates and Pythagoras still influences science today.

Women in Ancient Rome by Fiona Macdonald (NTC, 2000). Not all Romans were soldiers or senators. What was life like for the women in the Empire? This book provides a revealing look into girls' education, family life, women in the workplace, health and beauty, and famous Roman women—including Sulpicia, a poet, and Dr. Fabiola, a surgeon.

■ FICTION

D'Aulaires' Book of Greek Myths by Ingri and Edgar Parin d'Aulaire (Bantam Doubleday 1962). Stories of gods, goddesses, and heroes are brought to life with colorful drawings by this Caldecott-winning husband-and-wife team.

The Eagle of the Ninth by Rosemary Sutcliff (Oxford University Press, 1954). This classic historical novel by an award-winning author tells the story of a young Roman soldier who braves hostile northern tribes to recover the lost banner of the Ninth, a legion that mysteriously disappeared under his father's command.

For the Temple: A Tale of the Fall of Jerusalem by George A. Henty (PrestonSpeed Publications, 1998). This novel by a master of historical fiction tells the story of a youth who becomes the leader of a group of guerilla soldiers and endures slavery in his quest to save the Jewish temple from Roman invaders.

It's All Greek to Me and *See You Later, Gladiator* by Jon Scieszka (Viking, 1999; Viking, 2000). Join the "Time Warp Trio" in ancient Greece and Rome as they tangle with a triple-headed drooler, wear out their welcome on Mount Olympus, throw chicken bones at a big hairy gladiator named Horridus, and search for a vomitorium (it's not what you think).

Glossary

The glossary below is an alphabetical list of the underscored words found in the selections in this book. Some technical, foreign, and more obscure words in this book are not listed here, but instead are defined for you in the footnotes that accompany many of the selections.

Many words in the English language have more than one meaning. This glossary gives the meanings that apply to the words as they are used in the selections in this book.

Each word's pronunciation is given in parentheses. A guide to the pronunciation symbols appears at the bottom of each right-hand glossary page.

The following abbreviations are used:

     adj. adjective   *adv.* adverb   *n.* noun   *v.* verb

accusation (ak′yo͞o·zā′shən): *n.* charge of wrongdoing.
affirmation (af′ər·mā′shən): *n.* act of declaring to be true.
allegiance (ə·lē′jens): *n.* loyalty.
ally (al′ī): *n.* partner, especially in a formal agreement or alliance.
ambitious (am·bish′əs): *adj.* challenging; requiring much effort.
amble (am′bəl): *v.* to walk at an easy pace.
anatomy (ə·nat′ə·mē): *n.* science dealing with the structure of the body.
anonymous (ə·nän′ə·məs): *adj.* not known by name.
anthropologist (an′thrō·päl′ə·jist): *n.* scientist who studies human origins, including physical and cultural development.
appeal (ə·pēl′): *v.* to make a plea to; to request something of.
archaeologist (är′kē·äl′ə·jist): *n.* person trained in scientific study of earlier peoples, mainly done by digging up and examining remains of cultures.
archive (är′kīv′): *n.* document or record that is kept as evidence.
artisan (ärt′ə·zən): *n.* person trained to work at a trade requiring skill with the hands.
auction (ôk′shən): *v.* to sell to the highest bidder.
authoritative (ə·thôr′ə·tāt′iv): *adj.* official.

bar (bär): *v.* to keep out; to ban.
bias (bī′əs): *n.* discrimination; prejudice.
bribery (brīb′ər·ē): *n.* giving money to someone to do something illegal.
brutally (bro͞ot′l·lē): *adv.* in an unfeeling, cruel, or direct manner.
buoyancy (boi′ən·sē): *n.* ability of something to float.
catastrophe (kə·tas′trə·fē): *n.* widespread misfortune or disaster.
chaos (kā′äs′): *n.* confusion and disorder.
chronicle (krän′i·kəl): *n.* record of events as they happened in time; history.
circumference (sər·kum′fər·əns): *n.* distance bounding area of a circle or area suggesting a circle.
code (kōd): *n.* body of laws, principles, or rules.
collapse (kə·laps′): *v.* to fall down or to cave in.
commemorate (kə·mem′ə·rāt′): *v.* to mark or celebrate the memory of.
communally (kə·myo͞on′əl·lē): *adv.* sharing together as a group.
compassionate (kəm·pash′ən·it): *adj.* feeling or showing sympathy for the sorrow or suffering of others.
compose (kəm·pōz′): *v.* to create or produce, usually a musical or literary work.
compounded (käm·pound′id): *adj.* made up of various elements; complex.

comprehensive (käm′prē·hen′siv): *adj.* of wide scope; complete.
confine (kən·fīn′): *v.* to restrict.
conquest (kän′kwest): *n.* act of conquering and acquiring territory.
conservation (kän′sər·vā′shən): *n.* careful use and protection; preservation.
constellation (kän′stə·lā′shən): *n.* group of stars that has been given a definite name.
contradictory (kän′trə·dik′tə·rē): *adj.* opposing or opposite.
convert (kän′vurt′): *n.* person who changes from one religion to another.
courteous (kurt′ē·əs): *adj.* polite and considerate.
crescent (kres′ənt): *n.* shape like the moon when it is in quarter phase.
customary (kus′tə·mer′ē): *adj.* usual.
deceit (dē·sēt′): *n.* misleading by telling lies.
decipher (dē·sī′fər): *v.* to interpret the meaning of something.
decree (dē·krē′): *v.* to establish by command.
deity (dē′ə·tē): *n.* god or goddess.
depiction (dē·pik′shən): *n.* picture; representation.
deposit (dē·päz′it): *v.* to put into.
descendant (dē·sen′dənt): *n.* person who traces his or her family back to a certain ancestor.

---

at, āte, cär; ten, ēve; is, īce; gō, côrn, lo͞ok, yo͞o *as in pure,* to͞ol, yo͞o *as in you,* oil, out; up, fʉr; ə *for unstressed vowels, as* a *in adult or* u *in focus,* 'l *as in rattle,* 'n *as in flatten,* g *as in go,* j *as in jump,* hw *as in why,* chin, she, think, there, zh *as in measure,* ŋ *as in wing*

deterrent (dē-tûr′ənt): *n.* something that prevents or discourages someone from acting in a certain way.

dire (dīr): *adj.* horrible; feared.

disintegrate (dis-in′tə-grāt′): *v.* to break apart into small pieces; to crumble.

dispose (di-spōz′): *v.* to get rid of.

distinctive (di-stiŋk′tiv): *adj.* clear; marking a difference from others.

distraction (di-strak′shən): *n.* thing that draws attention away.

diverse (də-vûrs′): *adj.* made up of various people or things.

diversity (də-vûr′sə-tē): *n.* variety.

divisible (də-viz′ə-bəl): *adj.* capable of being divided.

dominate (däm′ə-nāt′): *v.* to control; to rule over.

dynamic (dī-nam′ik): *adj.* strong and energetic.

dynasty (dī′nəs-tē): *n.* period during which a certain family rules.

earnest (ûr′nist): *adj.* in a serious manner or with sincere effort.

ecology (ē-käl′ə-jē): *n.* pattern of relationships between living things and their surroundings.

efficiently (e-fish′ənt-lē): *adv.* in a manner that does not waste time, energy, money, or materials.

embark (em-bärk′): *v.* to set forth; to begin.

emerge (ē-mûrj′): *v.* to come out.

eminent (em′ə-nənt): *adj.* prominent; important.

encase (en-kas′): *v.* to enclose; to close in on all sides.

encumber (en-kum′bər): *v.* to block or obstruct.

endure (en-door′): *v.* to put up with quietly.

envious (en′vē-əs): *adj.* jealous.

eroded (ē-rōd′id): *adj.* worn or eaten away.

estimate (es′tə-mit′): *n.* rough or approximate calculation.

ethical (eth′i-kəl): *adj.* in keeping with moral standards and values.

excavate (eks′kə-vat′): *v.* to dig out; to hollow out.

excavation (eks′kə-vā′shən): *n.* act of digging; something uncovered by digging.

exercise (ek′sər-sīz′): *v.* to use; to put into play.

exhibition (ek′sə-bish′ən): *n.* display; public showing.

expedition (eks′pə-dish′ən): *n.* group of people making a journey with a definite purpose.

expose (ek-spōz′): *v.* to make visible or uncover.

extinct (ek-stiŋkt′): *adj.* no longer alive and having no descendants

extract (ek-strakt′): *v.* to pull out using great force or effort.

famine (fam′in): *n.* great shortage of food that can occur over large area for a long time.

fashion (fash′ən): *v.* to make or turn into.

feat (fēt): *n.* achievement.

flail (flāl): *v.* to move or beat wildly about.

forsaken (fər-sā′kən): *adj.* cast aside; abandoned.

fortified (fôrt′ə-fīd): *adj.* strengthened against attack by using walls or forts.

fortress (fôr′tris): *n.* stronghold; fort.

geometric (jē′ə-me′trik): *adj.* based on simple shapes such as a line, circle, or square.

glacier (glā′shər): *n.* huge mass of ice that flows very slowly down a mountain or over land.

glean (glēn): *v.* to gather.

grisly (griz′lē): *adj.* horrifying; frightening.

ground (ground): *v.* to have crushed into fine powder; past tense of grind (grīnd).

gruesome (groo′səm): *adj.* causing horror or disgust; repulsive.

heritage (her′ə-tij): *n.* beliefs or traditions handed down from the past.

hostilities (häs-til′ə-tēz): *n.* warfare.

humble (hum′bəl): *adj.* modest.

ignite (ig-nīt′): *v.* to catch fire.

imminent (im′ə-nənt): *adj.* about to happen.

implore (im-plôr′): *v.* to ask earnestly.

impression (im-presh′ən): *n.* 1. impact; effect; feeling. 2. visible mark made on a surface by pressing something hard into something softer.

inaccessible (in′ak-ses′ə-bəl): *adj.* not able to be accessed or known.

infestation (in′fes-tā′shən): *n.* destructive swarming.

infinite (in′fə-nit): *adj.* having no limits; vast.

initiate (i-nish′ē-āt′): *v.* to start; to begin.

innovative (in′ə-vā′tiv): *adj.* new and different.

inspiration (in′spə-rā′shən): *n.* bright idea or impulse.

intact (in-takt′): *adj.* whole or entire, with no part damaged or removed.

integral (in′tə-grəl): *adj.* essential.

invalid (in′və-lid): *n.* very sick person.

just (just): *adj.* upright; virtuous.

legacy (leg′ə-sē): *n.* something handed down from the past.

legislate (lej′is-lāt′): *v.* to bring about by making laws.

literally (lit′ər-əl-ē): *adv.* based on exactly what is said.

majestic (mə-jes′tik): *adj.* impressive; grand.

maneuver (mə-noo′vər): *v.* to skillfully move, manage, or manipulate.

massive (mas′iv): *adj.* huge.

melancholy (mel′ən-käl′ē): *adj.* sad; gloomy.

methodical (mə-thäd′i-kəl): *adj.* using strict, orderly system or method.

monitor (män′i-tər): *n.* student appointed to assist a teacher; person who warns or instructs.

mortally (môrt′l-ē): *adv.* fatally; causing death.

negotiate (ni-gō′shē-āt′): *v.* to bargain with others in hope of reaching agreement.

notion (nō′shən): *n.* belief.

oppress (ə-pres′): *v.* to treat harshly and unjustly.

overbearing (ō′vər-ber′iŋ): *adj.* arrogant or domineering.

pageant (paj′ənt): *n.* colorful show or entertainment.

paralyzed (par′ə-līzd′): *adj.* unable to move or feel.

plague (plāg): *n.* great trouble sent as divine punishment; calamity.

plight (plīt): *n.* bad or dangerous state or condition.

plundering (plun′dər-iŋ): *n.* robbing or looting.

poised (poizd): *adj.* balanced.

precedent (pres′ə-dənt): *n.* example to be followed.

predecessor (pred′ə•ses′ər): *n.* ancestor or person who came before.

prescribed (prē•skrībd′): *adj.* authorized; established.

preserved (prē•zʉrvd′): *adj.* unspoiled; undamaged.

principle (prin′sə•pəl): *n.* rule of conduct.

priority (prī•ôr′ə•tē): *n.* something that is first in importance or order.

privilege (priv′ə•lij): *n.* special favor.

prominent (präm′ə•nənt): *adj.* easily seen; obvious.

prosperity (präs•per′ə•tē): *n.* success; good fortune.

prosperous (präs′pər•əs): *adj.* successful.

protruding (prō•trood′iŋ): *adj.* sticking out from the surroundings.

provisions (prə•vizh′ənz): *n.* food and other supplies.

pungent (pun′jənt): *adj.* giving a strong, sharp sensation of smell.

quest (kwest): *n.* search or pursuit, usually of knowledge or some important goal or object.

recite (ri•sīt′): *v.* to answer questions orally or to read aloud publicly.

reckon (rek′ən): *v.* to figure; to calculate.

refuge (ref′yooj): *n.* safety or shelter.

regent (rē′jənt): *n.* person who rules when the ruler is too young, too sick, or otherwise unable to rule.

reluctant (ri•luk′tənt): *adj.* hesitant.

rely (ri•lī′): *v.* to depend on; to trust.

remains (ri•mānz′): *n.* ruins, especially of ancient times.

remnant (rem′nənt): *n.* trace; fragment.

renovation (ren′ə•vā′shun): *n.* repair.

replenish (ri•plen′ish): *v.* to provide with a new supply; to restock.

replica (rep′li•kə): *n.* exact or close copy.

restore (ri•stôr′): *v.* to bring back to a former condition.

reverberate (ri•vʉr′bə•rāt′): *v.* to echo back or resound.

revere (ri•vir′): *v.* to feel deep respect toward; to worship.

rudimentary (roo′də•men′tər•ē): *adj.* beginning; elementary.

ruthless (rooth′lis): *adj.* showing no mercy; cruel.

sacred (sā′krid): *adj.* holy.

sacrifice (sak′rə•fīs′): *n.* something precious, such as an animal or human life, offered to a god.

scaffold (skaf′əld): *n.* raised platform or framework to support people working high on a wall or building.

site (sīt): *n.* the place where something is located.

sloping (slōp′iŋ): *adj.* slanting upward or downward.

souvenir (soo′və•nir′): *n.* thing kept as reminder of the past.

specimen (spes′ə•mən): *n.* sample of something, or one person or thing of a group.

spectacle (spek′tə•kəl): *n.* dramatic public display.

spectator (spek′tāt′ər): *n.* onlooker.

spiritual (spir′i•choo•əl): *adj.* relating to the spirit or soul; supernatural.

stunning (stun′iŋ): *adj.* striking or remarkable.

suffocate (suf′ə•kāt′): *v.* to smother or to choke.

summit (sum′it): *n.* highest point or top.

supervise (soo′pər•vīz′): *v.* to oversee or manage others' work.

supreme (sə•prēm′): *adj.* greatest or highest in power or authority.

surveyor (sər•vā′ər): *n.* person who takes measurement and applies mathematical principles to determine boundaries, areas, and elevations.

sympathize (sim′pə•thiz′): *v.* to share or understand the feelings or ideas of another.

tatters (tat′ərs): *n.* rags; shreds.

thrive (thrīv): *v.* to grow, flourish, or prosper.

transcend (tran•send′): *v.* to go beyond; not to be limited.

translate (trans′lāt′): *v.* to lead to or result in.

transparent (trans•per′ənt): *adj.* clear; easily seen through.

triangular (trī•aŋ′gyə•lər): *adj.* shaped like a triangle, a three-sided figure.

verdict (vʉr′dikt): *n.* decision or judgment.

vicinity (və•sin′ə•tē): *n.* surrounding area.

vindicate (vin′də•kāt′): *v.* to clear of blame or suspicion; to justify.

vindictive (vin•dik′tiv): *adj.* desiring revenge.

---

at, āte, cär; ten, ēve; is, īce; gō, côrn, look, yoo *as in pure,* tool, yoo *as in you,* oil, out; up, fʉr; ə *for unstressed vowels, as* a *in adult or* u *in focus,* 'l *as in rattle,* 'n *as in flatten,* g *as in go,* j *as in jump,* hw *as in why,* chin, she, think, *th*ere, zh *as in measure,* ŋ *as in wing*

Acknowledgments

For permission to reprint copyrighted material, grateful acknowledgment is made to the following sources:

Archaeology's dig magazine: "March of the Terra-Cotta Soldiers" by Victoria C. Nesnick from *Archaeology's dig*, vol. 1, no. 5, December 1999/January 2000. Copyright © 2000 by Archaeological Institute of America.

Benchmark Books, an imprint of Marshall Cavendish: From *The Ancient Egyptians* by Elsa Marston. Copyright © 1996 by Marshall Cavendish Corporation. From "The Bible as History," and map "The Near East Around 2000 B.C.E." from *The Ancient Hebrews* by Kenny Mann. Copyright © 1999 by Marshall Cavendish Corporation.

Kent Bushart and Boys' Life: "Pytheas Finds an Icy 'Thule'" by Kent Bushart from *Boys' Life*, November 1999. Copyright © 1999 by Kent Bushart. Published by the Boy Scouts of America.

Carus Publishing Company: "The Wonders of the Pyramids" by Geraldine Woods from *Cricket*, vol. 10, no. 1, September 1991. Copyright © 1991 by Carus Publishing Company.

Cobblestone Publishing Company, 30 Grove Street, Suite C, Peterborough, NH 03458: "The Spread of Christianity" by Pamela Palmer from *Calliope: Early Christianity*, March/April 1996. Copyright © 1996 by Cobblestone Publishing Company. All rights reserved. "Alexander's Tutor" by Susanne Hicks and Duane Damon and "Science in a Hellenistic World" by Louise Chipley Slavicek from *Calliope: Alexander the Great and the Spread of Greek Culture*, December 1998. Copyright © 1998 by Cobblestone Publishing Company. All rights reserved. "Doing the Impossible: Hannibal Crosses the Alps" by Glenna Dunning from *Calliope: Hannibal Versus Rome*, January 1999. Copyright © 1999 by Cobblestone Publishing Company. All rights reserved. "A Vow to Conquer by Dhamma" by Jean Elliott Johnson from *Calliope: Ashoka: India's Philosopher King*, January 2000. Copyright © 2000 by Cobblestone Publishing Company. All rights reserved.

Curtis Brown Group Ltd., London, on behalf of the Griffith Institute: From *The Tomb of Tut Ankh Amen* by Howard Carter and A. C. Mace. Copyright © 1923 by Howard Carter.

Discover Magazine: From "Virtually Cro-Magnon" by Robert Kunzig from *Discover*, vol. 20, issue 11, November 1999. Copyright © 1999 by Robert Kunzig.

Discovery Communications, Inc.: From "Raising the Mammoth" by Dirk Hoogstra from *www.discovery.com*. Copyright © 2000 by Discovery Communications, Inc. From "Animal Mummies" by Jane Ellen Stevens from *www.discovery.com*. Copyright © 2000 by Discovery Communications, Inc. "Summer in the Pits—Going for the Goo" by Mark Wheeler from *www.discovery.com*. Copyright © 2000 by Discovery Communications, Inc.

Enslow Publishers, Inc.: Text and map of the Mideast from "Cities of the Indus Valley" from *Weird and Wacky Science: Lost Cities* by Joyce Goldenstern. Copyright © 1996 by Joyce Goldenstern.

David Getz: "Swimming into the Ice Age" by Dave Getz from *Muse*, March 2000, vol. 4, no. 3. Copyright © 2000 by David Getz.

James Cross Giblin: "The Great Wall of China" from *Walls: Defenses Throughout History* by James Cross Giblin. Copyright © 1984 by James Cross Giblin. Published by Little, Brown and Company.

Gloria Goldreich: "The Writings" from *A Treasury of Jewish Literature* by Gloria Goldreich. Copyright © 1982 by Gloria Goldreich.

Grolier Publishing Company: From "Astronomy and Timekeeping" from *Science in Ancient Egypt* by Geraldine Woods. Copyright © 1988 by Geraldine Woods.

Henry Holt and Company, LLC: "The Burning House" from *Buddha* by Demi. Copyright © 1996 by Demi.

Houghton Mifflin Company: Excerpt from *Bodies from the Bog* by James M. Deem. Copyright © 1998 by James M. Deem. All rights reserved. "Who Were the Gladiators?" from *Gladiator* by Richard Watkins. Copyright © 1997 by Richard Watkins. All rights reserved.

Alfred A. Knopf Children's Books, a division of Random House, Inc.: "Confucianism and Taoism" and "Judaism" from *One World, Many Religions* by Mary Pope Osborne. Copyright © 1996 by Mary Pope Osborne.

Lucent Books, Inc.: From "The Ancient Olympics" from *The Olympic Games* by Theodore Knight. Copyright © 1991 by Lucent Books, Inc. From *Greek and Roman Science* by Don Nardo. Copyright © 1998 by Lucent Books, Inc.

The Madison Press Limited: From *I Was There: The Buried City of Pompeii* by Shelley Tanaka, a Hyperion/Madison Press Book. Text copyright © 1997 by The Madison Press Limited.

Kenny Mann: From *African Kingdoms of the Past—Egypt, Kush, Aksum: Northeast Africa* by Kenny Mann. Copyright © 1997 by Kenny Mann.

Maryland Public Television: Series Overview of "In the Footsteps of Alexander the Great" by Michael Wood, from *http://www.pbs.org/mpt/alexander/journey*, accessed February 6, 2001. Copyright ©1998–2000 by Maryland Public Television.

The Millbrook Press, Brookfield, CT: "Hammurabi's Babylonia" from *The Babylonians* by Elaine Landau. Copyright © 1997 by Elaine Landau.

National Geographic Society: From "The Stadium of Life and Death" by Jerry Dunn from *National Geographic World*, March 1998. Copyright © 1998 by National Geographic Society. "What the Art May Tell" from *Painters of the Caves* by Patricia Lauber. Copyright © 1998 by Patricia Lauber. Published by National Geographic Society.

Newsweek, Inc.: From "Witness to the Creation: Mary Leakey, 1913–1996" by Sharon Begley, *Newsweek*, December 23, 1996. Copyright © 1996 by Newsweek, Inc.

Scholastic Inc.: "The Spartan Way" by Sean Price from *Junior Scholastic*, September 7, 1998. Copyright © 1998 by Scholastic Inc.

Bernarda Bryson Shahn: "The Monster Humbaba" from *Gilgamesh: Man's First Story* by Bernarda Bryson. Copyright © 1967 by Bernarda Bryson.

Hershel Shanks: "The Mystery of Qumran and the Dead Sea Scrolls" from *Muse*, vol. 4, no. 2, February 2000. Copyright © 2000 by Hershel Shanks.

Simon & Schuster Books for Young Readers, an imprint of Simon & Schuster Children's Publishing Division: From *Women of the Bible* by Carole Armstrong. Text copyright © 1998 by Carole Armstrong.

The Estate of John Snelling: "Siddhartha Gautama: The Buddha" from *Buddhism* by John Snelling. Copyright © 1986 by John Snelling.

The University of Chicago Press: From *The Sumerians: Their History, Culture, and Character* by Samuel Noah Kramer. Copyright © 1963 by The University of Chicago.

Usborne Publishing, 83-85 Saffron Hill, London EC1N 8RT, UK: Text and illustrations from *Who Built the Pyramids?* by Jane Chisholm and Struan Reid. Copyright © 1995 by Usborne Publishing Ltd.

Viking Penguin, an imprint of Penguin Putnam Books for Young Readers, a division of Penguin Putnam Inc.: "Writing and Alphabets" from *Alphabetical Order: How the Alphabet Began* by Tiphaine Samoyault, translated by Kathryn M. Pulver. Copyright © 1996 by Circonflexe. Translation copyright © 1998 by Penguin Books USA Inc.

John Wiley & Sons, Inc.: "Enheduana of Sumer" from *Outrageous Women of Ancient Times* by Vicki León. Copyright © 1998 by Vicki León.

Diane Wolkstein: From "The Courtship of Inanna and Dumuzi" from *Inanna: Queen of Heaven and Earth* by Diane Wolkstein and Samuel Noah Kramer. Copyright © 1983 by Diane Wolkstein and Samuel Noah Kramer.

Sources Cited:

Excerpt from *Mysterious Places: The Magical East* by Philip Wilkinson and Michael Pollard. Published by Chelsea House Publishers, Philadelphia, 1994.